PATHFINDERS
OF
WESTERN NORTH AMERICA

ROUTES FOLLOWED BY EXPLORERS

VANCOUVER

COOK

PEREZ

LEWIS & CLARK

HUNT

SMITH

STUART

MACKENZIE

THOMPSON

FRASER

MACKENZIE 1789

Great Slave Lake

MACKENZIE

Slave R.

1789

Lake Athabaska

FORT CHIPEWYAN

MACKENZIE 1793

R.

Athabaska

R.

Reindeer Lake

THOMPSON

FORT EDMONTON

North Saskatchewan

Lake Winnipeg

Lake Winnipegosis

ATHABASKA PASS

THOMPSON

ROCKY MOUNTAIN HOUSE

HOWSE PASS

1807

South

Saskatchewan

R.

STR. 1811

1809

Lake Windemere

R.

1808

1811

Koolenay

1808

AUG. 1809

1808

eille

1811

and

eille L 1809

KULLYSPELL HOUSE

KANE HOUSE

SALISH HOUSE

Clark Fork R.

e. R.

LOLO

305

PASS

Clearwater R.

LOLO TRAIL

CLARK 1806

LEWIS

CANYON

LEMHI PASS

Lemhi R.

Beaverhead R.

FORT HENRY

HUNT 1811

R.

SMITH 1826, 1827

FORT HALL

112

LEWIS 1806

Missouri R.

LEWIS 1806

LEWIS & CLARK 1805

FORT MANDAN
WINTER 1804-05

R O C K Y

Jefferson R.

LEWIS & CLARK 1806

M O U N T A I N S

Bighorn R.

Yellowstone R.

Horn R.

Big

HUNT 1811

CLARK 1806

Madison R.

TETON MTS.

PIERRE'S HOLE

Wind R.

STUART 1812

SOUTH PASS

BLACK HILLS

Scale

0   100   200   300 miles

North

Platte

Missouri R.

D1570719

Washington: A History of the Evergreen State

WASHINGTON:

A History

of the Evergreen State

MARY W. AVERY

UNIVERSITY OF WASHINGTON PRESS   SEATTLE & LONDON

Copyright © 1961, 1965 by the University of Washington Press
Library of Congress Catalog Card Number 61-8211
ISBN 0–295–95126–5
Printed in the United States of America
Second and third printings, 1967
Fourth printing, 1973

The present book is a revised version of the history section of
History and Government of the State of Washington,
published in 1961.

TO EMMETT, CHARLOTTE, AND BRAD

Preface

This volume is a revision of the history section of *The History and Government of the State of Washington* (1961), which is used as a text for the Washington history and government courses in both colleges and high schools within the state. A need has been expressed for a general history for the reading public who wanted a digest of the various phases of the area's development as a background for the increasing number of popular and scholarly treatments of some specific regional topic. This book is issued for that purpose.

As a result, many scientific and social areas of the region's development are included—geology, Indian culture, industries and cultural growth (except for literature and art). The remaining chapters on the early explorations, fur trade, missionary period, Indian wars, and political history are intended to be primarily narrative— to tell the story of the emergence of the state of Washington in as vivid a fashion as possible. In addition, I have attempted, to a limited degree, to show how these occurrences were related to movements in our country as a whole and to the international situation of the particular time.

During the twenty years of my working on some phase of Pacific Northwest history, so many of my colleagues and friends have aided me that I regard this as a cooperative effort with too many coauthors to name. The two who have given me such assistance for the longest period of time are Professor Emeritus Herman J. Deutsch, whose knowledge of Pacific Northwest history and generous advice enabled me to tackle my first publication in 1944, and my husband, Professor Emmett L. Avery, without whose encouragement I could never have written anything.

MARY W. AVERY, ARCHIVIST
WASHINGTON STATE UNIVERSITY LIBRARY

Contents

Illustrations

Maps

Washington: A History of the Evergreen State

Geology and Geography of the State of Washington

1

GENERAL GEOGRAPHICAL CHARACTERISTICS

Many states have some distinguishing feature automatically associated with their names, but the state of Washington contains so many contradictions that it is difficult to choose a typical characteristic. The slogan "Washington, the Evergreen State" is used to refer to the entire state, but actually, east of the Cascades, there is a wide area that is almost completely treeless. A person living on the coast would regard Washington as an extremely rainy state since, for example, the United States Weather Bureau lists 164.28 inches of rainfall as the figure for Amanda Park in the Olympic Peninsula in a typical year (1961). Someone living near Pasco in Franklin County or Ephrata in Grant County, however, would maintain from his own experience that Washington is practically a desert state. In 1961 Ephrata had 7.69 inches of rain and Richland, near Pasco, had 8.77 inches.

The same extremes are present in regard to temperature. In the dry southeastern and central section, the temperature in summer rises above 100 degrees and in winter drops to 30 degrees below zero occasionally, whereas in the coast region there is ordinarily no great variation in temperature the year round. For example, the Weather Bureau in 1961 lists the average temperature for Seattle as 46.5 in January and the average temperature for that city as 67.8 in July. On the other hand, in that year, Chewelah had a high of 110 on its hottest day and a low of 17 below zero on its coldest.

The differences in climate and topography have brought about similar variations in occupations in the state. The damp, mild climate of the coast has produced one of the heaviest stands of timber in the world. This natural abundance of timber made lumbering the state's chief industry for many years, and it is still extremely important to the state's economy. Manufacturing, in general, is now our greatest source of income; agriculture ranks second; tourist trade, third; and forest products, fourth. The *Annual Survey of Manufactures* by the United States Census Bureau for 1958 lists the value of the manufacturing of lumber and wood products as $293,345,000. Similar figures for pulp and paper products are $251,780,000. The coast climate is also suited to truck gardening and dairy production where agriculture is practiced.

The presence of the ocean plus coastal rivers and lakes makes fishing, too, an important occupation for the part of Washington west of the Cascades. In 1961 Washington ranked ninth among the states in the value of fish resources, 4.4 per cent of the value of fish and shellfish landed in the United States. Most of the Alaskan fisheries have their headquarters in Seattle, making it an even more important center for the processing and shipment of fish. It is the greatest halibut port in the world. Our salmon industry is even more valuable economically, and shellfish are also significant items. In 1961, Washington fishermen caught 29,984,621 pounds of salmon, according to the *Annual Report* of the Washington State Department of Fisheries. This is a low figure for odd-numbered years when pink salmon runs are ordinarily very high. The pink salmon run in 1961 was the lowest on record. The same bulletin lists the total pounds of all fish taken by Washington fishermen that year as having a catch value of $19,294,033 and a processed value of $38,033,210. In chapter 9, we shall discuss the problems facing the salmon industry because of the building of dams, which cut off migrating salmon from their spawning grounds, and because of stream pollution.

The dry and comparatively treeless eastern section of the state would obviously have to support entirely different industries from lumbering and fishing. Fortunately, throughout most of eastern Washington, there is sufficient rainfall for dry farming of wheat and other grains and for the raising of cattle and sheep. Irrigation in the central section provides water for fruit ranches, truck gardening, and dairy farming.

Thus, in general, eastern Washington can be regarded as agricultural and western Washington as industrial, by contrast. Up until recently, our industries have consisted mainly of simple processing of food and timber, but now the presence of cheap electrical power from Grand Coulee, Bonneville, and other dams is bringing about more complicated phases of manufacturing in the production of light metals, laminated wood products, and synthetic materials. The canning and freezing of food continues to be an important occupation, however.

WASHINGTON'S DISTINCTIVE FEATURES

Since the east and west sections of the state have no unity either from a geographical or occupational standpoint, the question arises: "Is there nothing then which can be called typical of the state as a whole?" One answer is that the position of our state in relation to the other states of our country and in relation to the Far East is unique. In fact, until very recently, our connections with Alaska and the Orient have been considered our most important attribute.

You have undoubtedly heard this area spoken of as the "Gateway to Alaska," the "Door to the Orient," the "Spring-board for China and Japan." European countries sent explorers to the Pacific Northwest in the eighteenth century to look for the "Northwest Passage," a river thought to connect with rivers in the eastern part of North America. If it could be found, ships could then cross the continent on their way from Europe to the Orient and avoid the long trip around South America to get from the Atlantic to the Pacific oceans. In the process of looking for such a river, the English acquired sea-otter skins from the natives and later discovered their value in the Orient. A valuable trade thus began between our coast and China, which continued even after the fur trade dwindled and the United States secured title to the region.

In the 1890's, gold was discovered in Alaska, and the town of Seattle mushroomed into a city as an outfitting center for the mines. As Alaska developed its resources—fishing, lumbering, and other metals besides gold—Seattle continued to be one of Washington's largest trade centers for the territory. Commerce with free Asiatic countries—particularly Japan—is still important, too.

The most dramatic result of emphasis on our nearness to the Orient and Alaska is the recent development of a regular schedule for airplanes carrying passengers and freight between Seattle, Anchorage, Tokyo, and other oriental points. Until the airplane made it possible to rise above the icy wastes of the Arctic, we regarded it as an impassable barrier between this region and the Orient or northern Europe. However, the Arctic is now becoming a main pathway, both for trade and defense, because of the great saving in distance as compared with the long voyage across the Pacific. An atomic submarine has also gone "under" the North Pole.

It is difficult yet for us to think of the northern sections of Asia, Europe, and our continent as forming almost a complete circle around the Arctic Ocean, but a study of a globe makes this relationship clear. The Arctic Ocean has been called the "Mediterranean of the Future"[1] because it forms a passageway between the two continents which lie around it in much the same way that Africa and Europe circle the Mediterranean.

When we depended largely on selling our raw materials almost in their original form, it was natural that people thought of Washington almost entirely as a "gateway" to some other place. We not only shipped our food, lumber, and minerals to Alaska and the Orient, but we sent them to cities in the Middle West and the East where further processing or manufacturing was done.

Although Washington continues to serve as a gateway for trade, the state has gradually developed its economic resources so that now important industries operate here. The first step was to start processing our raw materials in this area. By 1939 when the Bonneville Dam Commission published a list of leading industries in the Pacific Northwest, it became evident that we had entered that stage of industrial development. Major raw materials processed were lumber, wheat, fruits and vegetables, fish, and dairy products. Plywood, paper pulp, and other similar products were being made from lumber. Canneries and quick-freezing plants were preserving food for shipment, and grain and flour mills were increasing.

During World War II, however, a great demand arose for products that could not be made from raw materials found in this area—particularly steel and aluminum used in airplane manufacturing and shipbuilding. Because of the excellent harbors on the coast and the nearby forests, shipbuilding has always been an industry well suited to this area. In fact, we shall learn later something about John

[1] Vilhjalmur Stefansson, "Mediterranean of the Future," *Travel*, LXXXV (June, 1945), 11.

Grand Coulee Dam: Grand Coulee Dam is the largest concrete structure ever built. Its height equals a forty-six story building, its length twelve city blocks, and its width at the base is 500 feet. (Washington State Department of Commerce and Economic Development)

Meares, an English fur trader, who built a ship at Nootka Sound on Vancouver Island in 1788. Even now when ships are made almost entirely of metal, the very usable harbors make it worthwhile to continue building ships here, largely at the Bremerton shipyards. From the time of World War I, airplane manufacture has also been a major industry in Seattle. Some steel for the ships and planes is made in Seattle, but most of it is shipped in from Utah and southern California.

Aluminum plants were also set up in Spokane, Vancouver, Tacoma, Wenatchee, and Longview even though there is no bauxite, from which aluminum is made, in the Pacific Northwest. The great amount of cheap electrical power available from Bonneville and Grand Coulee dams made it feasible to ship in bauxite from the Southwest or from South America and process it here. Washington clays are rich in aluminum, but in a form that cannot be easily separated from the other elements in the soil. If present research yields an economical process whereby aluminum can be extracted directly from these clays, we shall have both the raw material and the cheap power for the manufacture of aluminum in great quantities.

In the past, manufacturing has been handicapped not only by our lack of iron ore and large amounts of hard coal, but by our distance from the markets of large eastern cities. The rise in the use of light metals has helped to offset the former, and a constant increase in our population is making the latter less important. If faster means of transportation across both the Pacific and Arctic oceans increase our trade in those areas, we shall have the advantage of our earlier contacts with Alaska and the Orient as well as our present industrial development.

GEOLOGY

Because of the great diversity of geographical features in the state, it is interesting to see how the various sections were formed and how their topography and climate have influenced their industry and culture.

Millions of years ago, the waters of what is now called the Pacific Ocean evidently covered all of the present state of Washington. The Bitterroot Range and the Blue Mountains represented the eastern rim of land at that time. Pressures under the ocean floor pushed it up at various points to the west of the existing ridge of land, forming islands here and there, some of which were mountains. At other points the ocean floor would be tilted up in such a way as to spill out the water, leaving areas of dry land. Over millions of years, this process went on until a series of mountains, lakes, rivers, and plateaus were formed in what is now the Inland Empire.

Ten to fifteen million years ago, successive floods of lava began to ooze out of cracks in the earth and to flow over this region. The lava pushed its way into a semicircle closed on the northern rim by the Okanogan Highlands and the high hills north and east of Spokane;

on the eastern rim by the mountains in western Idaho; and on the southeastern rim by the Blue Mountains. The lava flowed on through the opening west of the Blue Mountains down into Oregon almost to California.

The old mountains in the interior of this region were practically all covered by the lava, which reached an estimated depth of six thousand feet in some places. However, the tips of a number of the ancient mountains do still protrude above the lava deposits—Steptoe, Kamiak, and Wild Horse buttes, for example. Geologists have taken the name of the highest, Steptoe, to describe such a mountain sticking up through layers of lava that did not reach its top. Therefore, one sees references to steptoes (with a small *s*) in other parts of the world.

During the later lava flows, the Cascades were thrust up into a range of high hills, but not with their present volcanic peaks. In fact, they rose so slowly that the Yakima River could keep pace with their outlying ridges, cutting its way across them at each new level.

During the period of the lava flows, our climate varied from semi-tropical to temperate. Fossils of animals and plants and petrified wood are found to demonstrate this. For example, fossils of palm trees have been found. Petrified ginkgo trees may be seen near Vantage on the Columbia River where the living trees were buried over a million years ago in swamps sealed under the lava floods. Chemical changes occurred that allowed an opal-like substance to replace the cell walls of the tree and thus preserve it to the present time. The ginkgo tree is found growing in a natural state now only in China.

Fossils are found, too, of trees of a more temperate climate—oak, sycamore, maple, birch, beech, conifers, and so forth. The remains of animals of the period show the same variation in types known in both semitropical and temperate zones—rhinoceros, lions, camels, mastodons, mammoths, oreodon (a prehistoric animal seemingly related to the deer, camel, and hog), and dogs, wild cats, deer, saber-tooth tigers, broad-faced oxen, and mylodon (an early ground sloth).

Toward the close of the period of great lava flows, for reasons which are not yet clear to scientists, the climate began to get much colder, and glaciers crept down from the north into Washington. The snow-clad peaks of the Cascades came as a result of comparatively recent volcanic activity, but all of the major cones except Mount St.

Mt. Rainier across Tipsoo Lake: Mt. Rainier, 14,408 feet high, is the tallest peak in Washington and the third highest mountain in the continental United States. It lies in Pierce County. (Photo by Ella E. Clark)

Helens are thought to have been formed before the end of the glacial period. Those peaks in Washington are: Mount Baker (10,750 feet); Glacier Peak (10,436); Mount Rainier (14,408); Mount Adams (12,307). Geologists believe that Mount St. Helens (9,761) erupted after glacial times.

Anyone driving on U. S. Highway 195 between Spokane and Rosalia is aware of a fairly definite point at which evergreen forests end and the treeless Palouse Hills begin. That line marks the southernmost extent of any of the glaciers in eastern Washington. Areas to the south of this line were greatly affected by the glaciers, however, even though the ice itself did not cover them, because when the glaciers melted, huge floods occurred which formed large lakes, changed the course of rivers, and carried silt and rocks hundreds of miles beyond the ice cap.

The Columbia River itself is an example of this kind of action. Ice evidently dammed the river at a point approximately where Grand

Coulee Dam now stands so that the river had to flow round the obstacle and cut a new channel—the coulee called Grand Coulee or Dry Coulee. Then when the ice melted and the glacier withdrew, the river went back to its former channel, leaving the Grand Coulee dry. This change enables us now, of course, to use the coulee as a reservoir for water storage for the dam. While the ancient Columbia flowed through the Grand Coulee, it plunged over present Dry Falls, a drop of four hundred feet, three miles wide. The volume then would have equaled that of fifty falls of the size of Niagara.

Within the Columbia Basin area, the geologic history of the Palouse Hills has been puzzling to scientists. The bare hills look like solidified sand dunes, blown to this region, and geologists are convinced that the wind did play a part in their formation, but that the deep loess (wind-blown materials) lies on top of the lava layers. The surface soil, which varies from a few inches on the south sides of the hills to a few feet on the north slopes, has evidently been blown from the Cascade Mountains by the prevailing winds of the past several centuries. Under this top soil, however, there is a thick layer of dirt, 150 feet thick in some places, which was also blown in onto the earlier lava base. This second layer of wind-blown soil is not of the same chemical composition as that on top. Therefore, scientists think that it must have come from some place other than the Cascades, brought in by winds from another direction. Toward the west and northwestern parts of the Palouse region, the glacial floods washed away the loess, leaving the lava rock exposed in the form of the scablands extending from the present area of Lincoln, Adams, and Franklin counties west to the Columbia.

By the end of the glacial period, many of the animals had become extinct. To the north, remains have been found of a mammoth which had grown heavy woolly hair, but even this protection against the cold did not save the species. Another interesting phenomenon is that the small, prehistoric horse disappeared completely from this area, and, after the glacial period, there were no horses of any kind on this continent until the Spaniards introduced the modern horse into Mexico from Spain in the sixteenth century. Gradually they spread north from one Indian tribe to another, reaching the Oregon country probably around 1710 or slightly later.

Dry Falls, near Coulee City. At one time the Columbia River poured over these falls, creating a deluge that would dwarf Niagara. (Photo by Washington State Department of Commerce and Economic Development)

If we turn now to the development of the country west of the Cascades, we find that it followed the same pattern of that just discussed. The land rose slowly until the coast chain appeared as a low dike against the sea and then was thrust gradually higher into the Olympic Mountain Range and the Willapa Hills. Mount Olympus, the tallest of these mountains, is 7,954 feet high.

Before the beginning of the glacial period, Puget Sound was apparently a dry plateau, having numerous rivers and lakes. The first glaciers came down from the north and plowed through the former plateau. After these melted and withdrew, there was an interval when new rivers developed largely where the many fingers of the Sound now are. The last glacier then returned and cut across these former river valleys, changing the pattern somewhat, but leaving the many indentations approximately as they are now. As the glaciers melted finally, floods caused lakes to stretch over the Sound across the mouth of the Columbia, but when these receded, the river systems were visible again. Then somehow the sea flowed back into the Sound area, changing the old rivers into the main section of the Sound plus its many bays. The theory most generally accepted is that the floor of the plateau and rivers sank sufficiently to allow the ocean to enter and form the Sound as we know it.

Floods caused by the melting ice lobes also brought down gravel and sand from higher areas. These gravelly flat places are called *prairies*. They are particularly noticeable between Olympia and the Columbia River. A puzzle of the prairie sections is the Mima mounds. These are low mounds, some of which are seven feet high and seventy feet wide. Early theories were that they were Indian burial grounds or that they were thrown up by the burrowing of some prehistoric animal. The true explanation seems to be, however, that during the glacial period, the ground cracked in a fairly regular pattern of polygons and then ice formed in the crevices between these many-sided chunks of dirt. Areas frozen into such a design may be seen in parts of Alaska today. When the ice melted, the chunks remained, and then, as the thawing continued, the flood waters washed away the softer surface of the chunks, leaving the frozen cores rounded. An ice cube does the same when it melts since the edges melt faster than the sides.

Let us look now at the geographical and occupational features of the various areas of the state brought into being by the geological developments just described. For this it will be helpful to use the seven sections into which geographers divide the state: the Olympic Peninsula, the Willapa Hills, Puget Sound, the Cascades, the Okanogan Highlands, the Columbia Basin, and the Blue Mountains.

GEOGRAPHICAL DIVISIONS

The Olympic Peninsula

When we considered the differences between the west side and the east side of the state, we found that the west side was very rainy by comparison with the inland sections, and the Olympic Mountains represent the wettest part of the west side. At Oxbow on the Wynooche River, the average amount of rainfall over thirteen years was 150.73 inches, which gives it the distinction of being the wettest place in the United States. On the other hand, Sequim, which lies just sixty miles away on the east side of the Olympics near Juan de Fuca Straits, has an average of only sixteen inches a year, and the farms there require irrigation.

The fact that the Olympics lie between Oxbow and Sequim accounts for this great difference in precipitation. The prevailing winds come in across the Pacific Ocean warm and moisture-laden. As they

rise over the Olympic Mountains, the moisture is precipitated as the temperature falls in the higher altitudes. By the time that the winds cross the Olympics, they have lost most of their moisture in rain and so have only a small amount, comparatively, to drop on the eastern side of the mountains. In the lower altitudes, the winds are also able to carry more moisture because of the higher temperatures. As the winds move on over Puget Sound, they pick up more water and repeat the same process, to a lesser extent, of dropping rain on the west side of the Cascades and leaving the area east of that range quite dry.

Forests of spruce, fir, cedar, and hemlock cover much of the Olympic Peninsula, which includes the counties of Clallam, Jefferson, and parts of Grays Harbor and Mason, as far south as Grays Harbor itself. In the Olympic National Park, almost 892,000 acres of the densest timber stands are protected from cutting. In state and federal forests surrounding this central area, trees may be cut only by agreement with the State Department of Natural Resources or the United States Forest Service as to conservation practices to be met. A two-mile section of the Queets River is included in the park, in order to preserve one river in its primitive state; also a strip of beach along the ocean from the mouth of the Queets River north to Cape Alava.

Not only plant life, but also animals are protected in game refuges in the park. Roosevelt elk (named for President Theodore Roosevelt), which were becoming extinct in the early 1900's, are now increasing, to the great satisfaction of conservationists who hope that primitive areas of this type will be maintained for the pleasure of visitors and for safety measures in water supply, flood control, and soil conservation.

There are foot and horseback trails along with camps for the use of tourists, who may fish at various places. The famous Beardslee trout, a landlocked, steelhead trout, is found only in Lake Crescent, at the north end of the park.

This rain forest on the Olympic Peninsula is a part of Olympic National Park. (Photo by Washington State Department of Commerce and Economic Development)

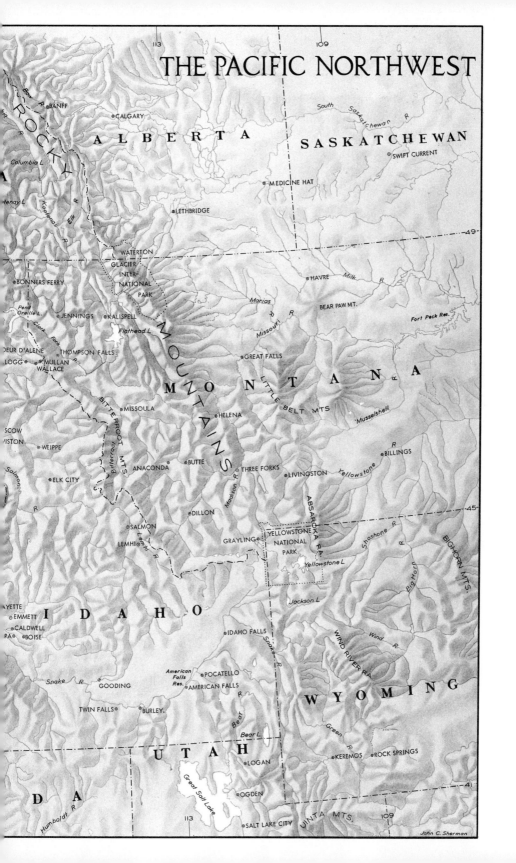

THE PACIFIC NORTHWEST

ROCKY

ALBERTA

SASKATCHEWAN

•BANFF
•CALGARY
South Saskatchewan R
•SWIFT CURRENT

Columbia L
•MEDICINE HAT

Kootenay L
Kootenai R
Elk R
Bow R

•LETHBRIDGE

49

WATERTON
GLACIER
INTER-
NATIONAL
PARK

•HAVRE
Milk R
Marias R
BEAR PAW MT.
Fort Peck Res.

•BONNERS FERRY

Pend
Oreille L.
•JENNINGS
•KALISPELL
Flathead L
Missouri R

M
O
U
N
T
A
I
N
S

DEUR D'ALENE
•THOMPSON FALLS
•GREAT FALLS
LITTLE BELT MTS.
Musselshell R

Clark Fork
LOGG•
•MULLAN
WALLACE

MONTANA

SCOW
ISTON
•WEIPPE
•MISSOULA
•HELENA
•BILLINGS

BITTERROOT MTS.
Bitterroot R

ANACONDA
•BUTTE
Madison R
•THREE FORKS
•LIVINGSTON
Yellowstone R

Salmon R
•ELK CITY

•DILLON

R

•SALMON
Lemhi R
GRAYLING•
YELLOWSTONE
NATIONAL
PARK

ABSAROKA RA.
45

LEMHI
Yellowstone L

BIGHORN MTS.

AYETTE
•EMMETT

IDAHO
Jackson L
Shoshone R
Big Horn R

•CALDWELL
PA•
•BOISE
•IDAHO FALLS

WIND RIVER RA.
Wind R

Snake R
American
Falls
Res.
•POCATELLO
•AMERICAN FALLS

WYOMING

Snake R
GOODING

TWIN FALLS•
•BURLEY
Bear R
Green R

Bear L
•KEREMOS
•ROCK SPRINGS

DA
UTAH
•LOGAN

Great Salt Lake
•OGDEN

41

Humboldt R
113
109

•SALT LAKE CITY
UINTA MTS.

John C. Sherman

Much of the terrain of the western side of the Olympics is so rugged that lumbering is too difficult, but where the timber is more accessible on the east side of the mountains near the Sound, lumbering has been carried on at a great rate. In the early days, the amount of timber seemed inexhaustible and therefore no precautions were taken to maintain forest growth. Forest fires, too, took an enormous toll of the wooded slopes. As a result of this waste, many towns on the Olympic Peninsula which were once flourishing lumber centers lost their source of income, particularly in the areas where the Douglas firs, the most desirable species, were vanishing. Examples are Shelton, Port Ludlow, Hoodsport, Potlatch, Eldon, Brinnon, and other small towns along Hood Canal.

These former "ghost towns" are being revived now to a considerable extent. For one thing, by the period of World War II, lumber operators realized that intensive conservation measures would have to be followed if the lumber industry was to continue profitably in this region. At the present time, therefore, both private companies and governmental agencies are planting thousands of acres with tree seedlings in cutover sections as the beginning of future timber stands. Care in cutting of trees, even on private land, is now required by law so that the wasteful logging methods of earlier times cannot continue. However, if a permanent stand of full-grown timber for the future were the only basis for the revival of lumbering towns, it would still be many years before the new trees had reached merchantable size.

The second factor aiding such areas is the development of industries based on small trees and waste products from sawmills. Such industries include: pulp, paper, paper products, fiberboard, "Prestologs," industrial alcohol and molasses for cattle from bark, battery separators and fluid, Venetian blinds, furniture of all kinds, plywood, and cellulose. On the Olympic Peninsula, these commodities are represented by pulp, plywood, and wallboard mills in Shelton as well as a plant which makes battery fluid from the waste liquors produced at the pulp mill. In Port Angeles, mills make plywood and various types of wallboard.

Agriculture is also possible on logged-off land, and on the Olympic Peninsula poultry-raising and dairying have proved to be the most practicable types of farming on cutover areas. Dairying requires better pasture land than will suffice for chickens, and most of the dairy farms are found along the Juan de Fuca Straits between Port Townsend and Port Angeles. Another small strip of dairy farms is situated in the southwestern corner of Clallam County.

Commercial fishing occurs, of course, along Juan de Fuca Straits and the ocean. Indians on the Makah, Ozette, Quilleute, Copalis, and Quinault Indian reservations on the coast do considerable fishing, but the headquarters for the main fishing firms are along Puget Sound and Grays Harbor. Oyster culture is carried on along Hood Canal, and Quilcene Bay is a particularly good place for raising oysters because of its sheltered position. The winds and tides do not disturb the young oysters greatly during the time they float loose on top of the water before attaching themselves to solid material.

Willapa Hills

South of Grays Harbor—the dividing line between the Olympic Peninsula and the Willapa Hills—lumbering, fishing, and farming are the main occupations, as they are to the north. In the Willapa Hills area, however, agriculture is much more advanced because the country is less rugged and the forests have been cleared to a greater degree than in the Olympics. The highest elevation there is below three thousand feet, and the rainfall is much less, the mean annual precipitation being seventy-five inches. Also there is much more open land in the eastern part of the Willapa area, where it merges into Puget Sound proper, than there is in the Olympic Peninsula. The Willapa Peninsula includes Pacific, Wahkiakum, and parts of Grays Harbor, Lewis, and Cowlitz counties.

The fact that Grays Harbor can accommodate ocean-going vessels makes Hoquiam and Aberdeen important shipping centers for the lumber and food products from the area. The port of Willapa Harbor on the outskirts of Raymond has also been dredged to allow ships to enter it.

Lumbering and its allied products follow the pattern in the Willapa Hills which was described above for the Olympics, but there are variations for both fishing and agriculture. For example, fish canneries pack salmon, tuna, and oysters in the Grays Harbor area. In fact, oyster beds are so numerous that a town on the North Peninsula, the long neck of land which makes the western boundary of Willapa Bay, is actually called Oysterville.

In the early 1850's when settlers were just beginning to move north of the Columbia River, beds of the small native Olympia oysters were found in the Willapa inlets and shipped to California, where the gold seekers were in need of food, at such a rate that the beds were fished out. Many years later, Japanese oyster seeds were introduced. They grew well except that a new supply had to be brought almost every year because the water was too cold for the oysters to spawn as successfully as they did in Japanese waters. During World War II, seed could not be secured, and an attempt was made to bring the native oyster beds back into commercial production. This has been sufficiently successful that oyster producers are optimistic about the prospect. Dungeness crabs, which are packed in the Willapa region, are regarded as another shellfish delicacy.

South of Hoquiam and Aberdeen, there is a swampy area that abounded in native cranberries during the pioneer period, and these are now produced commercially. Elsewhere in much of the cutover ground, the grass cover is sufficiently abundant to support herds of dairy cattle.

Puget Sound

The third geographical province is Puget Sound, which extends to the foothills of the Olympics and the Willapa Hills on the west and the foothills of the Cascades on the east. It includes San Juan, Island, Kitsap, part of Mason, Thurston, Lewis, Cowlitz, Clark, and parts of Pierce, King, Snohomish, Skagit, and Whatcom counties.

In this section, the basic industries of lumbering, fishing, and farming are carried on as described above, but, in addition, the presence of excellent harbors in the Sound plus the climatic and scenic attractions has resulted in the growth of cities. Neil Morgan, in his interesting study of our social and economic pattern, *Westward Tilt, the American West Today,* states that Seattle now has the greatest density of population of any western city; is the fourth largest city in the West; the nineteenth largest in the country; and claims to be the third largest market in the West (Los Angeles and San Francisco ranking first and second).

Seattle and the other coast cities form the state's manufacturing center, as well. Soft coal deposits along the east side of the Sound region are conveniently located for this purpose. Seattle, Tacoma, Olympia, Everett, and the other cities offer a market sufficient to encourage limited manufacturing of clothing, household equipment, and construction materials, such as bricks and cement blocks, which are too heavy in proportion to their value to be shipped profitably.

Although the amount of coal and iron ore in Washington has not been enough to warrant the manufacture of steel for export to the East, two steel rolling mills in Seattle supply some of the steel used in the Pacific Northwest. They have been able to compete with eastern mills in spite of having to import much of the necessary raw materials. A Seattle manufacturer also maintains a successful glass factory. The local advantage in glassware comes from the fact that it is uneconomical to ship it from the East because of the extra air space paid for in sending jars, bottles, and so forth. Flat glass is shipped so much more easily that it is not produced in the Pacific Northwest.

It was mentioned earlier that shipbuilding and aircraft manufacture are industries in the Seattle area. Airplane manufacture started in this area originally in 1916 because William Boeing, who had a small plant in Seattle at that time making his own private planes, was asked by the United States government to build them for use in World War I. The plant has remained there even though much material has to be imported for plane manufacture. Making such vehicles is profitable, however, because they do not depend on any other means of transportation for their distribution. They can be flown, just as the ships can be navigated on the water. The same principle applies to the railroad cars built in Renton. They can be attached to a railroad engine and towed away with other cars. At first, the manufacturers made railroad logging cars; then they expanded their factory to include refrigerator cars and other types of rolling stock.

Puget Sound has five of the eight aluminum plants built in Washington—three at Vancouver (a smelter, a wire and cable factory, and an extrusion mill), one at Longview, and one at Tacoma. Of the remaining three, one is in Wenatchee and two are in the Spokane suburbs.

The excellent shipping facilities by water, rail, truck, and air have added to the impetus for expanding the processing of lumber and food products on Puget Sound. Fish, fruits (including berries), vegetables, and meats are canned and frozen for wide sale; dairy and poultry products are shipped out; pulp, paper, and plywood products are made from wood at an increasing rate; flower bulbs are raised in great quantities for sale.

Cascade Mountains

The fourth geographic division of Washington consists of the Cascade Mountains, which narrow from one hundred miles in the north to around fifty miles in the south. The height of the ridges (except for the five volcanic peaks described earlier) varies from four thousand feet in the south to eight thousand feet in the north. As has been indicated, the precipitation on the west side of the mountains, an annual average of one hundred inches (much of it snow), is much heavier than on the east, with as little as fifteen inches in the eastern foothills. The Cascades include eastern Whatcom, Skagit, Snohomish, King, Pierce, Lewis, and Skamania counties and western Okanogan, Chelan, Kittitas, Yakima, and Klickitat counties.

Lumbering is an important industry in these mountains as well as in the Olympics because of the evergreen forests which tend more to a mixture of pines and firs, with fewer Douglas firs, than is true farther west. Because of the ruggedness of the land, there are few towns, and for the most part the trees are cut and hauled by truck to sawmills toward the foot of the mountains.

In addition to forests, there are valuable minerals in the Cascades. In fact, much of our mining is done there. The coal beds mentioned above extend through the Cascades, and, in addition, there are deposits of gold, silver, copper, lead, zinc, mercury, iron, manganese, chromium, and tungsten. In a later chapter, we shall discuss the development of mining throughout the state.

The grandeur of the scenery in the Cascades makes them, like the Sound and the Olympic and Willapa peninsulas, a superb vacation spot. The fact that there are excellent snow fields in the Cascades near Seattle and Tacoma draws hundreds of people from those cities to the mountains for skiing each weekend during many months of the year. The federal government has made Mount Rainier a national park, in which the plant and animal life are protected as in the Olympic National Park. Tourists from all over the country are attracted to western Washington by its recreational features.

In the foothills of the Cascades where the timber has been cut, there is some farming, but the west slopes are too steep even for much grazing. On the eastern slopes, poultry and cattle are raised on the cutover ground.

Okanogan Highlands Province

The Okanogan Highlands province, while not so high and rugged as the Cascades, is another mountainous area, ranging from four thousand to eight thousand feet high. This area includes Pend Oreille, Stevens, and Ferry counties and eastern Okanogan County.

Mining is important, particularly in the eastern part where gold, silver, zinc, lead, molybdenum, magnesite, and tungsten are found. In 1934, Ferry and Stevens counties produced 81 per cent of the gold of the state, and, for nine consecutive years, Ferry County was responsible for 52.3 per cent of the gold, silver, copper, and lead mined in Washington. In recent years, low prices for lead and zinc have caused curtailment of much mining of these metals in Stevens County, and the proportion of nonmetallic minerals has risen. In the 1961 *Minerals Yearbook,* the ores in the order of their dollar-yield for Ferry County were: gold, silver, sand and gravel, stone, copper; for Stevens, uranium, magnesite, stone, barite, sand and gravel, lead, zinc, gold, silver, and grinding pebbles. This is also the area where the clays are rich in aluminum and magnesium ores which, it is hoped, may some day be turned into aluminum and magnesium products.

Although the forested slopes do not equal those of the Cascades in quality and quantity of timber, lumbering is a prominent industry. The Okanogan, Sanpoil, Kettle, Columbia, Colville, and Pend Oreille (or Clark Fork) rivers cut down through the mountains from north to south. In these valleys, farming occurs, ranging from cattle and sheep raising on the dryer slopes to fruit and truck farming in the lowlands. Irrigation is used in some parts. Wheat is produced where the rainfall is sufficient. The precipitation varies from around fifteen inches in the western and southern parts to twenty-five inches in the eastern section.

Columbia Basin Province

The Columbia Basin province extends south from the Okanogan Highlands to the Blue Mountains and from the Idaho border to the edge of the Cascades on the west, including Spokane, Whitman, northern Garfield, Columbia, and Walla Walla counties; Franklin, Benton, Adams, Lincoln, Grant, and Douglas counties; and eastern Chelan, Kittitas, Yakima, and Klickitat counties.

The Columbia River is, of course, the chief geographical phenomenon in the region, and its importance is well-known to any Washington resident. It is one of the great rivers of the world; draining an area of 259,000 square miles, the Columbia is the ninth longest river in existence, approximately 1,200 miles long. Its immense possibilities for hydroelectric power come from the fact that it falls so rapidly from its source to its mouth. During its course of 520 miles in Canada, the Columbia drops 1,378 feet, and in the United States section 1,287 feet. It is estimated that the entire river contains over 30 per cent of the potential hydroelectric power of the United States.

We now have three dams in Washington and Oregon with a capacity of over one million kilowatts each: Grand Coulee, 1,944,000; Chief Joseph, 1,024,000; and The Dalles, 1,119,000. Bonneville dam produces 518,400 kilowatts. There are eleven smaller dams operating on the Columbia River system and five others under construction. This network will be described in greater detail in chapter 9. Much more power will still be required in the Pacific Northwest to supply the increasing domestic and industrial demand for electricity. The need is sufficiently great now that Congress in 1962 authorized the construction of a plant at Hanford for the production of electricity by atomic energy. By the end of 1965, it is expected that 900,000 kilowatts of firm power will be available from this source.

The topography of the eastern Palouse Hills and the channeled scablands to the west were described in connection with our geological development. The rainfall varies from a scant seven inches in the western part to twenty inches in the eastern part. The latter amount of rainfall is sufficient for the dry farming of wheat and peas, the chief products of the Palouse area. The western sections— the Walla Walla, Yakima, Ellensburg, and Wenatchee valleys—have for many years produced excellent fruits and vegetables by the use of irrigation. Wenatchee has long been famous for its apples, which are sold even in the East; Ellensburg for its dairying, potatoes, and grains; Yakima for its hops, sugar beets, potatoes, and soft fruits, including pears, grapes, cherries, and peaches; Walla Walla for its peas, asparagus, and other vegetables. Canneries and freezing plants in these areas have increased greatly since the beginning of World War II. With the construction of Grand Coulee Dam, water is being made available gradually to extend the irrigated area from Pasco to the bend of the Columbia on the north. Cattle ranches are numerous along the Snake River in the area west of the wheat country where water is not yet available for irrigation.

Spokane is the main city in the Columbia Basin. In fact, it serves an area called the "Inland Empire," an economic unit which is not limited to any one state, or even nation, but which has the same type of geography and industries. Its boundaries are usually given as follows: the northern edge running through the middle of Kootenai, Lower Arrow, and Okanagan lakes in British Columbia, Canada; the eastern boundary lying just east of Missoula, Montana; the southern line running south of Pendleton, Oregon; and the western edge extending slightly beyond Yakima and Ellensburg. Mountains shut in this region in such a way that railroads and highways funnel more easily into Spokane than into cities in the neighboring states and Canada. In a later chapter, we shall see that there have been proposals to make a state out of the Inland Empire. The name "Lincoln" has been suggested for it.

Because of its position at the end of an easy east-west pass, Spokane has been a shipping center from the fur-trade period to the present time. Wood- and food-processing plants are numerous there now, and it has been mentioned earlier that aluminum mills were located in the Spokane area at the time of World War II. One at Mead reduces the imported bauxite first to alumina (aluminum and oxygen) and then to pig aluminum. The one at Trentwood is a rolling mill that converts these chunks of aluminum into sheets, most of

which are shipped east for use in the final manufacturing of items requiring aluminum.

The Tri-City area of the Columbia Basin province (Pasco, Kennewick, and Richland) is growing at a very fast rate as a result of various aspects of the development of Grand Coulee Dam. For example, in 1943 the United States Atomic Energy Commission chose Richland as the site of the Hanford Atomic Works because of its nearness to the source of large amounts of electric power and because of the sparse population in the outlying area, which had to be removed to other places in the interests of secrecy and safety. The population of the Tri-City area was 6,078 in 1940; 42,143 in 1950; 52,314 in 1960. During the war years, it was even higher, since in 1944 sixty thousand workers were employed in connection with the Hanford project. Farming in the district has increased with the growth of population and with the extension of irrigation resulting from the completion of Grand Coulee Dam.

Blue Mountains

The seventh geographical section of the state is the Blue Mountains province, consisting of the part of Washington just north of the Oregon boundary—Asotin County and the southern parts of Garfield, Columbia, and Walla Walla counties. This region is probably most famous as a sports area where hunters and fishermen are attracted by the birds, deer, elk, and other game animals and by the trout in the rivers. The mountains, although not high by comparison with the Cascades and Olympics, are so rugged that very little farming is done, sheep and cattle raising being the principal forms of agriculture. For the same reason, the timber has been relatively inaccessible, also. With the prospect of opening up more sections of Idaho and Oregon along the difficult Hell's Canyon section of the Snake River, however, there will be greater resulting activity in the Washington part of the Blue Mountains.

The Grand Ronde River near the Blue Mountains. One can easily see why the pioneers found this to be one of the most difficult parts of the journey west. (Photo by the Washington State Department of Commerce and Economic Development)

Indian Culture

2

Most anthropologists are now agreed that the American Indians are of Mongoloid blood. The first bands probably crossed the Bering Strait to this continent from Siberia during the last glacial stage (called the Wisconsin), which began about seventy-five thousand years ago and lasted, with intermittent warm periods, until about nine thousand years ago. People ordinarily suppose that the ice was constant in the Arctic area during the many thousands of years when the various glaciers in our own region came and went. Similar fluctuations, however, did occur in the Far North, and geologists have evidence that the central interior of northern Alaska was never covered by glaciers. They also believe that a corridor along Alaska's Arctic Ocean boundary into the valley of the Mackenzie River was free of ice as early as twenty-five thousand years ago. This may have provided a possible route for the gradual extension of bands of Indians into the interior of the continent.

From the Mackenzie River Valley, the migrants could then have fanned out to the east and south in present Canada through whatever passages were free of ice. In due course, the descendants of these early tribes did reach all parts of North and South America, changing their culture over the centuries to fit the needs of the different environments.

The chain of Aleutian Islands between North Asia and Alaska was once considered the probable crossing place for the first migrants. The theory was that a group reached the first island in a crude boat, stayed there perhaps a hundred years or more, and then some of that generation moved on to the next island. This process could have repeated itself until the eastern mainland was reached. It was also thought that the islands at the time might have formed a continuous land bridge and that sections of it later collapsed, leaving the present islands. Geologists now think, however, that such a land bridge fell into the ocean before human life was present. They also believe that the earliest Indian tribes on this continent had not yet learned the use of boats. Therefore, the Bering Strait furnishes a more likely crossing place. In the winter, the ice becomes solid enough that groups of people could walk across it, carrying their Stone Age belongings. Another possibility is that enough ocean water was formed into the ice sheets (5,000 feet thick in some places) to lower the sea level 150 feet or more, an amount sufficient to allow people to cross the Strait on dry land. The presence of horses, elephants, and other large animals on this continent during part of the glacial period indicates that some land approach existed from Asia to this continent.

With the discovery of the heavy (radioactive) carbon method for dating remains of organic materials (plants or bones, for example), it has become possible to date with more accuracy than heretofore such objects dug up by archeologists. In the Pacific Northwest, radiocarbon tests have indicated that grass sandals found under Fort Rock Cave in south-central Oregon are from 8,700 to 9,300 years old, and burned bison bones in excavations made in Lind Coulee near Warden, Washington, are from 8,300 to 9,100 years old.

If these dates are accurate, prehistoric Indians were in this region much earlier than scientists used to think; therefore, they would have had to be on this continent many hundreds of years previously to have reached the Pacific Northwest by that time. They may even have approached this area by a route from the south if they came down from Canada through the Great Plains province east of the Rocky Mountains and then turned back north through another open section in present New Mexico, Nevada, and northern California. Research on the routes used by the early Indian tribes will continue, and from the location of dated artifacts, anthropologists may be able to trace the migrations. If a particular utensil appears, even in a changed form, in various areas, it may suggest routes by which the tribes advanced.

It is interesting to note that scholars used to think that if the cultures of two peoples in different parts of the world resembled each other, they must have been in contact at some early period in their development. Since the Indians showed certain cultural traits found not only in Asiatic groups, but in eastern Europe, Malaya, Egypt, and even in Celtic countries, several theories were advanced to try to explain how the Indians could have met peoples in these various places.

One theory was that the Indians were the descendants of one or more of the ten lost tribes of Israel mentioned in the Bible, who had wandered over Europe and Asia before crossing to this continent. Another theory was that the prehistoric Indian tribes had gone west from Asia across Europe and then had come via a land bridge to a once-existent continent in the middle of the Atlantic Ocean. From this continent (called Atlantis by many people), the Indians were thought to have continued to North America by means of another land bridge. After some of the groups had reached the Americas, the continent of Atlantis was believed to have fallen into the ocean, leaving North America separated from Europe as it is now. If such a continent ever existed, however, scientists conclude that it had disappeared before human life was present.

One man, who could find little similarity between language or physical characteristics of Indians and those of other races, advanced the theory that the Indians were a separate race, originating on this continent and having no relationship to any other. Both Biblical and scientific explanations of man's creation, however, point to a dispersion of early races from some central area, probably western Asia.

Several years ago, the Kon-Tiki expedition, which was made on a raft from the west coast of South America across the Pacific to the South Pacific islands, was intended to demonstrate that primitive boats could have made the trip. The Heyerdahl expedition made the return voyage eastward to the Pacific coast, a much more difficult feat in view of the prevailing winds. Some people who note the similarities of Pacific island culture to that of the American Indians think that our Indians came from one of the Polynesian islands in crude boats. Anthropologists believe, however, that whatever travel occurred in either direction came so much later than the arrival of the prehistoric Indian tribes that no modification of physical characteristics and scarcely any cultural change resulted from such contact.

Finding no acceptable evidence for the arrival of our first Indians by any of these Atlantic or South Pacific routes leaves us with the route from Siberia via the Bering Strait as the most feasible one, according to the information which scientists have at the present time.

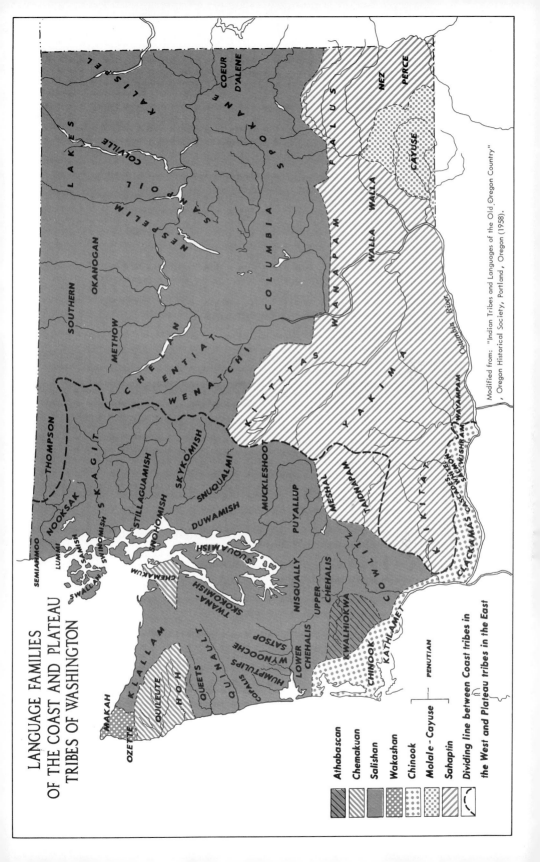

LANGUAGE FAMILIES
OF THE COAST AND PLATEAU
TRIBES OF WASHINGTON

Modified from: "Indian Tribes and Languages of the Old Oregon Country", Oregon Historical Society, Portland, Oregon (1958).

Athabascan
Chemakuan
Salishan
Wakashan
Chinook
Molale – Cayuse
Sahaptin

PENUTIAN

*Dividing line between Coast tribes in
the West and Plateau tribes in the East*

KALISPEL
COEUR D'ALENE
LAKES
COLVILLE
SPOKANE
OKANOGAN
SANPOIL
NESPELIM
SOUTHERN OKANOGAN
METHOW
CHELAN
WENATCHI
ENTIAT
COLUMBIA
PALUS
NEZ PERCE
CAYUSE
WALLA WALLA
WANAPAM
KITTITAS
YAKIMA
KLIKITAT
MESHAL
TAIDNAPAM
COWLITZ
TOPPENISH
WAYAMPAM
SKIN SALMON
CLACKAMAS
THOMPSON
NOOKSAK
SEMIAHMOO
LUMMI
SWALLAH
SAMISH
SWINOMISH
SKAGIT
STILLAGUAMISH
SKYKOMISH
SNOHOMISH
SNUQUALMI
DUWAMISH
MUCKLESHOOT
PUYALLUP
NISQUALLY
UPPER CHEHALIS
CHEMAKUM
SUQUAMISH
TWANA-SKOKOMISH
SATSOP
WYNOOCHE
LOWER CHEHALIS
COPALIS
HUMPTULIPS
QUINAULT
QUEETS
HOH
QUILEUTE
OZETTE
MAKAH
KLALLAM
KWALHIOKWA
CHINOOK
KATHLAMET
Columbia River

COAST INDIAN CULTURE

We have noted how the Cascades now divide the Pacific Northwest into two very different regions. In prehistoric times these mountains made a barrier so formidable that the culture of the Indian groups west of the Cascades differed greatly from that between the Cascades and the Rocky Mountains. Anthropologists call the tribes west of the Cascades *Pacific Northwest* or *Coast Indians* and those east of the Cascades *Plateau Indians*. Those east of the Rockies are called *Plains Indians*. Because the culture of the Coast Indians was oriented so completely toward water, they are also known as "Canoe" Indians, whereas the interior tribes were so associated with horses that they are called "Horse" Indians.

It is easy to see why the life of the Coast Indians was centered around water since they were on the edge of the ocean and had, in addition, many rivers and lakes near the sea. In fact, salmon was the foundation of their food supply, and they also ate many other kinds of fish—shellfish, lampreys, herring, smelts, cod, trout, halibut, and even whales. A dead whale was sometimes washed up on the shore, where it would be cut up and divided among the local Indians. The blubber would be edible even if the rest of the meat had spoiled. Tribes to the north, from British Columbia to southern Alaska, built canoes sturdy enough to go out to sea to kill whales, which were then towed back to shore. The tribes most adept at whaling were north of Washington, on Vancouver Island and Queen Charlotte Islands, but three of our tribes—the Makahs, Quinaults, and Quilleutes, just south of the entrance to Juan de Fuca Straits—did go out in the ocean to kill whales, and the Klallams along the south side of the Straits caught whales which came in there.

Not only did the coast region provide the Indians with fish, but also abundant wood from which canoes for fishing in the rivers and ocean were constructed. The canoes were used for practically all traveling, since the Indian villages were nearly always built at the mouth of a river emptying into the ocean where the people were near both salt and fresh water and where there were usually good beaches for landing canoes. There was very little inland travel, because the Coast Indians did not like to go through the dense forests that extended at nearly all points to the water's edge. For this reason, they had no need of horses, which were so necessary to the well-being of the inland tribes.

Houses

The Indians used wood to build their houses, which were surprisingly large in view of the kind of tools they used. Before the coming of the white man, the Indians had no metal implements. Adzes and hammers were ground from hard stone. A kind of jadeite that made particularly good blades was found on the Fraser River, and the Indians there traded it to other tribes. The blades were tied onto wooden handles with cord woven from cedar bark or spruce roots. The men used animal horns also as blades for chisels.

Red cedar trees were preferred for the posts and planks of the houses, but they were difficult to fell and transport by hand. A grove on the shore of a stream, where the trees would fall into the water when they were cut, was considered a great prize because the logs could be floated to the village. Much of some families' wealth came from their claiming such a grove of trees. This was particularly true on the west coast of Vancouver Island where red cedar trees, large enough for the great whaling canoes, grew at the edge of the water in some places. In our area, where there were not enough trees on water, even of house size, people used drift logs wherever possible. The remainder had to be felled and then rolled and dragged to the site for the house.

When a man felt the need of a bigger house and was wealthy enough to have the support of other members of his village, he persuaded them to help him. When they found a suitable tree of sufficient size, they cut away at it with their stone or horn chisels until it fell. On our part of the coast, they used fire in an ingenious manner to hasten the fall of the tree. Near the tree they started a fire and put stones in it until they became hot enough to char wood. They dug out a V-shaped niche toward the bottom of the tree and then, with wooden tongs, put a hot stone into the niche and scraped away the charred wood as it formed. If the wood became so hot that there was danger of fire starting, the men dipped seaweed or leaves into water and stuck them above and below the burning point. When the tree was almost burned through, a niche was cut on the opposite side of the tree at the correct place to cause the tree to fall at a point where it could be rolled down to a river or to the village itself. The branches were chipped off and the top burned off to give the right height for the post.

Fortunately, red cedar splits easily into planks, and the Indians could split planks from living trees if they did not need the trunks for posts. A man would chip away a niche near the base of the tree and then climb it to the correct height, chip another niche to the same depth, insert wooden wedges, and pry with a pole until the strip split off. (The Nootkan Indians were so skilled at this that they could split out a wedge big enough for a canoe. They dug the niches to the heart of the tree, inserted a pole, and went home to wait for the next big windstorm to break out the slab.) The thinner planks were used around a framework of posts to make walls for a house. When both a post and planks were needed, the men could split off planks from a fallen tree and leave the center of the log for a house post.

Even when the posts and planks could be floated down a river to the village, the Indians had to carry or drag them to the proper location and raise the posts to an upright position. Without modern tools, this would seem impossible. The Indians, however, used pieces of logs as levers in a clever fashion. First they dug a hole with one straight and one sloping side. They then pushed one end of the post down into the hole and rolled another log down the sloping side under the post at a right angle to it. As the log rolled down the incline, it automatically pushed the post into an upright position, and then the earth was filled in around it.

Posts were set around the area to be enclosed, which was very large since several families occupied one house. When the first white explorers appeared, they found that important chiefs had houses several hundred feet long. Ten families lived in Chief Seattle's one-hundred-foot-long house, which was much smaller than that of his brother. Either the planks were placed in the ground in an upright position around the house, making a vertical wall, or they were tied with cedar rope to the posts in a horizontal manner, overlapping each other (somewhat in the form of a present-day Venetian blind) to shed rain.

For very long, narrow houses, the Indians built a shedlike roof, sloping in one direction, usually from front to back. In wider houses, however, they used a gable, with crossbeams fitted into notches chiseled on top of the posts. Spruce root strips, which are strong, were also tied round the point where the post and the cross-beam joined to give added support. The builders then placed short-er posts on top of the crossbeams to which the ridgepole was fas-tened. Raising the extremely long ridgepole fifteen or twenty feet in the air was the most amazing feat in the housebuilding. The men did that also by means of levers. They placed one log across anoth-er in the form of a teeter-totter. When the high end was pulled down, the top of the ridgepole rose to the top of the post prepared for it. It was tied in place, and the other end was raised by the same procedure.

Posts were then slanted down from the ridgepole to the top of the walls, and planks were fastened across these to finish the sloping roof. The builders left the ends of the roof planks loose at various points above the spots where fires were to be built on the floor of the house so that smoke could escape through the openings.

Canoes

Making the dugout canoes required such specialized skill that the craftsmen believed they required the aid of powerful spirits to be successful. Popular guardian spirts were Axe, Wedge, Adze, Woodpecker, and Cedar Tree. If a canoe maker could find a hol-low log of the right size, he felt that his protecting spirit had been particularly helpful because he did not have to scoop out much of the log once it was split in two. The craftsman chose one half of the log and first shaped it roughly by splitting off pieces of wood. The inside of a firm log was then hollowed out by burning it slowly enough that successive layers of charred wood could be scraped away. Since the canoe needed to be wider in the middle than at the ends, the canoe-makers ingeniously stretched the center by filling the hollowed log with water, dumping in hot stones, and steaming the sides until they were pliable. They then dipped out the water and inserted yew poles of the desired width at various points. When the wood dried, it held this shape, and the poles were left in as seats in the dugout.

The big whaling canoes might be fifty feet long and over six feet thick. The Nootkan tribes on Vancouver Island made the best ca-

This sketch shows dugout canoes of Coast Indians and a wooden house of the type seen after tools of white settlers were available. (An etching in J. G. Swan's The Northwest Coast, *New York, 1857)*

noes, but our Makah Indians made some as well. People in other tribes sometimes hired the skillful canoe makers to build whaling canoes. These and smaller canoes meant for travel on the ocean had pointed ends that could cut through rough water. The ends were made from separate pieces of cedar and were attached to the body of the canoe with pegs. To make the holes into which the wooden pegs fitted, the canoe builder twirled a piece of bone round and round until it ground through the wood. Pegs chipped to the right size were then inserted or cedar rope was run through the holes and tied. The poles used as seats were fastened in the same way.

Canoes used in the rivers were called "shovel-nosed" canoes because of their blunt ends. This type was beautifully designed for shallow water and could be poled. The paddles were made from hard wood and sanded smooth with sharkskin.

Dishes

The Coast Indians made many other objects from wood, even dishes. They had no pottery, probably because wood was plentiful, and they had become so skilled in working with it that they did not need another medium. The men carved bowls from cedar in the form of miniature shovel-nosed canoes, small ones for the use of an individual and others several feet long for serving bowls. Wealthy chiefs had elaborate ones for feasts. Some preserved in museums are carved in the form of a man or animal. One example, done by a Kwakiutl Indian north of Washington, is of a man more than life size, lying down, the head carved and painted, the middle portion of the body hollowed out to form an enormous dish, the knees bent slightly up, supporting two small bowls, also carved in the form of miniature men and with another small bowl attached. The small bowls were used to hold oil pressed from candlefish, which was used to season food much as we use salad dressing at the present time. Indians south of British Columbia made large bowls for feasts, but the carving and decoration were less elaborate.

Ladles and spoons were carved from wood and also from horns of animals. The curved mountain-sheep horns were highly prized for ladles, and the Washington tribes traded for them farther north where they were more plentiful. When the horn was steamed, the bowl of the spoon could be easily cut out.

Totem Poles

The Indians in Washington did not make totem poles. It was the tribes farther north in British Columbia who carved the lavish designs in posts to tell the family history. Our northern tribes did, however, carve posts inside their houses. They also carved wooden masks, representing animals or mythical creatures, which were worn by people participating in ceremonial dances.

Baskets and Mats

In addition to working with stone, wood, and horn, our Washington Indians produced beautiful baskets and mats from tree and grass fibers. These were made by the women of a village who collected the necessary materials during the summer when they were on fishing or berry-gathering trips with the men of the tribe. The women also went out from their winter villages in pairs or larger groups to collect fibers.

Indian Baskets made by tribes in Washington State. (Washington State University Library)

Each woman brought back cedar and spruce roots, cedar bark, colored grasses, and many other plants. At home, she sorted these materials and stored them until winter, when she had time to work with them. First she dyed the grasses used for decoration. Swamp mud made them black; the root of the Oregon grape yellow. Wild cherry bark could be rubbed to a red color. Bear grass, which grew in the mountains, was very much desired for use in ornamenting baskets.

The next task was to prepare the fibers for weaving the basket itself. The basketmaker soaked the plant fibers until they were soft and then pulled them into threads that could be coiled round and round, woven in and out (plaited), or twined in a kind of braid to make the basket. The Makahs, for example, did particularly fine work with wide strips of cedar bark from which they made flat baskets, canoes, sails, and mats. The mats were used as bedding on raised ledges of dirt or wood running around the inside of the plank houses and as tablecloths under food set on the floor. They were also made into women's skirts and a kind of rain cape, which had a hole in the center for one's head.

For these items made from wide strips of cedar bark, the Makahs used the plaiting method, a form of simple weaving where the horizontal strands are woven in and out through the vertical ones—over one, under one. Decoration on these consisted of the rhythmic use of occasional strands dyed black. Tribes farther south laid cattails side by side and strung them together with fibers from nettles, using a big wooden needle.

The Chinooks, at the mouth of the Columbia River, excelled in making twined baskets from cattails and cedar bark. In this type, the vertical strands (warp) are laid side by side and then two horizontal strands (weft) are twined around and between them, crossing each other almost in a braided fashion.

The Indians along the Cowlitz River were noted for their coiled baskets in which the warp thread is not vertical, but coils round and round from the bottom to the top of the basket. The warp was ordinarily a bunch of cedar fibers.

Wool Weaving

Some of our Salish tribes from the southern end of Vancouver Island and along the Straits to the Fraser River and south into Puget Sound did a unique type of weaving from the wool of mountain goats and from a little woolly dog raised for that purpose by the Puget Sound Indians. The Salish people along the Fraser River killed mountain goats or, otherwise, in the spring they pulled hunks of wool off bushes which the goats had brushed against when shedding.

Woolly dogs were raised along the Sound and along Juan de Fuca Straits. They have died out now, but some of the early white explorers made paintings of them, and they resembled a Pomeranian. The Indian women raised the dogs for their wool, often keeping them on an island in the Sound or the Straits, paddling out to the island each day to feed them. Mussel shells were used as knives to clip off the wool. A woman worked it into strands by combing it with her fingers and rolling it against her leg. The next step was to spin it into thread by the use of a wooden spindle that consisted of a circular piece of wood with a hole in the middle pushed onto a long stick. She twirled it round and round against the wool, which was spun into yarn by the motion.

The loom was made from two upright posts set into the earth of the house floor. Two crosswise pieces were run through holes bored in the posts, and the warp threads, which could be cedar bark, nettles, or goat wool when it was obtainable, were strung over them. A woman wove dog- or goat-wool yarn in and out of the warp threads to make warm, fluffy blankets, called Salish blankets. If the weaver did not have enough animal wool, she extended it with feathers, milkweed fluff, nettle, or whatever she could get. The blankets were used as robes in cold weather and as bedding.

Clothing

The clothing of the Coast Indians differed greatly from that of the Plateau Indians, who wore the skin leggings, moccasins, and shirts regarded by most whites as conventional Indian costume. The inland tribes needed such clothing as protection in the more severe climate. On the coast, however, the need was not for protection against the cold so much as against rain. The cedar bark capes, mentioned above, were ideal for this purpose, and some of the tribes even added conical-shaped hats made of spruce root or grass fibers which served the same purpose as the plastic rain hats of the present time.

In winter, they wore the woven blankets of dog wool, already described, or robes made from animal skins. Wealthy men wore the beautiful sea-otter skins and bearskins. They also wore skin caps, sometimes made from birds. Poorer people used the skins of wildcats, raccoons, and other smaller animals sewed together. Holes were punched at the edge of a skin, and a thong of skin laced through the holes to tie the skins together.

In warm weather, the men wore only a breechclout or no clothing at all, as a rule. The women wore skirts of shredded cedar bark. The inner bark of the red cedar comes off in stiff sections, but the women used a wooden chopper to pound it into shreds that were comparatively soft and very light. These strips were tied in the middle to a cord made of nettles which was left long enough to tie like a sash at the waist. The result was a skirt of thick fringe which resembled somewhat the grass skirts of Hawaii.

Because the Coast Indians had their feet in water so much, they went barefooted. The Coast tribes who lived upriver from the ocean or the Sound, where they did a great deal more walking than the ones right on the sea, did wear moccasins, usually made from a single piece of deerskin with the fur worn next to the foot. The Indians living in the mountainous areas on the west slopes of the Cascades or in the Olympics adopted other features of Plateau culture which were suited to their weather conditions, such as skin shirts and leggings or skirts.

The wealthy Coast Indians liked to wear jewelry. They made necklaces, earrings, nose ornaments, and other pieces of body decoration from the materials at hand—shells, claws, animal teeth. Pieces of abalone shell were very popular because of its turquoise color. A small white shellfish, dentalium, was so highly prized that strings of dentalium shells were used as money as well as necklaces. Both men's and women's ears were pierced for earrings, not only on the lobe but around the edge of the ear so that the entire ear was decorated with many pieces of shells. Men wore ornaments in their nose by having the septum pierced and a shell pushed through the hole. Men of the northern Washington Coast tribes pierced their lower lip and wore a piece of shell in it, too.

Food

In connection with the making of canoes, we have mentioned the dependence of the Coast Indians on fish as the foundation of their food supply. They had many ingenious methods of taking the fish both from the ocean and from rivers. They made hooks for halibut from bent wood, tipped with bone. Salmon were harpooned or scooped up in nets in the rivers during their trip from the ocean to their spawning grounds. In those days the salmon runs were so large that at times sections of the rivers were almost filled by the fish.

If the river was not too deep, the Indians built platforms about four feet above the water on which they could stand to dip the fish

Rapids on the Columbia River. The wooden platform in the lower part of the picture was used by the Indian fishermen in the manner described in chapter 2. (Watercolor and pencil sketch by William Birch McMurtrie, 1816-72. Courtesy, Museum of Fine Arts, Boston, Mass. M. & M. Karolik Collection)

from the river or to spear them. Building platforms in a river was another feat that would seem impossible to us without modern tools. The Indians managed by cutting poles and scraping the lower end of each one until it was pointed enough that good divers could drive them into the bottom of the river. Poles were tied across them horizontally, making a fence across the river. A second fence was built parallel to the first, and planks were laid across from one horizontal bar to the other to make a platform. A kind of loose matting of sticks was then stretched along the upstream fence to hold the salmon near the platforms. This kind of fishing trap is called a weir.

Men climbed up onto the platforms with dip nets and harpoons. The dip nets were simply baskets made of nettles with a yew-wood rim. The bottom ends of two poles were fastened at either side of the basket, and the top ends of the poles were tied together to make a handle which the fisherman held as he stood on the platform. He used the nets to dip up fish if the water was too muddy to see them; if it was clear enough, he harpooned them.

The harpoon had two heads of elkhorn. Each one was scraped to a point at one end with a notch at the other and fitted on either side of a spruce pole. Thongs or bark were tied around the horn to hold the head firm. A long rope was also tied to the heads so that if the spearhead came off the wooden shaft when it entered the fish, it would still be attached to the rope, which could be used to pull the fish in.

Baskets with one closed end and a funnel-shaped opening at the other were wedged between logs in very narrow streams to catch fish as they swam upstream. In a river where the bottom was too rocky to allow posts to be driven in, men stood on shore or on rocks out in the river to take the fish. In large rivers like the Columbia, men dragged large nets between boats to catch fish. They could also harpoon fish from canoes.

During the salmon runs, all of the people of a village moved to a fishing site where they set up rectangular shelters made of poles covered with mats. Here the men fished and the women dried large quantities of fish on racks over a slow fire to preserve food for winter months.

Eight or more men, including a harpooner and a steersman, took canoes thirty or forty feet long on the ocean to harpoon whales. Since it was a difficult feat, a great deal of preparation had to be made. Only those men who had acquired the aid of "powerful spirits" could undertake the task.

Once the men in the whaling canoes had killed a whale, all of the canoes in the area formed a line, and the men in each canoe helped pull on the rope to tow the prize to the village beach. The harpooner received the choice piece of the whale, the hump, and it was his privilege to apportion the whole carcass among the crew and the others who had helped to take the whale, and to distribute the remainder as he wished. A celebration went on for several days, ending in a feast at which the villagers ate the blubber that had been boiled to extract the oil. The oil represented great wealth since people were eager to trade other possessions for it.

In addition to taking fresh water and ocean fish, the Coast Indians killed some land animals for food, although, because they were afraid of the forests, they did far less hunting than the Plateau tribes. Besides, the Coast Indians had such quantities of fish readily available that they did not have much need for other meat except for variety. They stretched nets between tall poles to catch ducks as they flew, and quite often, when a bear, deer, or elk wandered onto a village beach, the men could chase it out into the water where they shot it with bows and arrows. A few men in most of the Coast tribes, who were very brave and had "unusual spirit power," did enter the forest to shoot game with a bow and arrow.

Besides meat, the Coast tribes ate crab apples, nuts, various kinds of roots (such as camas), ferns, lupine, cow parsnips, thistle, skunk cabbage, and berries (such as thimbleberries, gooseberries, huckleberries, Oregon grapes, and blackberries). The women gathered these plant foods, either near the village or on special trips to places where they grew best. Neither our Coast nor Plateau Indians were farmers; they simply gathered what grew. On the coast, particularly, the vegetation was so abundant that there was no difficulty in getting enough to eat during the spring and summer plus a sufficient amount to dry for winter use.

Camas roots were baked, dried, pounded into flour, and mixed with water to make cakes, corresponding to our loaves of bread. They were stored for winter use, when slices were hacked off and served with fish or seal oil, much as we eat bread and butter. The candlefish, mentioned earlier, was sought after because of its large amount of oil which was used as butter. The Coast Indians also dried berries and served them with oil.

The cooking methods of the Coast Indians were much like ours today. When they were at their summer fishing grounds, the women cleaned the fish as they were caught by the men and broiled them by putting fresh fish steaks onto sticks which were stuck into the ground around a fire.

Another outdoor method of cooking fresh meat was steaming or baking, similar to our use of barbecue pits. They dug a hole and built a fire in it. Stones were laid on the fire, meat was placed on the stones, leaves were laid over the meat to keep it clean, and water was added if steaming was desired. They then filled up the pit with dirt and left it for the proper amount of time. This was also the process used in cooking camas or other tough roots to soften them to the point where they could be dried and pounded into flour.

The third method of cooking was boiling or steaming, usually done inside the house. The women who were very skillful in basketry could make watertight baskets which could be used for cooking. Inside the big frame houses on the coast, each immediate family had a hearth where a fire was built on the dirt floor. The women brought in round, smooth stones of the right size and kept a pile of them around their fire. When a woman was ready to cook a meal, she put the stones into the fire and partly filled a basket with water. When the stones were hot, she picked up some with a forked stick wedged to make a pair of tongs and put them in the water. As they cooled, she added more hot stones to keep the water boiling. Ordinarily the dried meats and roots were cooked in this fashion, although when fresh fish or game animals were killed during the winter, they could be boiled, too.

The Coast Indians also used wooden utensils as cooking pots. Boiling in baskets was done more toward the south of our state and in wooden buckets or trays more to the north. The wooden vessels were either dug out of a solid piece of wood or put together in the form of a box by steaming the wood until it was pliable enough to bend into a box shape.

Indians felt that personal cleanliness was important, and on the coast, where water was plentiful, they were strict about daily baths and washing of hands. In fact, their table manners were more exacting in some respects than those of the present day. Before they sat down around the table mats laid on the floor, they washed their hands in a bucket of water and dried them on a towel of shredded cedar bark which was passed around. They also rinsed out their mouths with water and took a drink of water, since they never drank during a meal.

The food was served from a big wooden tray into an individual tray for each person. Everyone used a ladle of wood or horn as a spoon to dip the food from his plate, and he was expected to sip daintily from the tip. If a family was too poor to have ladles, they used clam shells. At the end of each course, a bucket of water and the cedar towel were passed in the way that finger bowls and napkins are used today. If a family had guests, the men ate first and then the women.

Social and Economic Life

Now that we have seen something of the type of plank houses, canoes, house furnishings, clothing, and food used by the coastal tribes, let us consider their social and economic life.

To begin with, we should understand what we mean by the word *tribe* as it applies to both our Coast and Plateau Indians. When Governor Isaac Stevens came out in 1854 just after Washington Territory had been created by Congress, he set about making treaties with the Indians as though a tribe were a political unit with a chief or council that could control the tribe. In some parts of the East, this was true, but our western tribes had no formal political organization. Each village was a separate unit, and although two neighboring villages might speak the same Indian language and be related by blood, their relations with each other were ordinarily purely social. They visited back and forth, and their young people might intermarry, but they had no political organization corresponding to our county or state where a group of towns or cities form a larger governmental unit.

On the coast, the life of each Indian was geared to the amount of wealth he had. This emphasis on accumulating private property was stronger in our Coast Indians than in tribes any place else in North America. We think of the typical Plains Indians as holding much of their property in common and as having few personal possessions other than horses. This was not true at all on our coast. The wealthiest man in a village was chief, and he became wealthiest ordinarily because he had inherited the right to fish at a particularly good place on the river or to take berries from some unusually lush spot. He believed, of course, that he had the aid of powerful spirits in securing his possessions. The other members of the village respected such rights of an individual and did not try to encroach on them. It is true that much of the work of fishing and gathering was done as a group and the food divided, but the division was made often on the basis of the rank of the members of the group.

The other wealthy families made up what would be considered the aristocrats of a European society, and the poorer people were the lower classes who were treated like "poor relations." If they occupied one of the large houses with a wealthier member, they had less comfortable equipment and fewer social privileges.

The emphasis on rank based on wealth was carried to the point where the Coast tribes held slaves in a separate slave class. Our Plateau tribes took captives in battle who were made slaves of the captors, but they were often accepted into the victorious tribe as members. Even if a captive remained a slave, he did so as an individual, not as a member of a slave class. On the coast, the slaves were not supposed to marry anyone outside of their class, and, in some villages, their masters even used a different language in speaking to them. They were bought and sold, and, if a family was wealthy enough to own one or more slaves, they did the menial work around the house which was otherwise done by the wives and female relatives of the owners of the house.

The wealthy Coast Indians developed almost a mania for displaying their riches and proving to the members of their own and neighboring villages that they were wealthier than their rivals. One of the results of the desire to boast of their wealth was the *potlatch,* a unique feature of Pacific Northwest Coast Indian culture. The term *potlatch* has now been corrupted by usage to mean any kind of banquet. In its original form, however, a potlatch was a tremendous feast given by a wealthy Coast Indian at which he gave away most or all of his possessions to guests who were expected to give him, in return, presents more valuable than the ones received. It was actually a means of earning interest on one's holdings.

A potlatch made too heavy demands on the host to be undertaken lightly. A wealthy man might prepare for the event for years, since he had to collect food enough to take care of several hundred visitors for weeks. In addition, he had to have stores of canoes, slaves, mats, blankets, jewelry, baskets, carved wooden boxes and dishes, food, and other objects which would be given to the guests in order of their rank—the most valuable gifts going to the guests of greatest wealth.

The host sent out messengers to invite people in neighboring villages to come to the feast. They came in their canoes, dressed in their finest clothing. The host's family entertained the guests with songs and dances on the beach until they went to the host's house where they were seated according to their rank. Then began the

feasting and entertainment which might last for a number of days. An orator recited the family history of the host to impress the guests with the wealth and honors which had been accumulated by his ancestors and himself, and relatives sang and danced, acting out these stories for the guests. On the last day of the potlatch, the host distributed the presents. If he had sufficient goods, he might break up a canoe or other type of gift to show that he was wealthy enough to throw away valuable possessions. Early white explorers reported that sometimes slaves were killed on such occasions to demonstrate the host's tremendous wealth.

A person who received a gift at a potlatch was disgraced if he could not return one of greater value at a similar celebration in due course of time. Thus each host anticipated getting back more than he gave. Even if he did not, however, he would not be in want, since he still possessed fishing grounds, berry patches, and so forth from which he could immediately begin to accumulate goods for trading again.

The wealthy Coast Indians had other means besides giving potlatches to show people that they were of high social rank. One mark of social distinction was to have a "flattened" head. Actually, such heads were made pointed rather than flat by means of tying boards (which elongated the head as it grew) at the back and front of a baby's forehead. Slaves were not allowed to deform their heads in this manner.

The coast people whose heads were flattened must not be confused with the Flathead tribe of northern Montana, who did not "flatten" their heads, but let them alone to grow naturally as the other inland tribes did. Historians do not know how the one inland group got the name of "Flatheads." One theory is that some early fur trader saw some Coast Indians with deformed heads among the Montana Indians and assumed that they were part of the inland tribe. Another possible explanation is that just after the fur traders had come from the coast area, they named the inland tribe Flatheads because their heads were normally flat rather than pointed.

Membership in secret societies was another means by which a

Painting of a Chinook woman with flattened head by Paul Kane. (Royal Ontario Museum, Canada)

Coast Indian demonstrated that he was a man of power and rank. A secret society was made up of men who had the same guardian spirit. A study of the guardian spirit belief brings us to a consideration of Indian religion in general.

The Indians (both Coast and Plateau) believed that every animate and inanimate object had a spirit because everything had once been a living creature back in the beginning of time. Even a rock or a cloud was a spirit in this sense. Such a religion is called *animism* by anthropologists. These spirits could either help or harm a human being. Therefore, the most important thing in life was to secure the aid of a powerful spirit who became one's guardian and provided success in whaling, hunting, battle, securing wealth, or in whatever field this particular guardian spirit was gifted.

When each Indian boy on the coast (and occasionally some of the girls), was nearing puberty, he was sent out into some remote place to find his guardian spirit. In the whaling tribes, to have the whale as one's guardian spirit would be the greatest good which could come to a boy. In those tribes, a young boy went to some wild part of the beach to find his spirit. In the more southern groups, a boy was extremely eager to have the aid of some fierce animal like a bear, for example, which would make him a great hunter. In some tribes, the eagle was the spirit that made a boy a chief; the hawk the one who gave him success in gambling. Even fog was a helpful spirit power, since it taught a person how to get away from his enemies. The spirit of wind could teach a boy to sing.

From the time he was old enough to understand the principle of the guardian spirit quest, a boy dreamed of his own vigil. In the wintertime, he watched the members of the secret societies performing the songs and dances taught them by their particular guardian spirits. So by the time a boy reached his teens, he felt a great excitement at the prospect of his coming adventure.

He had to get ready for the quest by purifying himself with baths, sometimes rubbing himself with bark or nettles until his skin was bleeding to get himself so clean that the spirits would not be offended by any smell of grease which they disliked. Some member of the tribe acted as his adviser, and, when the older man thought the boy was ready, he told him where to go and gave him final instructions. He went to some mountain or lake which would take him at least five days to reach, and he ate nothing during that time. In addition to fasting, he was to keep awake as much as possible. We have noted that the Coast Indians were afraid of the deep woods. One can imagine the terror a young boy would feel out alone in the dark away from his village, faint from hunger, and believing that he was surrounded by thousands of spirits, some of whom were monsters who might eat him and another of whom, He-Who-Shouts-in-the-Woods, might frighten him into insanity simply by shouting with his terrible voice.

At night the boy built a fire and waited to see if he had won sufficient approval from the desired spirit for it to speak to him. If his place of vigil was near a lake, he would dive into the icy water a specified number of times, come out, rub himself with twigs or some other rough material, and dive again. The boy never knew how the spirit would appear. It might come as an earthquake or as ghostly hands pulling at him. It might appear in a dream while he lay in a kind of exhausted trance. If, in the dream, he saw canoes full of people, it signified that he had the aid of the spirit of wealth. People would come to his potlatches. Spirits who could cure disease were the most powerful of all, but they did not take the form of an animal.

We can understand how, after such conditioning, a boy would ordinarily have the experience of a vision of some sort. Sometimes, however, it took a number of trips before he was successful. People who sought spirits who could cure diseases, even when they thought their early expeditions were favored, kept on until they were middle-aged. In some cases, a person never did find a guardian spirit. When that was true, he could not expect to have much success in life.

If a spirit did appear to a boy, it made itself known in some way, often by singing or dancing for him. If this was its sign, the boy then had to learn the song or dance. He also had to be certain that he had identified the spirit correctly. Consequently, after he returned home from his quest, he did not talk openly of his experiences. If during the next few years the boy found that he did seem to have unusual skill along the lines of his supposed spirit's power, he began to be more certain that he actually had the aid of the spirit who had presumably appeared to him. Then he would try to prepare himself to take part in the winter spirit dances.

If his spirit power was actually taking hold of him, he would feel sick, and his family or someone who knew many spirit songs would try to help him remember the song sung by his spirit at the time of his quest. If it appeared that he was successful, his family invited the members of the village to a feast during which they hoped he would perform his spirit dance. His family prepared a costume and painted his face according to the directions which had come to him from his spirit. They also tied a rope of cedar bark around his waist so that they could hold onto him because when he put on the costume, if it was the correct one, his spirit would seize him to such an extent that he would run wildly around and might injure himself by dashing against a wall or tree. His friends took turns running with him until he was exhausted. Meanwhile, the other guests feasted, and those who had already demonstrated their spirit power sang their songs and danced their spirit dances. Finally the young man would leap into the room and begin his own dance, and the others would imitate his words and gestures carefully since this was an aid in attaching his spirit to him permanently through the song and dance.

We have mentioned that the most powerful spirits were those which brought disease. Therefore, the Indians with the greatest spirit power were those who could influence such spirits. Such a person is called a *shaman* by anthropologists or, popularly, a *medicine man*. We usually think of a medicine man as one who is actually a doctor—one who gives medicine. The Coast Indian shamans did try to cure certain types of ailments, ones which today are called psychosomatic diseases—of emotional rather than organic origin. Ordinary physical diseases were treated by women who were wise in the use of herbs.

If a person believed that a spirit had made him ill, he called in the medicine man who consulted his own guardian spirits to find out what the patient's trouble was. He got in touch with his spirits by means of a dance which he performed wearing a wooden mask and shaking a wooden rattle. The young men of the village who were testing out their guardian spirit power to see if they could become medicine men acted as his assistants. They repeated his song until he fell into a trance, a sign that his spirit was talking to him. When he awoke, he told the family what had happened.

The Indians believed that sometimes an evil medicine man shot an object or even a spirit into the patient's body. Whatever it was, it had to come out before the sick man could recover. One of the commonest methods of removing it was to suck it out. However, only certain medicine men had sufficiently strong spirit power to suck out the object or the evil spirit. Others removed it by rubbing the patient. If the shaman who made the diagnosis felt that he did not have the required power, he could advise the family to call in someone who did. No medicine man undertook to cure a person if he felt that he would be unsuccessful. Consequently, if one did treat a patient who then failed to recover, the doctor was under suspicion himself. Perhaps it was he who had caused the illness in the first place. If he had a large number of deaths among his patients, he might even be killed as a sorcerer. When we come to the study of the work of the white medical missionaries, we shall see how this belief in the magical powers of doctors to cause illness as well as cure it brought suffering and even death to them.

The Indians believed, too, that a person's own spirit (or soul, in the white people's sense) could leave his body. If it did, the person became weak and lost his zest for living. A successful medicine man could see the soul lying on the ground or on the branch of a tree, and he would then send his own guardian spirit helpers to bring back the soul. When the medicine man got hold of the soul, he put it back into the body of its owner by singing and magic gestures.

The medicine man also used his powers to foretell the future. If a village was planning to go to war against a neighboring village, for example, the medicine man would use his spirit power to determine whether or not the time was right for an attack. Sometimes he prophesied that a particular man would be killed, and, in that case, the doomed one stayed at home. There was hardly any occasion when the medicine man's advice was not requested. He was therefore a powerful person in his village, and, for that reason, there were always young men (and women in some tribes) who were willing to brave the dangers of the position for the sake of the influence it held. Ordinarily, some ambitious boy whose parents were not wealthy tried to secure shaman powers since he would not be likely to obtain prestige through wealth.

The influence of the medicine man was felt in many more phases of a Coast Indian's life than was that of the chief. On the coast the chief was the richest man in a village, and, if there were two men of great wealth, each could be regarded as a chief. In such a case, however, one usually was better liked and more popular than the other, so that he eventually gained a larger following. Two rival chiefs might also try to outdo each other in giving potlatches, with one winning out. The main function of a chief was to settle quarrels between members of his village. He had no police to enforce his decisions, but, if he had considerable influence, he was often able to get people to accept his point of view by arguing for it.

The Coast chief was also obliged to give feasts, take care of the poor people who were not supported by their relatives, and provide food for visitors. Usually a son or nephew of a chief succeeded him as chief because property rights were inherited through either the father or mother. The successor was not necessarily the oldest son, but the one who showed the most qualities of leadership. If no son was popular, it could be a wealthy man of another family.

It is obvious from the absence of control by any person or group in a village that the Indians had no law enforcement officials in the sense that we do. The Indians followed a much stricter code of conduct than most of us do, but they observed the rules because they were convinced that otherwise the spirits would punish them. In addition, they were afraid to harm a member of their village because either the victim or his family might persuade their guardian spirit helpers to attack the aggressor.

In spite of such taboos, people did do things which hurt others, sometimes accidentally, sometimes because of anger or greed. In many parts of our country, Indian tribes could settle such quarrels only by fighting, but because our Coast Indians had such a surplus of goods, they assessed fines for injuries done. It was the chief's duty, then, to hear both sides of the story, decide which person was in the wrong, assess a fine, and persuade the guilty party to pay it. If the injury was an accident, he decided the amount of damages which should be paid. If the defendant refused to accept the chief's decision, it was up to the victim or his family to take whatever action he wished.

If the offense was murder, the family of the victim could claim the amount in goods that had been paid for his mother by her husband's family as a marriage price. If the murderer came from another village, and the victim was a wealthy man, the chief went

along with the family of the murdered man to demand payment
from the murderer. If he was poor, but well liked by the members
of his village, they would pay his fine. If they did not like him,
however, and he could not meet the payment, they allowed the victim's family to kill him. If the murderer was not known, the victim's family would try to kill some member of his village of the
same rank and general circumstances as those of the victim.
Sometimes, of course, the two groups could not come to terms,
and a battle between the two villages might then be the result.

Preparations for battle varied in type from one village to another, but, in all of them, the men performed ceremonies to get the aid
of their guardian spirits before starting out. They painted their faces
black, sang the special songs of invocation, and danced the pre-
scribed dances. Then they departed in their canoes for the enemy
village. Sometimes they tried to arrive just before dawn to take the
village by surprise. They often threw burning cedar branches onto
the roofs of the houses and then tried to kill the villagers as they ran
out. There were never many casualties because bows and arrows
were not deadly enough at close range, and spears and clubs were
not effective at long range. Some of the tribes north of Washington
were extremely fierce and warlike, and they were often successful in
raids on their southern neighbors, taking slaves and other loot. A
few of our own tribes treated a battle like a modern athletic contest,
announcing to the enemy when they were coming to fight and
claiming victory on the basis of a certain number of casualties.

Life Cycle

We have noted many of the aspects of Coast Indian life, but we
have not traced an individual's life. The Coast Indians believed that
babies came from a land inhabited by infants and that they remembered the pleasant times they had there. If the parents did not make
a baby happy, it would return to babyland by dying. Since adults
enjoyed babies very much, they tried hard to keep them sufficiently
contented that they would remain on earth. During the day each
baby was fastened to a cradleboard lined with cedar bark shavings
to provide a soft bed, and the babies evidently got used to such
confinement and did not mind it. The mother carried the cradle-

board on her back when she walked around and hung it on a tree limb near her when she was working outside. Once a day she took the baby out, washed it, played with it, and put fresh cedar shavings in the board.

As soon as the children were big enough to walk, they were free to play, and the grandmothers and grandfathers took a great deal of care of them, telling them stories and playing games with them. From the age of six or seven, the men began to teach the boys the skills they would need when grown and tried to prepare them for their later ordeals by encouraging them to learn to fast, to ignore pain, and to do vigorous exercises. The women taught the little girls to dig roots, to gather grasses and cedar bark, to dry fish, and to do the countless other tasks of their housekeeping.

We have already described the guardian spirit quests made by boys when they approached puberty. The girls at that time were withdrawn from the general village life and kept in seclusion for a time on the grounds that while they were getting ready for marriage and childbearing, they had strong spirit power which could harm the other members of the village. In fact, from that time until a girl married, she was expected to avoid men other than her close relatives. Her parents arranged a marriage for her with the family of a boy—preferably a wealthy one from another village whose father would pay handsomely for her. When a match as made, the groom's relatives brought him to the bride's village where they were entertained at a feast and the bridal payments made. The bride's father gave them gifts in return. In some tribes, the two families staged a mock battle, the bride's family barring the house and the groom and his family pretending to try to break in.

After the specified length of time, the bride returned to her husband's village and lived with him in his parents' house. We have mentioned before that each family had a certain section of a house for its own, with a fire in the middle of the floor or in one corner, and raised bunks around the room for beds. Cattail mats were used to make partitions between the various compartments. After the young couple had enough children that the family compartment was crowded, they would be given their own compartment, and, eventually, if the family was wealthy, they might build another house.

Chinook lodge. (An engraving in Charles Wilkes's Narrative, *Philadelphia, 1845)*

An Indian could have more than one wife if he could afford it, but there were few fathers in a village who could pay for a number of wives for their sons. If a couple wished to separate, they could do so; but, since in that case the bridal gifts had to be returned, a divorce was a serious thing for the girl's parents because the groom's gifts were distributed by the bride's father to the relatives and friends who had helped with the wedding, and it was difficult to get them back. If a bride's family thought that the husband or his relatives had mistreated her, they would take vengeance personally or by paying a medicine man to have evil spirits attack him.

Both Indian children and adults liked many kinds of games that often involved gambling. A favorite was the hand game in which a man holds two sticks or bone cylinders marked differently. He moves them back and forth from one hand to the other very rapidly a number of times. His opponent then guesses which hand holds which object. There were endless variations of these guessing games, and the gamblers would stake more and more valuable possessions, including their slaves, as the games progressed.

There were also various athletic games—wrestling, playing tug of war, contests of shooting with bow and arrow, and a kind of shinny that resembled modern hockey, in which two teams tried to drive a ball (lump of bone) to each other's goal line. Sticks were used to drive the balls over the course, which was a mile long.

Middle and old age was a happy time for Indian men and women, particularly the latter. They were freed from much of the drudgery of their earlier years and were regarded with respect by the younger people. They spent much time instructing their grandchildren and telling them the legends of their tribe. They continued to sing and dance in the winter ceremonial dances.

The Indians regarded death with awe and fear. They believed that the dead went to a land much like the one they had known— a comfortable place. They were lonely, however, and would come back to try to find the soul of a relative or friend to take back with them. Consequently, the living did everything possible to break all connections with a dead person. It was a serious crime to mention the name of a dead man or woman because that could call him back.

Because the Coast Indians were fond of their relatives, however, they gave ceremonial funerals for their dead, but they usually hired someone outside the family to act as an undertaker. He then had to go through elaborate purification rituals to cleanse himself from his contact with the dead.

On the coast, the dead were ordinarily buried in canoes set up on posts or in trees. On the Sound, small houses were built as tombs. Usually an old person gave away his property before he died, except for his clothing and personal possessions. These were buried with him, but torn up or made useless before they were deposited. Puget Sound Indians occasionally killed a slave to send with his master.

Since the Indians believed that the spirit world was always present with them, it is easy to see how fear of the spirits influenced every act of their lives. Their explanation of how the spirit world had come to have its present form was a consistent part of the pattern. They said that in the beginning the earth was full of strange monsters who had tremendous powers of magic before the Changer came. Different tribes identified the Changer with various animals—the raven, fox, mink, and so forth. They agreed, however, that he transformed many of these ancient creatures into the animals, rocks, and trees that are seen today. The Changer gave them their present forms so that they could serve as food and shelter for the human beings who were to come. The salmon, for example, agreed to die and be eaten because their death would not be final. If their bodies were disposed of in a certain way, their spirits could go back to the salmon village where they would live happily again. Then they would return the following year for the release of death which would continue indefinitely to send them back to their village.

For this reason, the Indians thought they were actually doing what an animal wanted when they killed him. One of the whaling songs, for example, went as follows: ". . . we will cover your great body with blue-bill duck feathers . . . and with the down of the great eagle, the chief of all birds. For this is what you are wishing and this is what you are trying to find, from one end of the world to the other, every day you are traveling and spouting."[1]

They had to be careful then that they disposed of the carcass in the way that pleased the spirit of each animal. The procedures for these rituals were handed down orally from one generation to another, but if there was a question of the correctness of a ceremony or the suspicion that someone had not followed the rules, it was the medicine man who was called upon to get at the truth.

Because the salmon was the most important fish in terms of quantity taken, the salmon ceremonies were important to all tribes. The details varied from one tribe to another, but in general the rules were that the first salmon caught must be placed with his head upstream so that the ones following him would also swim upstream. Then the fisherman took the fish home to his wife and told the other members of the village that the salmon run had started. The wife used no water to clean the first salmon, only fern leaves. Lengthwise cuts, rather than crosswise, had to be made, and a stone or mussel-shell knife was the only implement which could be used. Either the fish could be broiled whole on a stick over a fire or it could be broken up and boiled. Pieces of the first salmon were distributed to the members of the village, and all of it had to be eaten before sundown. The bones had to be thrown onto a special place on the bank or in the water in order that the salmon would be able to go

[1] Ruth Underhill, *Indians of the Pacific Northwest* (Indian Life and Customs, No. 5, Washington, D.C.: U.S. Office of Indian Affairs, *ca.* 1944), pp. 39-40.

back to their village. The heart of the first salmon was burned in the fire. If these precautions were not followed exactly according to the ritual of a particular village, the salmon would not come back again.

PLATEAU CULTURE

In examining the life of the Plateau Indians on the east side of the Cascades, we find that their culture had many features similar to that on the coast. The villages of the inland tribes were independent units, for example, and their ideas of the spirit world were very much alike. Social organization, however, was much simpler. Because food was less plentiful inland than on the coast, the Plateau Indians had to spend more time in securing enough provisions. They therefore did not have either leisure or the materials to build up stores of wealth as the coast tribes did. Also, without a plentiful supply of food for the winter, they could not spend that season in feasting and dancing to the same degree.

Food

In fact, the topography and climate of the two areas were so different that the way of life in eastern Washington varied greatly from that in western Washington. Salmon was still the basis of food for the Plateau tribes, and they used weirs, traps, dip nets, and harpoons to catch them as the coast tribes did. Inasmuch as salt-water fish were lacking, additional meat had to be found, mainly from land animals—rabbits, deer, elk, and others—whose skins were also used as winter clothing.

Horses which were traded up the coast from Mexico reached the Nez Perce area of southern Idaho and eastern Oregon around 1710 and Washington around 1730. Before the inland Indians acquired horses, they were in a difficult situation. They could not cover a large area on foot, and they had to stalk their prey and shoot some unwary animal with a bow and arrow. Groups would try to surround a herd of deer or other large animals and drive them over a precipice where the wounded ones could be killed with a club or spear. They also made wooden traps and deadfalls. They raised dogs to help them in hunting, but even so it was difficult to store enough food during the summer to last through the winter. In fact, they did much of their hunting in winter.

After the Plateau Indians obtained horses, they were much better off. They could cover a larger area and pursue an animal at a much faster rate on horseback. The Nez Perces and some of the other tribes of eastern Washington and Idaho even began going across the Rockies to hunt buffalo as the Plains tribes did. Because buffalo meat and skins were eagerly sought after by all the Indian tribes, the buffalo hunters could trade the skins and dried meat to all the neighboring tribes clear to the coast. The Columbia River was the main trade route, and the Chinooks who lived at the mouth of the Columbia became wealthy and powerful because they acted as middlemen in trading goods coming down the Columbia to the Coast tribes along the ocean. In fact, the Chinook language became the basis of a trading jargon, which consisted of words from many other Indian languages. Later, English and French words were added by white fur traders, who called this "international" speech Chinook jargon.

The Plateau tribes added roots, berries, nuts, and seeds to their meat and fish diet, just as the Coast tribes did. In addition to camas, the inland tribes had bitterroot, which was also an article of trade. Their methods of cooking were the same as those on the coast (roasting or steaming in pits, broiling over an open fire, and boiling), except that, since there was little wood around many of the inland villages, they used more watertight baskets than wooden utensils for boiling. They did have wooden dishes and spoons as well as spoons made of horn and shell.

Clothing

The Coast tribes probably learned from the Plateau Indians some of the techniques of making coiled baskets. From various kinds of grasses the inland women then wove mats which they made into clothing. The Plateau men wore a fiber breechclout in summer and a fiber poncho, fur leggings, moccasins, fur cap, and skin robe in winter. The women wore a fiber apron and a poncho even in summer. After the Plateau tribes had considerable contact with the Plains Indians east of the Rockies while hunting buffalo, they began to imitate the dress of the latter. Hence, early white fur traders described the clothing of the Plateau tribes as leather skirts for men and leather dresses for the women. The Plateau tribes had decorated their original costumes with paint, feathers, and quill embroidery, but the ornaments and feather headdresses became more elaborate with imitation of the Plains Indians.

Houses

Because of a lack of wood, the inland tribes could not build the huge plank houses found on the coast. The winters were so cold, however, that they had to have more than a simple pole and mat shelter. Their solution was to make pit houses, which consisted of a circular hole five or six feet below ground with a flat or pointed roof of poles above ground. The poles were covered with planks if they were obtainable; if not, mats covered with grass or earth were used. They left a hole in the top for smoke from fires built on the dirt floor to escape. A ladder was used to get in and out of the pit. They piled mats or skins on top of grass for the beds. After contact with the Plains tribes, the Plateau groups, when hunting or berrying, copied the Plains tepee by setting up a circular pole frame and covering it with mats. At their fishing camps, however, they constructed a long, rectangular frame of poles which they covered with grass or mats on one or more sides, with one end left for drying salmon. A variation of this type, instead of a pit house, was also used by some tribes as a winter lodge. In that case, all sides were covered with layers of mats. Such lodges were meant for several families. Along the Snake and Columbia rivers, where there was more contact with the Coast tribes, more substantial wooden frames covered with planks were used for houses.

The inland tribes made dugout canoes of the shovel-nosed variety, but they were crude as compared with the coast canoes. They also used rafts sometimes in place of canoes. In winter, they traveled on snowshoes when necessary.

Social and Economic Life

As far as their social organization was concerned, each Plateau village had a chief, as did the Coast tribes, but the chief was chosen for his qualities of leadership and wisdom rather than wealth. In fact, horses were the only type of private property valued highly by the inland tribes, and some of our northern Plateau groups had few horses. The Nez Perces, however, had large herds of horses. The chief of an inland village had the same functions as a chief on the coast—to keep peace in the village, settle quarrels, decide guilt in case of wrongdoing, receive visitors from other villages, and see that all members of the village had enough to eat.

Since accumulation of wealth by an individual was not a matter of prestige, there was no upper class in an inland village. Neither was there a slave class nor the custom of head flattening. Each village had its assembly, which might consist of all of the men or even of all men and women. In any case, the chief presided over meetings in which important matters were decided.

Villages within a tribe rarely fought, and it was the chief's duty to prevent all fighting, if possible. If a tribe did go to war, a leader was chosen for the battle who was a "war chief" for the time being. He did not act as a modern general, however, since no Indian obeyed orders, and strategy was decided by the leading warriors.

The idea that everything had a spirit, either helpful or harmful to a human being, existed in the plateau as it did on the coast. Consequently, boys (and some girls) went on a guardian-spirit quest there, too. They looked only for animal spirits. A shaman did not have the protection of special spirits as he did on the coast. He simply had the aid of several animal spirits. If a spirit did appear to a boy on his quest, in some tribes the spirit came first in human form and gave him specific powers along with the accompanying forms. Then as the spirit departed, it changed into its animal likeness.

When the child got home after his vigil, he tried to forget all about his experience for several years. Then the spirit would return to confirm its first appearance, and the person would become ill, as was customary in the Coast tribes. Similar ceremonies followed in which the shaman revealed the true cause of the illness and helped the patient to remember his spirit song. At the next winter dance ceremony, the boy would sing his song and dance along with the other villagers. The Plateau tribes, however, had no secret societies.

There were ceremonies of various kinds to please the spirit of the salmon and other food animals. Although the details varied, they were similar to those on the coast. The Plateau people buried their dead in trees or in mounds of rocks, and they had taboos about mentioning the name of the dead person for a certain length of time. They believed that the dead went to a land in the sky; but if proper burial ceremonies had not been performed, the deceased might stay on earth as a ghost. If a person lost his spirit (soul) while alive, the soul became a ghost which could become a guardian spirit, but a dangerous one. Ideas of witchcraft in causing and curing disease were similar to those on the coast.

Smoking was more important to the Plateau tribes than to the Coast tribes, where it was done only occasionally by both men and women after a meal. In the plateau, all men smoked, but not all women. They smoked for pleasure and also as a ceremony. In both Coast and Plateau tribes, pipes were made of stone with stems of bird bones or plant stems. Kinnikinnick was the common herb serving as tobacco.

In the plateau, the sweathouse was also much more important than it was on the coast, where it was not used at all by some tribes. Those who did have sweathouses used them merely as a bath house, not as a form of ceremony. The Coast tribes believed that the spirits were pleased by dives into cold rivers or lakes, as we saw in connection with the guardian-spirit quests on the coast.

The inland tribes, who had much less water around them, made a purification ceremony of sweating in these huts. Ordinarily, they followed the sweat bath with a cold bath in whatever stream ran near their village. In fact, some inland tribes believed that the spirit of the sweat lodge was very powerful, corresponding to the white conception of a divine creator. These groups believed that if they took sweat baths regularly and prayed to the sweat-lodge deity, he would answer their prayers.

The sweat lodges were huts covered with sod or brush just large enough for one person to enter. Hot stones were placed on the floor, and the bather stepped inside and poured water on the stones, letting the steam surround him until he was thoroughly cleansed.

Maritime Fur Trade

3

SPANIARDS ON THE PACIFIC NORTHWEST COAST
Trade between Mexico and the Philippines

The first Europeans to skirt the coast of Washington were Spaniards who had settled in Mexico shortly after Columbus discovered the West Indies. After they were sufficiently established in Central America to venture on across the Pacific, they conquered the Philippines in the 1560's and found that these islands gave them an excellent base for trading with oriental countries. Chinese merchants, for example, brought oriental silks, spices, porcelains, and other luxuries to the Philippines, where the Spaniards could pay for them with the gold and silver they mined in Central America.

The trip from Acapulco, Mexico, to the Philippines was fairly easy because of westerly trade winds, but the return voyage was extremely difficult, for the winds were against the ships. The return route ran north through the Philippine Islands almost to Japan before turning east toward the Pacific Northwest coast to approximately the present boundary between California and Oregon. When the ships were in sight of California, they turned south and let the northwest winds take them on down to Acapulco. From there, the oriental goods were shipped to Europe for sale at a large profit.

The return voyage often took over seven months, and, since no means of canning food was known at that time, salted meat made up the crew's diet for much of that time. Accounts of sailing voyages during the sixteenth and seventeenth centuries mention eating meat or broth "teeming with maggots." Vegetables were consumed within a few weeks, and most of the men on board developed scurvy, a disease that we now know is caused by a lack of vitamin C. By the time the Spanish ships got back near our shores, some of the crew might be dead and many others in a serious condition. Consequently, the Spaniards needed a port on our coast where fresh food and water could be obtained, but the coast was so rocky that the ships did not dare try to land until explorers had found a safe harbor. The Spaniards were also afraid of the Indians.

The Spanish officials in Mexico tried at first to send expeditions north along the coast. In 1542, before the Philippine trade had begun, Bartolomé Ferrelo sailed as far north as Cape Mendocino, and his log indicates that he may have reached Oregon. The techniques used in those days to determine latitude and longitude were not sufficiently developed to make accurate identification of points mentioned. Again in 1603, Sebastian Vizcaino and Martin D'Aguilar were sent north to find a suitable rest stop for the Philippine traders.

They were also instructed to look for the Northwest Passage or "Strait of Anian," the mythical river which people firmly believed ran from the Atlantic to the Pacific. At that time, it was thought that North America was a very narrow continent. If such a river could be found, Spain could avoid the long trip by sea around South America or the difficult overland trek across the Isthmus of Panama. England and France were also looking feverishly for the eastern end of the Strait of Anian on the Atlantic Coast. Vizcaino got as far as the present southern boundary of Oregon, probably to Port Orford, and D'Aguilar in another ship went somewhat farther north. He named a point Cape Blanco, and the name was later retained for a point in Oregon thought to be the one D'Aguilar mentioned. Neither of these ships tried to land.

For over a hundred years, Spain did nothing more about exploring the Northwest coast. Inland explorers had reported that there was no gold in California, the product of most concern to the Spaniards. Reports were circulated that whole islands of gold and silver did exist just off the coast of Japan. The Spanish government decided that if their exploring expeditions could find those islands, they would not only provide rest stops for the Manila galleons on their way home from the Philippines, but add more gold to the Mexican supply. Another obstacle to Spanish penetration of our coast was that Spain was so far away from Mexico that the home government was never very well informed about the real situation. Moreover, the Spaniards were not allowed to encourage ordinary individuals to trade. In fact, no one was allowed to engage in trading without a license from the king to do so. Such a practice prevented the development of business and the increase of immigration from Spain to Mexico.

Juan de Fuca's Voyage

One other voyage of this period should be mentioned before we turn to the appearance of other European nations on our coast—that of Juan de Fuca. His is what is called an apocryphal voyage, one which may not have taken place. In 1596 Michael Lok, an Englishman, met an old Greek in Venice whose real name was Apostolos Valerianus, but who had taken the Spanish name of Juan de Fuca. The old man told Lok that he had worked for the Spaniards in Mexico for forty years, and he mentioned specific trips between the Philippines and Mexico. In 1592 he was sent on a tour of exploration northward to find the Strait of Anian. He described his voyage, saying that he sailed up the coast to 47° of latitude, where he found a vast strait in which he sailed for twenty days, passing many islands. He also mentioned "a great headland or island, with an exceeding high pinnacle, or spired rock, like a pillar, thereupon" which stood on the north side of the entrance to the strait.

Juan de Fuca went on to claim, however, that he followed this strait into the Atlantic Ocean and that the land along the strait was "rich of gold, silver, pearls and other things, like Nova Spania." When he returned, the Spanish officials refused to reward him for his discovery; so he went back to Greece. He told Lok that he would be willing to guide the English to this Strait of Anian if they would pay him to do so. Lok was impressed with the old man's story and published an account of it in England, hoping that the British government would hire Juan de Fuca to make a second expedition to the area. Nothing came of this plan, however.

Over two centuries later when the English fur traders, William Barclay in 1787 and John Meares in 1788, saw a large strait in the vicinity where Juan de Fuca had described it, they were certain that it was the one he had seen, and Meares gave it his name. A hundred years after that, however, when historians were trying to reconstruct the story of the discovery of our coast, they began to look for references to Juan de Fuca in Spanish archives in Mexico and Spain, but none was or has been found. Since part of Juan de Fuca's story was obviously false—the claim that he reached the Atlantic Ocean after sailing through the Strait for twenty days—most scholars decided that his whole tale was fictitious and that he had never been near our coast.

Some historians at the present time, however, think that his description of the entrance was too accurate to have come from his imagination and that the chances are that he did reach the present Juan de Fuca Strait. His calculation of latitude was off only one degree, which is accurate for that time. It is true that there is no pillar of rock at the northwest entrance to the Strait, but one supposition is that he was referring to Mount Olympus and that Lok misquoted him as to its direction from the entrance.

The fact that the Spaniards did not mention his voyage is not proof that he did not make it, since they were eager not to let other nations know of their discoveries. If Juan de Fuca's claim is true, he obviously did not bring back gold from a plundered city as the Spanish officials had hoped; consequently, they may have thought the expedition a failure and have tried to keep the Spanish court from knowing that they had spent money on the trip.

As for Juan de Fuca's claim of reaching the Atlantic, he may have said that deliberately to impress the Spanish officials, or, since he did not know what the East Coast looked like and since people then thought that it lay close to the Pacific, he may actually have believed that he had reached it.

RUSSIAN EXPLORATIONS

After the sixteenth- and seventeenth-century explorations, Spain did nothing more about examining our part of the coast until she realized toward the end of the eighteenth century that Russia controlled present Alaska. Spain was afraid that the Russians would work their way on down the coast until they might threaten her hold on Mexico. Consequently, she decided to make a real effort to establish herself farther north, but, before she could succeed, not only Russia, but England and the United States were disputing each other for control of the Pacific Northwest coast.

Bering's First Voyage

In 1728 the Russian emperor Peter the Great hired Vitus Bering, a Dane by birth, to lead an expedition across Russia to the Siberian coast and there to build boats to explore the coast. Peter wanted him to find out if North America and Siberia were joined together and, if not, what kind of strait or ocean divided them. Bering spent the rest of his life on two trips to the Alaskan coast and died of scurvy and exposure on an uninhabited island off the Siberian coast in 1741.

The story of his experiences is a thrilling account of voyages made under seemingly impossible conditions. On the first trip from 1725-28, Bering and his men had crossed four thousand miles of dense forest, mountains, and treeless plains (largely without roads) in terrible cold, pulling wagons loaded with equipment for building a boat in addition to food and supplies. By the end of 1726, they reached Okhotsk, a collection of native huts where a few Russian fur traders also had quarters on the central Siberian coast opposite the Kamchatka Peninsula. They made earth shelters for themselves and stayed there while they built a boat which they had ready in July.

In it, Bering and his men crossed the Sea of Okhotsk to western Kamchatka. They crossed the peninsula on foot, cut timber, and built another small boat, the *St. Gabriel,* in which they sailed north for a month along the Siberian coast in dense fog in what they believed to be the Arctic Ocean. However, because the fog never lifted, they could not see the American shore to the east and could not be completely certain that they had sailed between the two continents. With winter approaching, they had to go back to Kamchatka, where they spent the winter of 1728.

In the spring they sailed east from Kamchatka hoping to see the American coast, but the fog hid even the islands around them, and their boat was not sturdy enough to risk more dangerous waters. Hence they turned back, sailed around the southern end of Kamchatka and on across the Sea of Okhotsk to the port of that name, which they had left two years before. From there, they made the long overland trek back to St. Petersburg, reaching it in 1730.

Bering's Second Voyage

The Russian government sent Bering out again in 1732, but this time the expedition was to be large—over a thousand men. Orders were sent to the Russian fur traders in Yakutsk, a village seven hundred miles west of Okhotsk, to have houses and food ready for Bering, but there were neither men nor resources to provide them.

As a result, Bering's men had to build sod shelters and depend on supply lines back to Russian settlements to secure much of their food. They were in Yakutsk three years before Bering's patience gave out. Then he took a small party with him and went to Okhotsk. The others went home.

In 1741 the remainder of the expedition sailed from Okhotsk in two ships which they had built, the *St. Peter* with Bering in charge and the *St. Paul* under Chirikov. The two ships were separated in a storm, and Bering lost valuable time searching for Chirikov, who had reached the coast of Alaska. Some of his men who put off in a small boat to get water on shore never returned, and Chirikov had to hurry back to Kamchatka because hardly any water was left on board. His men were in misery from thirst, but they did arrive safely and got back to Russia.

In the meantime, Bering was ill with scurvy and depressed by what he thought was the loss of Chirikov with his ship. Bering let the officers turn north instead of east, as he wanted them to, and they did not sight land until they reached an island in Prince William Sound off the southern coast of Alaska. They managed to send a boat to land for water, but they laughed at a German botanist, Steller, who wanted the men to collect leaves and berries. He meant to cook them as a protection against scurvy, but the men thought he was simply making a scientific collection. As a result, he took on board only what he could carry himself.

Bering sailed back along the Aleutian Islands, but because of the constant fog, he thought he was at the edge of a long peninsula. All the crew except Steller became so ill from scurvy that no one could handle the ship, and the trip became more and more of a nightmare. A number of men died, and the remaining ones realized that they could not reach their Kamchatka port. Consequently, when they next saw land, they anchored as best they could in their weakened condition, and the few men who were strong enough to lower the small boat went ashore in it. Gradually, they brought the sick off the ship and made covered trenches in which to spend the winter.

They found that they were on an island uninhabited by humans. The animal life was abundant, so that fresh meat was available, but there were no trees on the island, and the men had to go long distances to get sufficient driftwood for fires. During the winter the snow was deep and the cold so intense that keeping alive was a constant struggle, and many did not survive. Bering died in December.

In the spring, those who were left built a small ship from the remains of the *St. Peter,* which had begun to break to pieces, and they sailed back to Kamchatka. Gradually, most of the survivors made the long trip back to Russia where the journals kept by Steller and some of the officers were preserved. The story of the valiant and tragic effort to chart the Siberian and Alaskan coasts was learned from them. The news of the vast numbers of sea otters and fur-bearing land animals in the Aleutian Islands made the Russian trappers around Okhotsk and Kamchatka eager to use the directions given by the Bering group for getting to these islands. The traders found Bering Island, the one on which Bering and his men had spent the winter, and in the following years they progressed through the Aleutian Islands. The flow of furs back to the Russian cities was great enough that more and more fur traders left civilization for the wilds of Siberia. Within fifty years, the Russians were in control of the Alaskan coast, establishing fur-trading posts as they went along.

LATER SPANISH EXPEDITIONS
Perez' Voyage

Spanish ambassadors at the Russian court heard of the advance of the Russian fur traders down the Alaskan coast and warned Spain that she had better send an expedition at once to take possession of the Pacific Northwest. In 1774, therefore, Juan Perez started out from Mexico with instructions to go as far north as the sixtieth parallel (southern Alaska) and then sail back down the coast, noting the best places for possible settlements.

By the time Perez reached the area of the Queen Charlotte Islands, his men were already beginning to show signs of scurvy; consequently, Perez decided to start back. On the west coast of Vancouver Island, he found a protected harbor which was later given its Indian name, Nootka Sound. Perez found, to his surprise, that the natives there wanted to trade and that they had knives and iron tips on their arrows, a fact which indicated previous contact with white trade goods.

Anthropologists believe that either the metal had been traded from tribe to tribe down the coast from Russian posts or it had come from vessels blown off their course and shipwrecked on our coast. Perez, however, had few goods that the Indians wanted, and the potential value of bringing goods to trade for furs apparently did not occur to him. The Spaniards had accustomed themselves to thinking only of gold and silver as important natural resources. On his way south, Perez sighted Mount Olympus, which he called Santa Rosalia.

Heceta's Voyage

The next year, 1775, the Spaniards sent another expedition north to add to Perez' discoveries. Bruno Heceta and Juan Francisco de la Bodega y Quadra each commanded a ship. Quadra sent a boat ashore to get water at the mouth of the Hoh River, the first known landing made in what now is the state of Washington. It turned out tragically in that the Indians seized the boat, a fight developed, and the Spaniards were killed. Heceta then turned his ship back toward Mexico. At the forty-sixth parallel, he saw the entrance to a large river, but the weather was too stormy for him to enter. Since his men showed signs of scurvy, he hurried on down to Acapulco. He described the opening which he had seen, however, and on subsequent maps, it was labeled "Heceta's Inlet." It was, of course, the Columbia River, discovered later by the American, Robert Gray. Quadra continued north to Alaska before he went back to Mexico, but he made no contribution to the knowledge of our particular region.

BRITISH EXPLORATIONS
Sir Francis Drake

Before the Spaniards could follow up the discoveries of Perez and Heceta, the English appeared on the scene in 1778. Previously another Englishman, Sir Francis Drake, had spent the winter of 1578 in a bay near San Francisco, and scholars used to think that he might have gone as far north as Oregon, or even farther. The evidence seems convincing now, however, that he did not get north of California. Drake, after having come from the Atlantic into the Pacific through the Strait of Magellan at the southern tip of South

America, had seized and plundered Spanish ships along the coast of South and Central America. He was afraid to go back by the same route because he was certain the Spaniards would be lying in wait for him. Consequently, after wintering near the present San Francisco, he sailed across the Pacific and around Africa to return to England.

Captain Cook

Two hundred years later, the British government sent Captain James Cook to make a determined effort to find the Strait of Anian or Northwest Passage, as the elusive river was called by then. Cook was already a veteran explorer, having made one trip—from 1768 to 1771—during which he discovered the Society Islands and New Zealand and another trip—from 1772 to 1775—during which he charted an enormous part of the South Pacific. He rendered a great service to all sailors at that time with his discovery that vegetables could be pickled slightly and used for months in that form as a preventive for scurvy. Cook used cabbage, making a mild sauerkraut soup from it on the voyage, and none of his men developed the disease.

In 1776 Cook started from England on his third voyage to try to locate the entrance to the mythical river from the Pacific side. He came up through the South Pacific islands again and this time discovered the Hawaiian Islands, which he named the Sandwich Islands in honor of the Earl of Sandwich. From there he turned northeast in 1778 and hit the Pacific coast at 44° north, in present central Oregon. As he sailed on up the coast, bad weather prevented his sighting either the mouth of the Columbia or the Strait of Juan de Fuca, although he did sight Cape Flattery, to which he gave that name because it had "flattered" (deceived) him by promising to be the location of the great river, whereas he could not find one there. Cook went on north past Alaska and through the Bering Strait until the ice became too thick to proceed. He returned to Hawaii for the winter, and there he was killed by a native.

His officers brought the ship back to the North American coast the following summer (1779) to continue their explorations along the Alaskan coast and then proceeded across the Pacific to China and from there around Africa back to England. While the ship was touching along our coast, the men saw the beautiful sea-otter skins used as robes by the Indians, and they were eager to obtain some for use as bedding. They found that the natives wanted iron so badly that they would trade skins for the knives or scraps of iron which the men could find on the ship. By this means, the sailors acquired a number of skins.

When they reached China, they found that the Chinese were willing to pay fantastic prices for the sea-otter skins, even though they were dirty and worn by that time. The men sold them for so much money that the commanding officer had a hard time persuading them to go on to England as their orders required; they wanted to return to the Pacific Northwest coast with enough merchandise to trade for as many skins as possible. When they reached England, they reported the possibility of this lucrative trade, and, within a few years, scores of Englishmen were on our coast, collecting furs from the Indians and taking them across the Pacific to China and other oriental countries for sale. Cook is therefore credited with the discovery of the maritime fur trade which opened up the Oregon country to Europeans and Americans, although he himself died before the value of the furs was made known.

At first, the profits were unbelievably high. An ax meant to an Indian that he could cut down a tree in one tenth the time he could burn through one, and he was therefore willing to give any number of sea-otter skins (which were plentiful) for one iron tool. A few nails or a hammer were extremely precious in the same way, whereas to the white traders they were absolutely worthless by comparison with the price received for one sea-otter skin. As more traders appeared on the coast, however, competition made the Indians realize that the whites would give them a great deal more in the way of goods than they had asked at first. So their prices went up. Moreover, they began to spend all of their time hunting sea-otters and other fur-bearing animals, and the herds were slaughtered at such a rate that it was soon hard to secure the finest skins.

Captain Barclay

Some of the English traders are interesting to us because of explorations which they made or events in which they were involved.

For example, Captain Charles William Barclay (or Berkley) arrived at Nootka in 1787, and his wife was among those on board ship. She is the first non-Indian woman, so far as is known, to visit the Pacific Northwest coast. Barclay happened to send a boat from the ship to get water at the mouth of the Hoh River where Quadra's men had been killed by the Indians, and the natives grabbed Barclay's boat and murdered those men also. Barclay named the river Destruction River for that reason, but in later years the Indian name of Hoh again came into use for the river. The name "Destruction," however, has been retained for the island just offshore. Captain Barclay also found the Strait of Juan de Fuca, where Cook had said it did not exist.

British Trading Licenses

The British trading system was partly responsible for a quarrel which almost brought England and Spain into war. The English kings had followed the policy of giving a monopoly on the trade of a certain area to their friends, who formed a trading company. The East India Company had the right to all the English trade in the Orient, and the South Sea Company had the monopoly for trade on the west coast of the Americas. Any Englishman making a trading voyage in either area was required to have a license from one company or the other, and from both if he engaged in the fur trade between our coast and the Orient.

Since these licenses were expensive, many traders tried to manage without them by means of what we call black-market practices today. An English trader would go to a Portuguese operator (or to a person from some other country important in international trade) and pay him to make out false papers stating that the ship belonged to certain Portuguese who would then accompany the Englishmen in their ship. If the illicit English ship met a ship of the East India Company, the Portuguese would then appear when the captain came on board to inspect the ship, show him the papers, and pretend to be the owners or officers of the ship. As soon as the inspection was over, the Portuguese returned to their cabins and continued as passengers until some further danger of detection presented itself.

Captain Meares

John Meares, a British trader, started out for our coast in 1786 without a license from either company. He reached Prince William Sound in southern Alaska too late to continue trading and decided to spend the winter there, apparently not realizing how severe the weather would be. His ship was completely locked in by ice; his men developed scurvy from lack of fresh food, and more than half of them died.

Nathaniel Portlock and George Dixon, who had licenses from both the East India and the South Sea companies, came into the area to trade in the spring of 1787 and found Meares in his desperate condition. Portlock and Dixon, of course, resented having poachers secure furs without having spent the money for license fees which they themselves had paid. Consequently, according to their story, they gave Meares fresh food in return for which Meares signed a note saying that he would not trade any more on the Pacific Northwest coast on that trip.

Meares returned to China and had false papers prepared for two ships, the *Felice* and the *Iphigenia,* claiming that they belonged to a Portuguese and that the captains of the ships were two Portuguese who went along. Actually, Meares commanded the *Felice* and William Douglas the *Iphigenia.* The capital for the venture was put up by Meares and a number of other financiers who gave the captains instructions that they were not to let any Russian, English, or Spanish ship seize them and, if attacked, were to capture the aggressor, if possible, and bring the ship to China as a pirate vessel.

Meares reached Nootka Sound in the spring of 1788 and started building a ship, the *Northwest America,* near the village of Chief Maquinna. He had brought Chinese laborers with him to do the work. This was the first ship built on the Northwest coast. While the men were constructing it, Meares traded along the coast and looked for the strait located by Barclay the previous summer. Meares found the strait and named it for the old Greek who had presumably seen it first—Juan de Fuca. Meares was unscrupulous in his statements about his accomplishments and claimed in his logbook that he was the one to rediscover it.

He continued down the coast and discovered Cape Shoalwater at the entrance to Willapa Bay, but he could find no evidence of Heceta's St. Roc River (the Columbia) and called its entrance Deception Bay for that reason. He added in his journal, "We can now with safety assert that there is no such river as that of St. Roc exists, as laid down in the Spanish charts." This is extremely ironical, since he was in the entrance to the river at the time.

Meares went back to Nootka, loaded onto one ship the furs that had been collected, and took them back to China; he sent the *Iphigenia* and the new ship, the *Northwest America*, to Hawaii for the winter. Their captains were instructed to return to Nootka the following year for continued trading.

While Meares was in the Orient, he decided that his operations had grown to the point where he would do better to take out the required licenses from the East India and South Sea companies than to continue pretending that his ships were Portuguese. Consequently, he sent out two additional ships from China in the spring of 1789 with correct English papers. The two captains left in Hawaii did not know of this change and returned to Nootka in 1789, using the Portuguese subterfuge as they had the previous year.

Nootka Sound Controversy

In the meantime, when a version of Cook's journals was published in 1784, the Spaniards became thoroughly alarmed over the prospect of an influx of Englishmen on our coast. Consequently, the Spanish government sent an expedition under the command of Estevan Martinez and Gonzalo Haro up the coast to make an actual settlement at Nootka. When they reached Nootka, they found not only the *Iphigenia* and the *Northwest America* (Meares's two ships from Hawaii), but also the ships of Robert Gray and John Kendrick, the first American traders on our coast. Martinez seems not to have considered the Americans a threat to Spain's claim to the coast. However, when he read the Portuguese papers produced by the alleged owners of the English ships, he seized them on behalf of Spain because of the instructions to take Spanish ships, if necessary, and bring them to Macao as pirates.

When Meares's additional ships from the Orient arrived in Nootka, Martinez also captured one of them, but the second got away, and its captain hurried back to China to report to Meares that Mar-

Friendly Cove, Nootka Sound. (An etching from Captain George Vancouver's A Voyage of Discovery in the North Pacific Ocean, and Round the World, *London, 1798)*

tinez had taken three of his ships and was on his way to Mexico with them.

Meares immediately returned to England to report this outrage against the British government (as he viewed it). He was such a forceful speaker that, although the first ships seized had been trading in violation of English law, he was able to rouse the British people to such a pitch that they demanded war against Spain. The Spaniards tried to insist that they had absolute right to the use of the entire coast and that neither British nor Portuguese could trade there. Since neither the Spanish nor the British government actually wanted to go to war when the French Revolution was causing alarm to all European monarchies, they signed a treaty called the Nootka Agreement.

In this treaty, Spain conceded that England could trade any place on the Pacific coast north of the forty-second parallel (the present boundary between Oregon and California). She also agreed to allow England to set up posts at any place in that area where Spain did not already have a settlement. Spain also promised to restore Meares's ships and any buildings or other property taken at Nootka.

Although Spain did not give up her claim to ownership of the Northwest coast, for all practical purposes the Nootka Agreement meant the end of her hold on our coast, because English and American fur traders soon established a firm grip here.

Spain did try to plant a settlement at Neah Bay after the Nootka Agreement was signed in order to keep a foothold on the coast north of California. Bricks were unloaded at Neah Bay, at least, whether or not the Spaniards built any houses. In recent years, people have dug up Spanish bricks in that area, and they are presumably some of this building material. Neither the fur trade nor the northern climate appealed to the Spaniards, so that maintaining a post here was too much of an ordeal for them.

Place names along the Strait of Juan de Fuca and the San Juan Islands show Spanish influence, and such names were given by the Spaniards from 1790 to 1792 when an attempt was made to compete with the English in establishing posts. Samples of ones that remain are Haro and Rosario straits and Camano Island. Many other Spanish names were replaced by English ones used by Captain George Vancouver and later Americans.

Captain George Vancouver

Because of the difficulty of settling claims for property damage under the Nootka Agreement in Europe without first-hand information, Spain and England sent representatives to the Pacific Northwest coast to attend to details on the spot. Captain George Vancouver was appointed commander of the British expedition, and the Spanish government named Quadra as its commissioner. England directed Vancouver not only to conduct negotiations with Quadra over Meares's claims as to buildings seized at Nootka, but to chart the Pacific Northwest coast and to make a determined effort to find the elusive Northwest Passage.

Vancouver was one of the world's great explorers, and his mapping of our coast and of Puget Sound still remains an outstanding achievement. In fact, over fifty of the place names of the Sound area in use today were chosen by Vancouver, and three places in the region still bear his name—Vancouver Island (originally called Island of Quadra and Vancouver); Vancouver, British Columbia; and Vancouver, Washington.

As a young man Vancouver had sailed on Captain Cook's two last voyages, so that he was already familiar with the coast. On his own voyage of exploration, he reached the California coast in April, 1792, and sailed north, examining the coastline carefully around the latitudes where Heceta had reported a great river and where Meares had said that it did not exist. Vancouver repeated Meares's experience in regard to Deception Bay and Cape Disappointment and noted in his journal that he did not consider "this opening worthy of more attention" and sailed on past the entrance of the Columbia River, proceeding north toward the Strait of Juan de Fuca.

On the way, he met the American Captain Gray on his second fur-trading voyage to the Pacific Northwest. Gray informed Vancouver that he was certain a large river did exist where Heceta described it and that he was going back to that point to make another attempt to get across the bar. Vancouver went on into the Strait of Juan de Fuca and anchored in a protected bay which he called New Dungeness. He gave the name Mount Baker to a lofty mountain visible in the distance for one of his officers, Lieutenant Baker, who sighted it first.

Vancouver sent various smaller ships into the arms of the Sound (which he named for Peter Puget, one of his lieutenants), and, after charting many of them, Vancouver took his ships north through the Strait of Georgia to Queen Charlotte Sound and then back down the coast to Nootka to meet Quadra, who was waiting there for him.

Quadra told Vancouver that Gray actually had crossed the bar into a large river and had named it the Columbia for his ship. Vancouver was chagrined that he had not persisted in his attempt to find the river. Consequently, in October he sent Lieutenant W. R. Broughton in a smaller ship to examine the river while he went to San Francisco. Broughton explored the river as far as the site of present Vancouver, Washington, although he had to use a cutter (a small ship) and finally a row boat to get that far. He maintained that the river proper began fifteen miles upstream and that Gray had not gone beyond the bay which is the mouth of the stream. The

Deception Pass from Deception Pass Bridge: Deception Pass, an inlet on the west side of Whidbey Island, was so named by Vancouver in 1792 because it deceived his assistants, who discovered it, by appearing at first to be too narrow and rocky for navigation and by not cutting through to the east side of the island. (Photo by Ella E. Clark)

argument about whether Gray or Broughton should be considered the discoverer of the Columbia played an important part in the subsequent contest between England and the United States over possession of the Oregon country, as the land west of the Rockies between California and Alaska was later called.

AMERICAN EXPLORATIONS

We have mentioned that Martinez found American as well as English ships at Nootka in 1789 when he seized Meares's ships. In addition, Gray took some of Meares's crews and the Chinese laborers, who were stranded by the Spanish capture of their ships, with him from Nootka in order to carry them back to China. Let us now trace the story of the American entrance into the fur trade of the Pacific Northwest coast.

Before the American Revolution, the Americans had become great seamen and importers, but as British subjects their trade was largely with the West Indies. At the close of the Revolution, they no longer had the benefit of favorable trade relations with Great Britain. In fact, England set up restrictions on American commerce with the West Indies and other English possessions. Consequently, the American traders had to find some new source of trade, and they turned to the Orient for that purpose.

Some went around South America and across the Pacific by way of Hawaii; others went the opposite way across the Atlantic and around Africa to reach the Asiatic ports. Although oriental silks, spices, porcelain, carved ivory, tea, and other luxury items sold well in the United States, there were few American products desired by the Asiatics. Consequently, the American merchants had to have sufficient capital to pay cash for practically all of the oriental goods they purchased. The merchants realized that they needed to find some commodity which the Chinese wanted as much as the Americans wanted the oriental merchandise.

John Ledyard

The sea-otter furs on our coast turned out to be that commodity, and it was the results of Captain Cook's voyage which made American merchants aware of their commercial possibilities. An American, John Ledyard, went to England as a young man and sailed from there with Captain Cook on his trip to the Northwest coast. When he saw how eager the Chinese were to buy the sea-otter skins which Cook's men had taken with them more or less accidentally, he realized that Americans could make a fortune by trading furs for oriental goods, which could be carried back to the United States for sale.

When the Cook expedition reached England, Ledyard went on to America and wrote an account of his trip with Cook, which was published in 1783. Ledyard tried to interest merchants in New York, Philadelphia, and Boston in his plan, pointing out that the trading ships could start out with cheap produce—knives, hammers, nails, woolen cloth, mirrors, beads, and other trinkets—and exchange them for the valuable furs. By this means, the initial cost would be low and the margin of profit enormous. Interested merchants delayed their expeditions until Ledyard, who was an intense, impatient person, could not bear to wait any longer; he went back to England in 1784 to see if someone there would outfit him for the Northwest coast.

Captain Robert Gray

Whether it was Ledyard's campaign or the accounts of Cook's voyage that finally won over the American merchants, we do not know. However, in 1787 a group of Boston businessmen did outfit an expedition under the command of Robert Gray and John Kendrick, who were sent on exactly the trading tour envisaged by Ledyard. They left Boston with cheap trade goods for the Indians and reached the Northwest coast in 1788.

As he sailed north, Gray noticed at latitude 46° 10' the entrance to what he thought was a large river, which he tried to enter, but the water was too rough even though he waited for nine days. He continued up the coast to Nootka, and, when Kendrick arrived, the two captains spent a year trading for furs.

As we have seen, Gray was at Nootka in 1789 when Martinez captured Meares's ships, but for some unknown reason Gray was not molested by the Spaniards. At least two Spaniards of that time were as puzzled by Martinez' friendly relations with Gray as scholars are now. Father Luis Sales, a Dominican priest stationed at San Miguel Mission in Lower California wrote long letters to a friend in Spain which were published in 1794. In one of the letters, he says that the viceroy of New Spain found out that the Kendrick-Gray expedition was on its way to Nootka and wrote to all of the Spanish missionaries on the Pacific coast telling them that if the "American Englishman" (Kendrick) with two ships put in at any of their ports, the missionaries should try hard to seize him.

Sales enclosed a report of the Nootka incident by Josef Tobar y Tamáriz, Martinez' first mate. In it Tamáriz says that when Martinez met Kendrick and Gray, the Spanish commander did not consider it desirable to intern either of their ships, "why I do not know, unless because of their superiority of force he was persuaded that encountering them with his lesser strength, as we confirmed, he would have been taken prisoner; but not considering the special decree the Commander let the ships referred to go free, as I am informed since leaving Noka."[1]

Gray took his furs to China, sold them, bought oriental goods, and sailed back to Boston via Africa and the Atlantic. Thus Gray became the first American captain to sail his ship around the world. His backers were disappointed in their profit, however. English traders had by that time flooded the Chinese market with furs, and the Americans again had plenty of tea—a commodity they could not get during the American Revolution. The merchants, however, agreed to outfit another expedition, and Gray started out again in 1790, intending while he was on our coast to make another try at entering the river he had seen.

He reached Nootka in the summer of 1791 and spent a year trading to the north. Then in April, 1792, he started south to look again for his river. As we have mentioned, he met Vancouver's ship near Juan de Fuca Strait just after Vancouver had passed and missed the entrance to the Columbia River.

Gray followed the coast and discovered Gray's Harbor, where he anchored and traded with the natives for three days. Then he hurried on south, and, at four o'clock in the morning on May 11, 1792, he saw again the entrance of the long-sought-for river. Like Meares and Vancouver, Gray could see no opening through the rough breakers, but the fact that he could see muddy water eddying out from shore convinced him that the dark line represented a river; consequently, he gave orders to sail into it, and the ship was soon over the bar and into a large fresh-water stream.

So many Indians came out in canoes from both sides of the river to trade that Gray stayed there buying furs from them for nine days. Then he went upstream, but entered the wrong channel. After about fifteen miles, the ship ran aground. When the men got it clear, Gray turned back down the river and spent some time trading near its mouth before he put back to sea for Nootka. There he told Quadra about his discovery and drew charts for him which, as we have seen, Quadra gave to Vancouver when he arrived at Nootka to negotiate the details of the Nootka Agreement. Vancouver's *Voyage of Discovery,* which was published in 1798, was the first

[1] Luis Sales, *Observations on California, 1772-1790,* trans. and ed. Charles N. Rudkin (Los Angeles, Calif.: Glen Dawson, 1956), pp. 101-5.

notification to the public that the American Robert Gray had found the great river, or, as Vancouver claimed, its mouth, but no more.

Many other American fur traders followed Gray in his round-the-world venture. In fact, the Americans soon outnumbered the English fur traders, and by 1812 there were hardly any British traders on our coast. The success of the Americans was partly due to the tremendous geographical advantage which they had—the source of cheap trinkets at home for the first lap of the voyage; the large quantity of precious furs at the next stop which could be secured in exchange for the trade goods; the disposal of the furs for equally precious oriental commodities on the next lap, China; and after having circled the globe, the sale of the Chinese goods at Boston or New York.

By contrast the English fur traders plied their fur trading back and forth across the Pacific from China to Nootka, neither of which was their home port. Moreover, the Indians were not attracted by oriental goods. The English traders had to circle half the globe from England if they wanted to bring more desirable objects to the Indians.

In addition, the Americans did not have to have a license to trade. Anyone who had capital enough to outfit a ship could make such a voyage, whereas the British traders were hampered by the requirements for licenses from the East India Company and South Sea Company. After the War of 1812, the British again came into control of the Oregon country, but that was largely a result of the overland fur trade, which we shall discuss in the next chapter.

Overland Fur Trade

4

The overland fur traders entered the Oregon country from the east just as the maritime fur traders had penetrated it on the west. Sea-otter skins were the water-animal furs most prized by the coast traders, and beaver skins were the land furs of most value to the overland traders.

HUDSON'S BAY COMPANY (EARLY HISTORY)

As soon as the first Englishmen and Frenchmen landed on the east coast of North America in the seventeenth century, they began to trap fur-bearing animals for their skins, which they used as winter clothing and bed coverings. The Indians soon found, as they did later on our coast, that they could trade furs for the white man's goods, and trapping became a full-time occupation for them. One of the richest early fur areas discovered extended from northern New York through the St. Lawrence Valley and on northwest of Hudson Bay. By the 1660's the possibilities of the fur trade in northeastern Canada were evident to the British; consequently, in 1670 Charles II, the English king, gave a charter to a group of English noblemen, allowing them the monopoly of trade in the region drained by Hudson Bay. At that time, no explorer had penetrated far enough to the west to know what the boundaries of the Hudson Bay drainage area were. Most people thought, however, that it ran to the Pacific Ocean.

The English nobles took the name of the Hudson's Bay Company for their enterprise, and within a few years they had forts established around the rim of Hudson Bay. In return for its charter, the company was expected to explore the region west of Hudson Bay, but the managers (factors) at the posts on the Bay found that they did not need to go into the interior to get furs. The Indians were so eager to trade that the tribes farther inland gathered skins during the winter and in the spring brought them in canoes down the rivers flowing into Hudson Bay. Thus the company officials made their posts on Hudson Bay as comfortable as they could with furniture and supplies from England and lived there, receiving an enormous quantity of furs each year from the Indians and forwarding them to the company office in London for sale. The profits were so great that there was no incentive to push farther into the wilderness.

FRENCH FUR TRADERS

Competition did emerge, however, from the French fur traders along the St. Lawrence River who liked to explore and who made excursions to the west and the north, gradually going beyond the Great Lakes and into the Lake Winnipeg region. From there, they pushed on to the Saskatchewan country. Their trading ventures were beginning to cut down somewhat on the volume of furs reaching Hudson Bay when the Seven Years' War between England and France occurred. At its close in 1763, France surrendered her Canadian holdings to England, and the St. Lawrence River area was thus opened to British fur traders.

Since the drainage system of the St. Lawrence River is completely separate from that of Hudson Bay, the Hudson's Bay Company's monopoly on trade did not extend to it. Independent British traders (many of them Scotsmen) therefore quickly entered the fur-trading business along the St. Lawrence, using the French fur traders who were already familiar with the interior wilderness as trappers and boatmen.

Voyageurs

In exploring the interior, the French had traveled with bands of Indian hunters and had soon intermarried with Indian women. As a result, the French-Canadians were almost all people of mixed French and Indian blood. These "voyageurs" became the famous boatmen of the fur trade, who paddled the birchbark canoes for twelve to sixteen hours a day (beginning at 2:30 or 3:00 A.M.) and carried the canoes over long and difficult portages along with ninety-pound packages of trade goods, one or more strapped to the back of each man. In doing this incredibly hard work, they wore gay, colorful costumes and sang lustily as they rowed. Along some stretches, they had nothing but fish to eat. At other times, they were allowed large quantities of melted animal fat (pork grease, usually) mixed with Indian corn, like our hominy.

In the September, 1963, issue of the *National Geographic Magazine,* there is an interesting article by Sigurd F. Olson, "Relics from the Rapids," in which the author tells of the recovery of articles lost by the voyageurs in Canadian rivers. It occurred to E. W. Davis of Minnesota that divers should be able to bring to the surface the guns, kettles, and other sturdy pieces of trade goods which often went to the bottom of the chain of rivers from Montreal to the Rockies. He hired divers who searched the bottom of the Basswood and Granite rivers between Lake Superior and Rainy Lake and succeeded in recovering relics—including iron axheads, ice chisels, brass kettles, clay pipestems, flintlock muskets, and spears. As such operations continue, a more vivid picture of the life of the early fur traders will emerge.

NORTH WEST COMPANY

The Scotsmen hired as many of the French-Canadians as they needed to send trading expeditions into the interior, but these groups came into competition with each other as well as with the Hudson's Bay Company. They realized that they would not need to pay the Indians so much for the furs if they were not bidding against each other. Consequently, they began combining in a sporadic fashion for particular expeditions, and in 1784 nearly all of the independent traders merged into the North West Company. From that time on, except for occasional periods when it split up into rival factions, the North West Company was the only important English competitor of the Hudson's Bay Company.

Alexander Mackenzie

Since it was to the advantage of the North West Company to catch the Indian brigades with their furs in the interior before they were close to Hudson Bay, their explorers pushed farther each year toward the present Canadian Northwest. As they went along, they established posts at some of the important river junctions where a few white men would be left to guard the trade goods, sell them to the Indians in exchange for furs, and do what trapping they could themselves. By this process, one of the company's ablest men, Alexander Mackenzie, found himself in charge of Fort Chipewyan on Lake Athabasca, half way between Hudson Bay and the Pacific and two hundred miles south of Great Slave Lake. Indians had told him that a river connected the north end of Great Slave Lake with a large body of water which Mackenzie hoped might be the Pacific Ocean. Consequently, in the spring of 1789, Mackenzie took men in three canoes to find out. The body of water turned out to be the Arctic Ocean, which cut off the possibility of a "Northwest Passage" in that direction. Mackenzie did find the area north of Great Slave Lake rich in beavers.

Mackenzie felt that he would have recognized earlier that he was approaching the Arctic rather than the Pacific Ocean if he had had more training in mathematics and astronomy in order to take latitude and longitude readings easily. Therefore, he went back to England, studied for a year, and returned to make a second attempt to reach the Pacific. He left Fort Chipewyan in October, 1792, with companions and two canoes loaded with trade goods and supplies and spent the winter in camp on the Peace River near the summit of the Rockies. In May, 1793, he went up the Peace with one canoe, ten men, and three thousand pounds of baggage. From the source of the river, the men carried the canoe and gear over the crest of the mountains and started down a river which they again hoped was the great "River of the West."

It was, actually, a tributary of the river later named the Fraser. As they proceeded downstream into the Fraser proper, the men found narrows and rapids so rocky that the boat was damaged when they stayed in the stream. The cliffs at the sides were so steep that carrying the canoe and baggage over them was backbreaking work. When Indians along the way told Mackenzie that the river got worse farther on, he decided to work his way back up stream to a point where an Indian trail went overland to the ocean.

They gathered bark, made a new canoe (since the old one was beyond repair), and went back up the river to its junction with the Blackwater River. Indians then guided the party overland to the Bella Coola River, where they borrowed Indian canoes and proceeded in them to the Pacific Ocean, which they reached on July

20, 1793. Mackenzie thus became the first European, so far as is known, to cross the North American continent north of the Spanish possessions. He spent a few days exploring among the islands between Vancouver Island and the mainland. When he was ready to leave, he painted the following statement on a rock in Dan Cove: "Alexander Mackenzie, from Canada, by land, the twenty-second of July, one thousand seven hundred and ninety-three." The inscription was found in 1913 by R. P. Bishop, who was surveying the area for the British Columbia provincial government.

Mackenzie and his men returned overland to Fort Chipewyan, and Mackenzie went on to Montreal and then to England where in 1801 he published his journals along with a history of the Canadian fur trade. While he was working on them, he learned that Gray had discovered the Columbia, which he assumed to be the difficult river that he had given up for the overland trip. Mackenzie also learned that Vancouver had been at the mouth of the Bella Coola just a few weeks before he reached the Pacific at that point, but for some reason the Indians had not told Mackenzie that another British explorer was in the area. When he came back to Montreal, he was active in the North West Company as a director, but he did not go again into the wilderness as an explorer or trader. In 1808 he withdrew from the fur trade and returned to Scotland to live.

Mackenzie was knighted by the British government for his explorations. He was a paradoxical figure, being equally at home in a London drawing room and in the wilderness. His companions reported that he would stay to care for a sick Indian guide when the delay might be disastrous to him. He was also known to sit all day with a gun on his knees, waiting for an Indian to return some tool that he had stolen.

Simon Fraser

The North West Company sent more and more traders into the Saskatchewan regions, but it was not until 1808 that one of them again tried to follow to its mouth the river which Mackenzie thought was the Columbia. This explorer was Simon Fraser, who crossed the Canadian Rockies in 1806 and spent two years trading in the Peace River country. In May, 1808, he started out with twenty-three men in four canoes to follow the turbulent river abandoned by Mackenzie fifteen years earlier. The canoes were swirled around in the rapids, and time after time the men thought they as well as their boats would be lost. Finally, they agreed that they would have to leave the river and carry their baggage. Fraser gives the following description of their situation:

> . . . I have been for a long period among the Rocky Mountains, but have never seen anything like this country. It is so wild that I cannot find words to describe our situation at times. We had to pass where no human being should venture; yet in those places there is a regular footpath impressed, or rather indented upon the very rocks by the frequent travelling [by Indians]. Besides this, steps which are formed like a ladder . . . by poles hanging to one another and crossed at certain distances with twigs, the whole suspended from the top to the foot of immense precipices . . . furnish a safe and convenient passage to the natives; but we, who had not had the advantage of their education and experience, were often in imminent danger when obliged to follow their example.[1]

They succeeded, however, in following the river almost to its mouth and then cut overland to the ocean. Fraser could tell from the latitude that this river was not the Columbia, since he knew the position of the mouth of the Columbia from Vancouver's reports of the discoveries there by Gray and Broughton. The river Fraser explored was named for him.

David Thompson

While Fraser had been exploring the Peace and Fraser River regions, another able member of the North West Company, David Thompson, was busy along the Saskatchewan River and the section of the Columbia flowing north from its source in Canada before it makes the first big bend and turns south on its course to the Pacific.

David Thompson had worked for the Hudson's Bay Company for thirteen years when he was a young man, and he proved to be intelligent and resourceful. His main interest, however, was in exploring rather than in fur trading. In his expeditions he was often hampered by his superiors, who would grudgingly authorize him to spend his time making maps instead of trading and then refuse to

---

[1] T. R. Masson, *Les Bourgeois de la Compagnie du Nord-Ouest* (Quebec: A. Côté et Cie, 1889) I, 190-91.

supply him with instruments or reverse their orders. When his term of service expired in 1797, he therefore left the Hudson's Bay Company and joined the North West Company, whose partners were eager to employ explorers as well as traders.

By 1807 he had surveyed much of the Athabaska, Saskatchewan, and Peace River country and turned his attention to the Columbia. When he first reached its eastern section flowing north, he believed it to be an unknown river and called it the "Kootenay" River. In 1807 he built Kootenay House (a fur-trading post) on this river, about a mile from Lake Windermere, where he spent the winter trading with the Kootenay Indians and mapping the area.

In the spring of 1808, Thompson crossed to what we now call the Kootenay River (McGillivray's River in his terminology) and descended it in a canoe to a point near present Bonner's Ferry, Idaho. He spent the winter trading with the Flathead Indians, taking the furs back to the East in the spring. In August, 1809, he and a few of his men returned to the Flathead villages in northern Idaho. Purchasing horses from them, he rode overland to Pend Oreille Lake where he built a fur-trading post (Kullyspell House) on the east side of the lake about a mile and a half from the mouth of Clark Fork River. After exploring the area for two months, he went up the Clark Fork River and built another post (Salish House) near the present Northern Pacific Railroad stop, Woodlin, in northern Montana.

When Thompson returned to the East during the summer of 1810, he learned that an American, John Jacob Astor, was organizing an expedition to go to the mouth of the Columbia where he planned to build posts and enter the fur-trading business in competition with the North West Company. Thompson quickly prepared to return to the Columbia area, and statements he made to men at Hudson's Bay posts along the Saskatchewan River indicate that he was trying to beat Astor to the Pacific via the Columbia in order to prevail on the Indians to sell furs to the Canadian rather than the American company. By this time, he had learned from Indians along the Kootenay and Pend Oreille rivers that what he had called the Kootenay River was actually the northern end of the Columbia.

Bad luck prevented his reaching the Columbia that fall, however. The Piegan Indians were angry because white traders had crossed the Rockies and were selling guns to enemy tribes, particularly the

Kootenays, who could not defend themselves without the white man's firearms. Consequently, the Piegans set up such a constant lookout for white traders that Thompson could not use the Howse Pass to get across the mountains and had to turn north in January, 1811, to find a new pass. He discovered the Athabasca Pass, which later became the main route for the fur brigades from Hudson Bay to the Columbia. Once through the pass, Thompson found the snow too soft to proceed. With a few men he built a shelter and spent the winter at the tip of the Canadian bend of the Columbia, a spot later called "Boat Encampment," where the Wood and the Canoe rivers join the Columbia.

In the spring the group made a canoe of split cedar sewed together with strips of pine roots, and Thompson with three men started back to Salish House to find men to accompany him to the Pacific. On the way up the Columbia toward the Kootenay River, Thompson hired four eastern Indians from a group he met. The party followed the Columbia to its source, portaged to the Kootenay River, and went down it for about 240 miles to a point near present Jennings, Montana, where they bought horses from some Indians. From there Thompson proceeded overland to Salish House on the Clark Fork River.

Thompson and his men then built a canoe, went down the river to Pend Oreille Lake, crossed it, and went down the Pend Oreille River to a point near the present town of Cusick, Washington. There they transferred again to horses and went to Spokane House, which had been built in 1810 while Thompson was in the East. The post was at the junction of the Spokane and Little Spokane rivers nine miles northwest of present Spokane, and this site later became one of the major fur-trading posts for both British and American fur traders.

From Spokane House, Thompson and his men continued by horse to Kettle Falls on the Columbia. Here they built another canoe from cedar boards, and, on July 3, 1811, they started down the Columbia on the last lap of their journey to the Pacific. Thompson had heard on his recent trips east that an American exploring party (Lewis and Clark) had reached the mouth of the Columbia in 1805, and Thompson was undoubtedly eager to make a better claim to the area for England than Lewis and Clark had made for the United States. As evidence of this, he stopped at the site of present Pasco, set up a pole, and tied to it a sheet of paper on which he had written: "Know hereby that this country is claimed by Great Britain as part of its Territories, and that the N. W. Company of Merchants from Canada, finding the factory for this people inconvenient for them, do hereby intend to erect a factory at this place for the commerce of the country around.   D. Thompson." "Factory" was a term used at that time for any business establishment, such as a fur-trading post.

Thompson made it a point to establish friendly relations with the Indians, as Lewis and Clark had done before him; consequently, the tribes along the Lower Columbia greeted him warmly, and he and his men ate and smoked with the various groups of Indians along the way.

When he reached the mouth of the Columbia on July 15, 1811, he found that the Astor sea expedition had already arrived and that the men had built four log huts. They called their post Astoria in honor of the American financier. Many of the Astorians had formerly worked for the North West Company and were already acquainted with Thompson. They would have been delighted to see any white men and were doubly so to meet one of their friends. Consequently, they entertained Thompson and his men as hospitably as they could until July 22, when Thompson started up the Columbia to return to Montreal. Thompson was never again in the Oregon country, but he continued to work on maps of the areas he had covered. They were so accurate that upon publication they became the basis for the cartography of this region for many years.

THE AMERICAN OVERLAND ADVANCE

While members of the North West Company were penetrating the Oregon country, the American fur traders were also trying to reach the Pacific by an overland route in order to extend their trade in beaver and other land furs. They carried on a brisk fur trade in northern New York and other sections of the East, and, as we have seen, they supplanted the British sea-otter traders along the Northwest coast. They realized that the Canadian fur traders were reaping great profits from beaver in northwest Canada and that the Americans were not taking advantage of the beaver trade to the west of the Great Lakes.

During the 1790's, however, the new United States government was handicapped in encouraging American fur trade in the west by the fact that Spain claimed central North America from the Mississippi to the Rockies plus the southern part of the section between the Rockies and the Pacific. Spain also, as we have seen, disputed England's claim to the region between California and the Russian posts in Alaska. She was just as unwilling to let explorers or traders cross the Mississippi-Missouri region as she was to let them into her Pacific borders; consequently, her possessions made a barrier for the Americans in any overland trip to the Pacific.

Thomas Jefferson and John Ledyard

Even before Thomas Jefferson was President of the United States, he was concerned over the exclusion of Americans from the western beaver trade. He tried to interest private organizations in sponsoring scientific excursions to the Oregon country. He even became involved with the same John Ledyard who had urged the Boston merchants in 1784 to send him on the kind of round-the-world trade in sea-otter skins which Gray accomplished a few years later. When Ledyard failed to get backers for his project in the United States, he went back to Europe where in 1786 he met Jefferson, who was then minister to France. Ledyard's obsession with the American fur trade appealed greatly to Jefferson. They conceived the idea that if Ledyard went overland across Europe and Russia to Kamchatka, he could cross to the Russian posts in Alaska in one of their ships and then walk down the coast to some point from which he could strike out for the Mississippi River from the west. The Spaniards could not very well be overly severe with one lone American walking across their land to get home.

Ledyard started out in December, 1786, by boat and reached Stockholm where (because he had no money) he expected to walk across the Gulf of Bothnia on the thick ice which ordinarily covered it during the winter. That year, however, it had not frozen solid enough for foot travel, but had patches of ice too numerous for the passage of a boat. Ledyard could either wait until spring or walk across Finland to St. Petersburg, and, with his usual disregard for hardship and dangerous journeys, he started out on foot. In intense cold, through deep snow in an area where there were few villages, he walked an average of twenty-five miles a day and reached St. Petersburg in seven weeks.

There he did succeed in getting a Russian passport, and he rode in a horse-drawn coach or in a boat in fair comfort, accompanying various Russian officials across Siberia. However, while he was waiting at Yakutsk for the weather to permit the next lap of the journey to Okhotsk, he was arrested and taken back to St. Petersburg. The accepted version of the incident has been that the Empress Catherine sent an officer after Ledyard because the Russian-American fur company advised her not to let an American travel with the Russian fur traders and thus learn of their activities and the extent of their trade.

A different version, however, is given by a contemporaneous Russian, Gawrila Sarytschew, who was a member of an exploring expedition under the leadership of Joseph Billings. Catherine sent the group to explore the Siberian coast in 1785, and in 1806 a translation of Sarytschew's record of the trip was published in London under the title *Account of a Voyage of Discovery to the North-East of Siberia*. He says that when the Billings expedition reached Yakutsk, Ledyard was there and was behaving badly. He picked a quarrel with the Russian commanding officer in whose home he was staying and was abusive to him and others. As a result, when Billings had to return to Irkutsk, he took Ledyard with him along with a letter of accusations from the commander to the governor-general. The latter then took him into custody and sent him on to St. Petersburg on a charge of disorderly conduct. Whatever the circumstances, this was the most crushing disappointment in the series of frustrations which Ledyard met. When he got back to London, he was offered the chance of exploring in Africa; he got as far as Cairo on that expedition when he died.

Lewis and Clark Expedition

Thomas Jefferson, as President, continued to plan secretly for an overland expedition to cross the United States from east to west, and he asked his private secretary and friend, young Meriwether Lewis, to be ready to command the venture when it materialized. In 1802 he learned that France, which had secured the area between the Mississippi and the Rockies from Spain in 1800, might be willing to sell a part of this region, called Louisiana. Jefferson wanted to see what the country was like before he bought any of it, but he had to keep secret the fact that he was negotiating with France until he had a definite commitment. Therefore, in January, 1803, he asked Congress in a secret message to appropriate $2,500 for an expedition to the Pacific, and Congress granted his request. To Jefferson's amazement, France shortly sold the entire region between the Mississippi and the Rockies to the United States. There was no longer any need to conceal the fact that the expedition was on its way to explore the Louisiana Purchase for a usable route to the Pacific and to open the West to the American fur trade.

Lewis had fought in the Indian wars along the Ohio and Mississippi rivers in the 1790's along with William Clark, who was one of General Anthony Wayne's officers during several campaigns. Lewis and Clark became friends and kept in touch with each other after Clark had gone back to his family home in Kentucky and Lewis had become Thomas Jefferson's private secretary.

When Jefferson asked Lewis to lead an exploring expedition to the Pacific, the latter invited Clark to accompany him as co-captain of the company, but when Clark received his commission after they were on their way, he found that he had been given only the rank of second lieutenant. Clark was disgruntled, and Lewis was very much disappointed. He assured Clark that as far as he was concerned, they were equal in authority, and Lewis never let anybody else in the expedition know that Clark did not actually have such a position. The harmony between the two leaders during the entire hazardous trip was remarkable. Their only disagreements were over things which could hardly affect the welfare of the expedition—the taste of dog meat and the need for salt in one's diet.

Thomas Jefferson, in addition to his desire to capture a part of the western fur trade for the United States and perhaps even to push American settlement to the Pacific, was vitally interested in the plants and animals to be found in the unknown country, the customs of the natives, the types of soil, and weather conditions—even the geology. He apparently halfway believed that certain species of dinosaurs or other prehistoric animals still lived in the western wilderness. Consequently, he gave instructions that each officer of the company was to keep a daily journal in which he recorded whatever details he noticed in the country through which the expedition passed. Moreover, Jefferson made it clear that the Indians were to be treated with great consideration so that they would be inclined to gather furs for the American traders who would presumably soon follow Lewis and Clark to the Pacific.

Lewis and Clark spent the summer and fall of 1803 recruiting officers and men for the expedition (including interpreters, hunters, carpenters, and blacksmiths), buying military equipment, food, clothing, medicine, trade goods for the Indians, and other necessities for wilderness travel.

As soon as recruits were secured, they were sent to a camp on the east bank of the Mississippi almost across from St. Louis. Here Clark drilled them during the winter, weeding out those who appeared to be physically or emotionally unfit for the dangerous and rigorous journey ahead. Lewis was in camp occasionally, but he spent most of the time rounding up supplies and men. He happened to be in camp on March 8, 1804, and went over to St. Louis to witness the ceremony of the transfer of Louisiana from France to the United States.

The expedition started up the Missouri River on May 13, 1804, in three river boats. Hunters brought in game from the woods, and some of the men herded horses along the shore. The party spent the winter of 1804-5 among the Mandan Indians about twenty-five miles north of present Bismarck, North Dakota, in a camp of log cabins which they built and called Fort Mandan. It was while they were at Fort Mandan that Sacajawea, the famous Indian woman of the expedition, joined them.

The story of her life reads like fiction. Sacajawea and two other Shoshone girls had been captured as children by the Minnetarees, an enemy tribe. They were sold or traded in gambling games from one tribe to another, but one of the little girls escaped their captor one night. The accepted version of this occurrence is that the three thought their owner would be drunk after a big celebration and planned to slip away while he was in a stupor. Sacajawea and one other girl woke up, but they could not wake the third without making a noise which might arouse someone. Sacajawea is supposed to have refused to leave the sleeping girl alone and hence stayed in captivity with her while the third started back for the Shoshones alone.

Sacajawea and her companion had been traded to a French-Canadian trapper by the name of Toussaint Charbonneau by the time Lewis and Clark reached the Mandan country. They were extremely eager to find an interpreter to accompany them who knew the Indian languages west of the Missouri River. When the explorers heard that two Shoshone women were in the Mandan country, they sent for Charbonneau, who agreed to accompany the group with one of his wives (Sacajawea) and leave the other girl behind. Lewis and Clark were delighted to find that Charbonneau knew the Indian languages along the Missouri and could act as interpreter as far as the Rockies, where, presumably, Sacajawea could take over.

While they were in camp, Sacajawea's first child was born, and when the expedition started on up the Missouri in the spring of 1805 with thirty-two people, Sacajawea carried the baby. Clark became very fond of him and nicknamed him Pompey. In fact, both Sacajawea and the baby endeared themselves to the expedition, but Charbonneau was merely tolerated. He was considered cowardly and disagreeable. One time Clark interfered in a fury when Charbonneau was beating Sacajawea.

When they came to the forks of the Missouri (present Three Forks, Montana), they had to examine each branch to determine which one led toward the estimated source of the Columbia River. They decided that the north branch, which they named for Thomas Jefferson, went in the right direction. Although Sacajawea was of little help in identifying places she had crossed as a child, she did recognize the area east of Three Forks as Shoshone country and pointed out a creek where her tribe had come to collect white earth for paint. She could not, however, tell Lewis and Clark which fork to take or how to get through the mountains to the Columbia.

When the Jefferson branched, Lewis and Clark again divided the expedition into two reconnaissance groups to find the best route from that point. Because of a series of frustrating mishaps, it was August before the expedition was reunited. The captains knew that they must get through the mountains quickly before the passes were blocked by early snow. They had to find Indians who knew the trails, however, because they could not possibly find their way through the Rockies without a guide. They also had to have horses, for when they came to the end of the navigable rivers, they would have to take more supplies and trade goods than the men could carry on their backs.

They had seen smoke signals for several weeks, which indicated that Indians were near and that they had seen the white men; but the expedition could catch no sight of an Indian. They found out later that the Shoshones ran from the white party as soon as they saw it approaching, and the fires were lighted to warn other bands that some kind of dangerous-looking group was coming. The Shoshones hurried toward the higher ridges of the Rockies as fast as they could, where, ordinarily, hostile Indian tribes did not pursue them.

Lewis decided to go ahead of the boats on foot to look for the elusive Indians, and he left a note for Clark on a pole, telling him which fork of the river to take. This time Lewis was careful to fasten the note to a dry willow pole, which would not tempt a beaver. On a previous occasion when he had tied a note to a green willow pole, a beaver had evidently eaten note and all, and Clark had not received the message.

Near present Grayling, Montana, Lewis set off with Drouilliard and Shields, and the three separated to look for Indians. When Lewis saw an Indian on horseback about two miles away, he looked through his telescope and found that the Indian was dressed differently from the Plains Indians; Lewis therefore concluded that he must be a Shoshone.

The Indian saw Lewis when he was about a mile away and halted. Lewis hurriedly grabbed a blanket from his pack and waved it above his head before bringing it to the ground, a friendship sign which he had learned. Drouilliard and Shields, who had been hidden in the underbrush, came into the open just then and continued to move toward the Indian on both sides of the trail, making it appear to the Indian that Lewis was leading him into a trap. Lewis finally signaled to the men to stop, but Shields did not notice the sign. When the armed man came closer to the Indian, he wheeled and rode away to save himself from this apparent ambush.

Lewis was heartsick, because the whole success of the expedition depended on making contact with Indians who had horses and who knew the trails through the Rockies. The next day they crossed the summit of the divide, and Lewis wrote in his journal that he tasted the waters of the Columbia for the first time. The river he saw was the Lemhi, but it does drain into the Columbia eventually. Finally, on August 13, the explorers stumbled onto three Indian women who had not seen them coming because of a hill. One ran away, but an old woman and a little girl were not quick enough.

They bent over, expecting the men to cut off their heads. Lewis, of course, quickly showered presents on them and tried to make them understand that he wanted to be friends with their tribe. Drouilliard used sign language, understood by all the tribes, to ask the old woman to take them to her camp. She agreed, but on the way they met sixty warriors of her band coming to rescue the two from what they thought was a hostile tribe. Lewis threw down his rifle, and, as the advance guard of the Shoshones came up to them, the old woman rushed up to show her presents and to assure the warriors that these strange beings were friendly. The chief, whose name was Cameahwait, then got down off his horse, embraced Lewis cordially, and took the men to his camp.

Lewis had the difficult job of persuading the Shoshones to stay with him until Clark and the rest of the party could come up the river in the boats. Since the Indians had only berries to eat and were half-starved, Lewis sent out a hunter who managed to shoot a deer, which they devoured as fast as possible. Small groups of the Shoshones then began to disappear until Lewis was afraid that his chance to get horses and guides was lost. However, just at that moment, an Indian came back from the river to announce that he had seen the canoes coming.

In the meantime, Clark, Sacajawea, and Charbonneau had left the canoes to walk on ahead. Suddenly, Clark saw Sacajawea begin to dance and suck her fingers which in sign language meant that she had met her own tribe, the Shoshones. Clark then recognized Drouilliard among the Indians and realized, with great joy, that Lewis had found Indians and horses. The next incredible thing which happened was that one of the Indian women rushed forward and embraced Sacajawea. She was the girl who had left the other two captives, and although it seemed absolutely impossible, she had worked her way alone back to her own people.

As though this were not already too much of a coincidence, when the whole party gathered for a conference with Cameahwait, Sacajawea was asked to help interpret. After a few minutes, she rushed over to Cameahwait, weeping. She had recognized him as her own brother. Lewis and Clark had stumbled onto the one band whom Sacajawea's presence made it most helpful to meet.

Even though they were eager to move on into buffalo country for their fall hunt before the Plains Indians got there to drive them off, the Shoshones stayed with Lewis and Clark for several days to help them round up horses from neighboring bands of Shoshones. In return, the captains promised them that they would tell the fur traders in the East to use the Shoshone country as their crossing place, so that the traders could bring them guns with which to fight their enemy tribes in buffalo country. Until 1805 the Shoshones had been cut off by mountains and difficult rivers from the Coast tribes, who got white goods; and the hostile tribes to the east of the Rockies kept them from receiving the eastern trade goods. This promise therefore delighted the Shoshones so much that they sent guides along with Lewis and Clark to lead the party to the Lemhi Pass.

Once across the Bitterroot Mountains at that point, the expedition followed the Indians' directions to go north along the range up to Lolo Creek where they could again cross the same range of mountains, which bends there to the northwest. This part of the trip was most difficult. They had only berries to eat at one point, and nothing but bear grease and candles at another. In addition, the weather was very cold, and they were in danger of having their feet freeze in their thin moccasins. Clark took some men on ahead through present Lolo Pass and soon struck Nez Perce camps on the Clearwater River. He bought salmon and dried camas roots from them and sent the food back by messenger to Lewis and the rest of the party. From that time on their food problems were over, except that the change to a fish diet upset their stomachs and some of the men were quite sick.

They followed the Lolo Trail to the south branch of the Clearwater and traveled along it to its junction with the north fork halfway between present Weippe and Lapwai, Idaho, where they made a camp to rest and to build canoes for the rest of the journey to the Pacific. A Nez Perce story persists to the present time that the first Nez Perces who met the white men decided that they ought to kill them, but that Wat-ku-ese, a Nez Perce girl, persuaded them to treat the white people as friends. Wat-ku-ese is supposed to have escaped with her baby from an enemy tribe and to have been aided by some white people on her way home. This sounds so much like a garbled version of the Sacajawea story that one wonders if it is not just that. In any case, however, the Nez Perces were extremely friendly and helpful to the white party.

In fact, the men were hindered in their work by the desire of the Indians to feast and dance. They were particularly intrigued by Clark's Negro servant York. Having never heard of black men, they at first, like the tribes to the east, licked their fingers and tried to rub off his color, thinking that he was painted black as a means of appeasing some spirit. Another member of the expedition, Cruzat, had brought along his violin, and all along the way the men had done square dances in the evening to his music. The Indians, of course, had never heard stringed instruments, and they loved to listen to his music and to watch York and the others dance. Then they, in turn, wanted to perform some of their own Indian dances. Since Lewis and Clark had instructions to do everything possible to please the Indians, they spent a great deal of time in such festivities.

To continue their journey, they made dugout canoes, using fire to char the wood as the Indians did, since there were no trees suitable for bark canoes. When they had finished five canoes, they branded their horses with an iron brought by Lewis, left them in the care of the Nez Perce Chief Twisted Hair, and set off down the river.

Wherever they stopped to camp along the Snake and the Columbia, large groups of Indians appeared to enjoy the sight of these strange people whom Indian messengers had described. The men had to dance and entertain the throngs. The Indians believed, of course, that the guns of the white men were strong magic. Indians who were then children told stories many years later of the sights which they or their parents saw. One account is that a member of the expedition made a loud noise which was such powerful medicine that it brought a swan down out of the sky and that he also knew magic which would call fire down from the sky. In his journal Clark tells of shooting a swan and of lighting his pipe with a sun-glass at that place.

The Nez Perces were also amazed that the white men would eat dogs, which the Columbia River Indians would not touch. They raised dogs for hunting. The explorers got so tired of a fish diet that they varied it with dog meat, which some of the men liked very

much. As was mentioned earlier, this was one point of disagree-
ment between Lewis and Clark: Lewis enjoyed it, whereas Clark
could not stand it.

When the Indians told them that they were near the junction of
the Snake and the main river, Clark went out on a side trip to explore the forks, going as far as the mouth of the Yakima River before returning to the canoes, which were hurrying down the main
Columbia. They soon began to see white trade goods among the
Indians, but the Indians indicated that the white traders from the
coast did not come up the river that far. The Coast tribes traded the
white goods from one to another of the bands farther inland. As
Lewis and Clark got nearer the Pacific, they found that the Indians
began to steal goods from them at the portages which they had to
make around rapids. These Indians were obviously used to the
white sea-otter traders and were beginning to think that they were
justified in taking from the whites as much as they could.

In early November, the expedition reached the Pacific and chose
a spot near the ocean about seven miles south of the mouth of the
Columbia for their winter camp. The men were almost as miserable
as they had been at any time on the journey, because cold raw rain,
which kept their clothes and bedding wet, fell constantly while they
were cutting trees and putting up cabins. Since they could not find
any game for food, they were reduced to the Indian diet of roots
and fish, and for these the Coast Indians demanded high payment.
They had their cabins up by Christmas, but meat was still scarce,
and the journals record a dreary Christmas Day with "spoiled elk
meat" for the gala dinner.

Sacajawea had continued to endear herself to the members of the
expedition, both because her presence had enabled them to get
horses and guides from the Shoshones and because she was a
charming and courageous person. During the winter when she
heard that Clark was taking a group to a beach where the Indians
were cutting up a dead whale that had been washed ashore, she
begged to go along, saying that it seemed unfair that, after she had
come all this way, she should not be allowed to see the ocean or the
huge fish. Clark obligingly took her along.

As soon as they thought they could get back through the mountains, they started for the East—March 23, 1806. Chief Twisted
Hair produced their horses in good condition when they reached

the Clearwater. After they crossed the Lolo Pass, the captains separated. Clark took some of the men south along their inward trail as far as Three Forks and then cut overland to the Yellowstone River, following it to its junction with the Missouri. As soon as the Yellowstone was navigable, Clark built canoes for use on the return trip to St. Louis. Lewis with the rest of the party headed northeast from the Lolo Pass and hit the Missouri north of present Great Falls, Montana, instead of retracing their path along the Bitterroot River and down Jefferson River to Three Forks. The two groups met at the junction of the Missouri and the Yellowstone and proceeded downstream to St. Louis. They were greeted as men returned to life, because people had supposed them dead. A messenger hurried off with the news to President Jefferson, who had almost given up hope of their return.

The Lewis and Clark expedition had accomplished an extraordinary task under difficult circumstances with the loss of only one man and that from sickness. They not only had strengthened the claim of the United States to the Oregon country, but had succeeded to a remarkable degree in creating an atmosphere of friendliness with the Indians west of the Rockies which enabled American fur traders to take advantage of the route found by the explorers. The party had also taken voluminous notes on the natural history and nature of the Indian tribes which gave the public a vast amount of scientific information about the region. The captains are regarded as among the most able and admirable leaders in our history.

Winship Venture

When the news of the return of the expedition reached people in the East, it aroused their curiosity about the region west of the Mississippi. Fur traders were particularly eager to take advantage of the new route to the Pacific Northwest. It took considerable capital, however, to embark on such a venture, and it was not until 1809 that one was undertaken. The Winship brothers, Jonathan and Abiel, outfitted a ship that left Boston in 1809 and sailed round South America to Hawaii where the men spent the winter. In the spring of 1810, they sailed to the mouth of the Columbia and went upriver about forty-five miles to a spot where they planted a garden and began to put up buildings. The spring floods, however, soon covered the site; consequently, they had to move to higher ground. Before they got well under way in their second attempt, the Indians showed so much hostility that they abandoned the attempt.

The Indians did not want these men to set up a post because they had become the "middlemen" in selling trade goods, supplied by white coast traders, to the interior tribes farther up the river. If the white men established a trading post east of the Indians' location, the latter would then be deprived of their position as merchants.

John Jacob Astor's Expeditions

While the Winships were engaged in their unsuccessful undertaking to build a fur-trading post on the lower Columbia, a New York merchant, John Jacob Astor, was organizing a similar venture on a much grander scale. He had vast amounts of capital which he had made partly by trading in furs along the St. Lawrence River. He had become well acquainted with the partners of the North West Company and visited with them on his trips to Montreal. They had a club where they enjoyed lavish dinners, and, since their conversation naturally turned to their fur-trading expeditions into northwestern Canada, Astor learned of the wonderful beaver country in the Saskatchewan, Athabasca, and northern Columbia regions, as reports of Mackenzie's, Fraser's, and Thompson's discoveries were discussed in his hearing.

Astor realized that the North West Company was put to a great deal of unnecessary expense in carrying furs from present British Columbia across Canada to Montreal. It occurred to him that the sensible thing to do was to build a post at the mouth of the Columbia River. If posts were established at intervals from St. Louis along the Missouri, the Snake, and the Columbia rivers, beaver pelts collected west of the Rockies could be floated down these streams to the mouth of the Columbia and held there until ships sent round South America could pick them up and take them on to Asia and Europe via the Pacific or back to New York via the Atlantic. In addition, such ships could pick up sea-otter furs, and thus profits could be realized from both sea furs and land furs, something previously not attempted to any extent.

Astor's imagination was excited by such a prospect, and he also conceived of making his post an agricultural one. Food could be raised and sold to the Russians in Alaska. Lewis and Clark had reported on huge stands of timber on the coast, and lumber from these could be sold in Alaska or even the Orient.

Moreover, Astor's troubles with British tariffs made such a plan seem enticing. After the American Revolution, restrictions on American trade with British colonies had increased, and as we have seen, were often very severe. During some years, if Astor bought furs in Montreal, he was required to have them shipped in British ships first to England and then back to New York. This made the freight charges extremely high, and Astor was eager to avoid them.

Because Astor needed experienced traders for such a venture, he first proposed a joint partnership with the North West Company, but was refused. Deciding to go on with the project alone, Astor did persuade twenty-seven of the North West Company's employees to resign and join him. He named this group the Pacific Fur Company. It was this news which David Thompson heard when he returned from the Columbia in the summer of 1810, and, as we have seen, he hurried back to the Pacific Northwest to start on his own trek to the mouth of the Columbia.

Astor organized a sea expedition under the command of Captain Jonathan Thorn and a land expedition under the direction of Wilson Price Hunt and had them both ready to start in the fall of 1810. In spite of his shrewdness in business dealings, Astor was a poor judge of personality, and this trait was one of the causes of the tragedies that occurred in both groups. Let us first trace the story of the group going by sea on board the *Tonquin*.

Captain Thorn was a United States Navy lieutenant, on leave to command Astor's expedition. Thorn was, of course, used to enforcing the strict naval discipline of that day. A ship's captain still had the authority to flog sailors for disobedience, and he expected absolute compliance with his orders. Thorn undertook the voyage in this frame of mind. The former employees of the North West Company, on the other hand, were used to acting in an extremely independent fashion. In fact, a person was not likely to survive long in the wilderness unless he was resourceful, fearless, and able to act decisively. Consequently, when Captain Thorn ordered Duncan McDougall, Donald McKenzie, Alexander McKay, Robert Stuart, and the other

Astor partners to put out the lights in their cabins at eight o'clock, not to "fraternize" with the hired men of the expedition, to exercise on deck at stated times, and to keep their bunks ready for inspection, they grew rebellious. They regarded themselves as passengers on a merchant ship and felt that Thorn had no right to demand that they observe any naval discipline.

By the time the *Tonquin* reached the mouth of the Columbia on March 22, 1811, after having stopped at the Hawaiian Islands for food and water, the feeling between Thorn and the passengers was so hostile that he was interested only in getting rid of them. Consequently, five men were lost in the first ill-considered attempt to enter the river.

After other unsuccessful attempts to get boats through the breakers, Thorn ordered the men to push out a small ship carried in the hold, and four more men started out in it ahead of the *Tonquin*. Favorable winds just then pushed the *Tonquin* in across the bar, but the smaller ship upset, and two of the men in it drowned. After the unnecessary loss of seven of their party, the remaining men felt such hatred for Thorn that they quickly chose a site where the cargo could be unloaded so that they could leave the ship.

The spot they chose was on the south side of the Columbia, ten miles up the river—present Astoria, Oregon. As soon as buildings could be built to protect the cargo, the goods were put on shore, and Thorn sailed on up the coast. He planned to trade for sea-otter skins, to visit the Russians in Alaska to make arrangements for selling produce to them, and to return home via the Orient. Unfortunately, Alexander McKay, one of the ablest of the Astorians, and a crew to man the ship went with Thorn.

All that is known of the *Tonquin*'s fate comes from Indian stories, but enough details gradually drifted back to the Astorians to make it fairly certain that the following incidents occurred. Thorn stopped on Vancouver Island near Nootka (probably Clayoquot Sound) to trade with the Indians. He expected to be able to buy skins from them quickly, but they wanted to spend considerable time bargaining. They demanded more payment than Thorn had anticipated because they had been trading with white ships since the 1780's and had learned the value of the furs to the white traders.

Thorn grew impatient, of course, and became surly with the Indians. Moreover, he disregarded McKay's advice to let only a few Indians on board at a time. Finally, Thorn struck one of the Indians. McKay and the others were convinced that the Indians would return to avenge this insult, and they urged Thorn to leave, but he refused. The next day the Indians returned to the ship and killed all men on deck, including Thorn and McKay.

Five men who were in the hold apparently escaped notice, and four of them left the ship in a rowboat that night, intending to try to get back to Astoria. The wind must have driven them on shore, however, because the Indians found and killed them. The fifth seems to have stayed in the hold until the Indians came back on board the next day to loot the ship, whereupon either by design or accident he blew it up. At any rate, the ship exploded, killing a hundred or more Indians.

An Indian interpreter, who had been on board the *Tonquin,* made his way back to Astoria and reported what had happened. The Astorians were so badly frightened that Duncan McDougall, the partner given command of the post by Astor, did a very foolish thing. He told the Indians around Astoria that he held the spirit of smallpox in an empty bottle, and that if the Indians threatened to harm the whites in any way, he would let loose the smallpox spirit which would then attack them. This threat simply alarmed the Chinooks and other tribes at the mouth of the Columbia who had been friendly. We shall see how this notion of releasing evil spirits to cause disease became one factor in the Indians' desire to kill Marcus Whitman, one of the Protestant missionaries.

When the Astorians heard from Indians that white men had established a trading post on the Spokane River, they knew that it would belong to the North West Company. Even though the overland group had not yet arrived, they decided to send David Stuart with a few men to set up a rival post in the Spokane territory. Stuart was just ready to depart when David Thompson with eight of his men arrived at Astoria on July 15, 1812, as we have seen.

After a week's visit with the Astorians, Thompson started back east, and David Stuart with eight men, including two Hawaiians, accompanied them part way up the river. The Astorians decided to locate their first trading post at the junction of the Okanogan and Columbia rivers where they left Alexander Ross in a small fort

Astoria, Columbia River. (An engraving in Charles Wilkes's Narrative, *Philadelphia, 1845)*

which they built to trade with the Indians during the winter. Stuart went north in the Thompson River country to encourage the Indians to start collecting beaver skins there.

While these events were going on, the overland party under the direction of Wilson Price Hunt was having almost as bad a time as the *Tonquin*'s passengers had had in getting to Astoria. Hunt was the only American among the partners and, as such, was made Astor's proxy. He was a loyal, intelligent man, but he had had no experience in wilderness travel and so was not well prepared to lead the group. Donald McKenzie, another member of the expedition, was an experienced North West Company trader who was somewhat irked because Astor had at first made Hunt and him co-captains and then had sent a messenger after them with a notice that Hunt was to be in complete charge.

They had so much difficulty in hiring the required number of men that they had to spend the winter of 1810 in camp 450 miles up the Missouri River from St. Louis. In the spring they continued up the river in boats as the Lewis and Clark party had done. They soon met three Kentuckians (Edward Robinson, John Hoback, and

Jacob Rizner) who had gone out with Andrew Henry three years before to trade in the Rockies. To get away from hostile Indians, they had crossed the Rockies and built a shelter on Henry's Fork of the Snake River in present Idaho—the first American post west of the Rockies.

The three men were returning with the intention of leaving the fur trade permanently, but, when they met the Hunt party, they turned around and went back in order to show them an overland trail to the Rockies which would avoid the Missouri country of the Sioux and Blackfeet Indians who had made trouble for other traders. Therefore the Hunt party (consisting of sixty-one men plus the wife of the interpreter, Pierre Dorion, and their two small children) bought horses from Indians in South Dakota and went on through the Black Hills, the Big Horn, the Wind River, and the Teton Mountains to the log cabins built by Andrew Henry.

Thinking that they could float down the Snake from there to the Pacific, they made the mistake of building canoes. They left a few men at the shelter with the horses, and the rest of the party started out in mid-October in the boats. Of course, as they proceeded, they discovered that the river was too turbulent for canoes and the canyon sides too high and steep for portaging. They went on for 340 miles before Hunt sent a few of the men back to try to reach the shelter and return with the horses. However, the route was too difficult to manage in the winter, and they had to return to the main party on foot.

The company then formed small groups in order to find game more easily. Donald McKenzie with five men cut away from the river to the northwest. When they hit the Snake again near Hell's Canyon, they crossed the river and worked their way through the Blue Mountains to the Columbia. They were weak from lack of food when they reached Astoria in late January, 1812, but their hardships were slight in comparison with those of the remaining members of the party.

They broke up into two groups, with Hunt leading one down the north side of the Snake, and Ramsay Crooks the leader of the other on the south side. They worked their way down the river until they came to the beginning of Hell's Canyon where their way was completely barred on both sides. The Indians whom they had met had little food and few horses or dogs to sell, and the Astorians were weak from hunger, having had only an occasional fish or beaver to eat. In this condition, they had to work their way back up the river until they could find Indian camps and procure horses. Hunt found Indians who had horses to sell, and the men killed some for food.

When they were almost at the end of their endurance, Hunt's group came upon some Indians who agreed to guide them through the mountains. They cut away from the river and with somewhat more food (although still very little) made their way across the Blue Mountains. Hunt and around thirty of his men reached Astoria in February. Some of the party had preferred to stay with the Indian bands whom they had met, hoping to regain their strength before coming the rest of the way.

During all of this time, Mrs. Dorion had kept her two children alive, had given birth to a third who died, and had kept up with the men, part of the time on foot. When Dorion had managed to buy a horse, he let the children ride on it, and, even when it was the only horse left, the men refused to kill it for food so that Mrs. Dorion could have it as a pack horse. Her courage and cheerfulness endeared her to the men as Sacajawea's similar traits had done to the Lewis and Clark party. The following year Mrs. Dorion went through even a worse ordeal after an Indian attack, keeping her children alive through deep snow and blizzards until she could get help for them.

After Hunt arrived, the Astorians decided that John Reed should go back East with dispatches for Astor; that Robert Stuart should take supplies to the Okanogan post; and that Russell Farnham should go back to pick up supplies that Hunt had cached along the way. The three groups started out together, but they were attacked at the first portage by Wishram Indians who stole the dispatches and some of the supplies. All of the men therefore joined forces and went together to the Okanogan post where they picked up the twenty-five hundred beaver skins which David Stuart had gathered during the winter, and from there started back to Astoria.

After passing the site of present Pasco, they heard somebody call to them in English. They saw two naked white men—Ramsay Crooks and John Day—who had finally managed to get across the Blue Mountains and then had been robbed and stripped by the Indians around Celilo Falls. They hurriedly took the men to Astoria to recuperate. To their added joy, they found that Astor's second ship, the *Beaver,* had arrived at Astoria the previous day, bringing more supplies and trade goods.

They were now ready to outfit additional trading posts and to try again to get dispatches to Astor. On June 29, 1812, Robert Stuart set out to try to reach New York overland, accompanying the trading parties as far as the fork of the Columbia and Snake rivers. Stuart and four other men then bought horses from the Walla Wallas and started back along the route by which they had come the preceding year. By another series of amazing coincidences, Stuart's party met several of the Astorians who had not yet reached the Columbia. In trying to guide him over a less difficult trail than the one along the Snake, they got lost, and their horses were stolen by Indians.

When they finally got to the ridge of the Rockies on foot, they discovered that they were on a wide, easy pass leading to a plain which they crossed to the Platte River. Here they met Indian traders from St. Louis, bought canoes, and went on easily down the Platte and Missouri rivers to St. Louis and on by ship to New York.

When Stuart's party got there, they reported that they had found an easy route through the mountains, and in *Niles Register,* a magazine of that period, there was an article predicting that wagons would some day follow this path to the coast. Many years later when the Oregon Trail did actually coincide with much of Stuart's trail, people tried to figure out exactly where he crossed the continental divide. It has been decided that he was in South Pass or on the edge of it—the low, easy gap through the main spur of the Rockies which made it possible for settlers to cross them in wagons.

In the meantime, the Astorians had built a number of fur-trading posts, many of them close to the rival establishments of the North West Company. For example, Spokane House, the North West Company post built by David Thompson's men in 1810 was only a few yards from Fort Spokane, built by the Astorians in 1812. It was here in January, 1813, that North West Company messengers from Montreal brought the news that the War of 1812 had broken out between the United States and England and that a British warship was on its way to seize Astoria. The Astorians at Fort Spokane hastily returned to Astoria to warn the others.

Wilson Price Hunt had left in the *Beaver* to complete arrangements with the Russians in Alaska for the sale of food, lumber, and other products. He had not returned because the ship was damaged and went directly to Hawaii where Hunt intended to meet Astor's next ship as it stopped there on its way to Astoria. The ship, unfortunately, sank, and it was August, 1813, by the time Hunt could find one to take him back to the Columbia.

When he reached Astoria, he found that the other partners were determined to abandon the Astor posts for fear of the British. Hunt returned to Hawaii to find a ship in which he could take Astor's supplies back home, but while he was gone the second time the Astorians sold all of the posts to the North West Company. When Astor learned of the sale, he maintained that they had deliberately wrecked his enterprise to aid their former employer, the North West Company.

Some of the Astorians went back to work for the North West Company and stayed in the Oregon country; others returned home. The British warship *Raccoon* did reach Astoria in November, 1814, and its commander, Captain Black, seemed to regret that the post had already been sold to the Canadian company so that there was nothing for him to seize. He did, however, go through the ceremony of claiming the fort for Britain and renamed the post Fort George. In the end this turned out to be a fortunate thing for the Americans because the Treaty of Ghent, ending the war in 1814, specified that any property taken by either country from the other was to be returned. A United States ship was sent to take possession; however, since the property had been sold as a commercial transaction, the seizure was only a formality, and the North West Company continued in possession. The transfer did give the United States the basis for another claim to the region.

The sale of Astoria to the British put an end to American trade in the Oregon country for many years except for an occasional ship that sailed up the coast looking for sea-otter skins. The oriental market for those furs had declined so much, however, that this trade was slight in comparison with its early years.

The North West Company expanded its beaver trade in all directions as soon as its competitor was gone. The Spokane post became increasingly important. It is thought that the Canadian company left its own building (Spokane House) to move into the more com-

modious Astorian structure (Fort Spokane) and later enlarged it
into a third post used finally by the Hudson's Bay Company. Archeologists have made diggings at the site nine miles northwest of
present Spokane and have uncovered house posts in a pattern which
seems to confirm this theory.

HUDSON'S BAY COMPANY IN THE OREGON COUNTRY

Although the North West Company was rid of competition from
the Americans, the Hudson's Bay Company began to assert itself in
central and northwest Canada until the friction between the two
companies resulted in actual warfare. The bloodshed and violence
finally reached the point where both companies realized that their
profits were disappearing in the fight. Moreover, the British government had become concerned over the rivalry. Consequently, in 1821
the two companies merged, keeping the name of Hudson's Bay
Company in order to enjoy the benefits of that firm's monopoly of
the trade in the Hudson Bay region.

John McLoughlin

John McLoughlin was chosen by the Hudson's Bay Company to
be in charge of the fur trade in the Oregon country, and he became
one of the most important figures in our history. He was the son of
a poor Catholic family living on the St. Lawrence River in Canada.
However, his maternal grandfather, a Protestant, had considerable
money and educated young John. The grandfather was eager for
him to become a doctor, but John's imagination was excited by the
stories of his fur-trading uncles, and he longed for the adventure
and romance of a fur trader's life.

It turned out that he was able to combine the two occupations
since, after he had studied to be a physician, he was made a post
doctor for the North West Company at Fort William on Lake Superior. He did as little doctoring as possible, and as much trading. He
was such a successful trader and able manager that when the North
West Company decided to unite with the Hudson's Bay Company,
John was named as one of the representatives of the former company to go to London to arrange the details of the merger.

In 1824 McLoughlin crossed the continent from Hudson Bay to Fort George (Astoria) by canoe. After he and the Hudson's Bay Company governor, George Simpson, explored both sides of the Columbia River, they decided to move the main post from Fort George to present Vancouver, Washington. There were several reasons for the change. By this time, England was becoming convinced that she could not hold the area south of the Columbia, but she still wanted to get title to the region north of the river. Therefore, it would be more sensible to have the main post of the British company north of the Columbia. The site had to be near enough to the ocean to be reached by the largest ships, and it should be surrounded by farming country so that the men could raise sufficient produce to make the post self-supporting. The location of Fort Vancouver satisfied all of these purposes, and it was also near rivers giving access to Puget Sound to the north, the Willamette Valley to the south, and the fur country through which the Columbia and Snake rivers flowed.

Under McLoughlin's able direction, Fort Vancouver developed into a large establishment, eventually housing from five to seven hundred residents. A wall of posts twenty feet high enclosed an area 250 yards long and 150 yards wide which contained over thirty buildings, including warehouses, carpenter shops, smithies, a bakery, store, schoolhouse, chapel, living quarters for the men, and McLoughlin's house in the middle where the gentlemen dined. McLoughlin had many pieces of elegant furniture brought from England over the years, and, as the farms and livestock herds increased, the food served was excellent. Outside the fort were rows of wooden houses where the workmen lived, and many Indians were usually camped there.

The Indians came to respect the Hudson's Bay men because McLoughlin required that the Indians be treated with consideration. He kept his word with them, and they were eager enough for McLoughlin's trade goods to trap beavers as a means of payment. The Hudson's Bay Company men covered the entire river system north of California and west of the Rockies, trapping and trading for furs which were taken in canoes or on packhorses to the nearest port. Then in the spring the brigades came from the East along the network of rivers from Hudson Bay to the Columbia, portaging where necessary as the early voyageurs had done before them. The canoes brought mail and such supplies and trade goods as they could and then returned east with the bundles of furs. Ships came round the Horn from England with heavy equipment and additional supplies. Although the wilderness life was still rigorous and dangerous, the era from 1824 to 1834 was one of relative peace and expansion of the trade.

LATER AMERICAN OVERLAND TRADERS

Until the 1830's McLoughlin had little competition to contend with. During the War of 1812, the St. Louis traders had had to keep out of the way of the British to the north, and even after the close of the war they stayed east of the Rockies for several years. Then in the 1820's, they began to cross the mountains again and tried to challenge the Hudson's Bay Company men in their control of the fur trade in the Snake River country. In 1825 Peter Skene Ogden, a famous Hudson's Bay Company trader, ran into a group of American trappers belonging to the Rocky Mountain Fur Company on his Snake River expedition. He got many fewer skins than usual, and a large number of his men deserted him and joined the Americans.

Jedediah Smith

In 1828, a member of the Rocky Mountain Fur Company and one of the great American traders and explorers, Jedediah Smith, reached Fort Vancouver. Earlier he had attempted to buy furs and trap in the Southwest, but the Spaniards drove him out of California. He decided to go northward and explore the country between California and the Columbia River. While camped along the Umpqua River in Oregon, he left briefly to reconnoiter for a good river crossing. When he returned Smith found that Indians had attacked his camp, killing a number of his men. Not knowing if the missing men were dead, he hastened up the coast to Fort Vancouver where he found the three men who had survived the attack.

McLoughlin entertained the Americans graciously and sent some of his men to warn the Indians that he would not permit them to molest any white men. The Hudson's Bay Company men forced the Indians to return as many of the stolen furs as they could find, and when they returned to Fort Vancouver with the furs, McLoughlin bought them from Smith at the current market price. Smith was so astonished at this generous treatment from a rival trading outfit that he decided not to challenge the Hudson's Bay Company further. He therefore returned east of the Rockies to trap. Unfortunately, while on a trading expedition in the Southwest a few years later, Smith was killed by an Indian. For our own area his achievements included leading the first white group overland from California to the Columbia River and making maps which were of great aid to later explorers.

Benjamin Bonneville

Captain Benjamin Bonneville was another American trader who tried to compete with McLoughlin without success, but his reaction to the Hudson's Bay Company was far different from Smith's. Bonneville secured a leave of absence from the War Department in order to try his hand at fur trading, but he was supposed to keep a record of his travels and report to the United States government on whatever geographical and scientific discoveries he made.

In 1832 Bonneville hired 110 men, loaded twenty wagons with traps and trading goods, and followed the path of the Rocky Mountain Fur Company, whose members had used wagons to transport their goods along the Platte and Sweetwater rivers to South Pass. Bonneville is notable for taking his wagons on through the pass to Pierre's Hole in the Teton Basin of present Idaho where the rendezvous for the fur trade was held that year.

The American fur traders did not build many permanent posts like those of the North West and Hudson's Bay companies. Instead, they trapped in small groups during the winter, building temporary shelters or using Indian tepees. Most of them were accompanied by Indians wives who helped the men in tanning leather, making clothes from the skins, drying meat, roots, berries, and other types of food for winter use. In fact, some of the trappers became very much attached to their Indian wives; but many of the unions were temporary.

Each summer the American traders and the Indians in the entire Rocky Mountain area would meet at a place agreed upon the preceding year for a period of two or three weeks. This gathering, called a *rendezvous,* was a very colorful affair. Pack trains came from St. Louis with flour, sugar, coffee, liquor, and other items not available in the wilderness. The trappers, in turn, brought to the rendezvous the skins they had gathered during the winter and exchanged them for the trade goods.

Many of the men had not tasted city foods since the last rendezvous, and they were ravenous for the civilized delicacies. Hundreds of Indians came to the rendezvous with their finest horses. The days were spent in trading, horse racing, feasting, and general visiting. Dancing and gambling were popular sports that sometimes went on through the night and day. Oftentimes, a trapper spent all of the money from the year's catch for the food and drink consumed during the rendezvous, so that he went back to another winter's trapping with nothing to show for his previous year's work.

After the 1832 rendezvous, Bonneville built a post on the Green River and sent out trapping parties. The other traders were able to outbid him for furs, however, because they got many skins from Indians who were better acquainted with the country and could find richer beaver grounds. Bonneville realized that he would need more trade goods, and he went to Fort Walla Walla, the Hudson's Bay Company post near the site of Wallula (which is now under water), to try to buy them. Pierre Pambrun, the factor there, entertained him graciously, gave him food and necessary supplies, but refused to sell him anything that could be used as trade goods.

This infuriated Bonneville, who went back to his post determined to succeed in a second year of trading. He could not compete, however, with the Rocky Mountain Fur Company, the American Fur Company (another Astor organization which operated east of the Rockies), and the independent trappers who were used to the area. Bonneville again visited the Columbia, but McLoughlin had instructed the Indians not to trade with Americans. After another year's struggle, consequently, Bonneville gave up and went home in 1834. He blamed the Hudson's Bay Company for his failure and gave the picture of the company as a hateful monster which Washington Irving used in *Adventures of Captain Bonneville.*

Old Fort Walla Walla, called Fort Nez Perce by the North West and Hudson's Bay companies, was built at the junction of the Walla Walla and Columbia rivers. The lithographs were made by J. M. Stanley, artist with Isaac Stevens' party on his railroad survey from the Mississippi to the Pacific, 1853-55. (In Supplement to Volume I of Reports of Explorations and Surveys [Ex. Doc. No. 46, 35th Cong., 2nd Sess.], Washington, 1859)

Nathaniel Wyeth

Another independent American fur trader who in 1832 and 1834 tried unsuccessfully to compete with McLoughlin on the Columbia was Nathaniel Wyeth, an ice dealer in Cambridge, Massachusetts, who was intrigued by the tales of profits made in the Oregon country fur trade. The winter before his first trip, a ship trading in sea otters on our coast had also taken back to Boston some barrels of salted salmon from the Columbia. They sold so readily in the East that Wyeth conceived the idea of doing business on our coast in salmon as well as in furs. He therefore raised enough capital from friends and relatives to outfit a land and a sea expedition as Astor had done, and he accompanied the overland group himself.

He made overly ambitious arrangements for the trip—putting uniforms on his men and teaching them to drill in military formation. He also had built a boat with wheels, which he thought he could use on both land and water, but it proved to be too heavy for the mountains. Fortunately, at Independence, Missouri, he met William Sublette, one of the Rocky Mountain Fur Company's leaders, and Sublette showed the party how to put packs on mules and how to camp and hunt. Wyeth was very intelligent and was soon able to manage the trail himself.

When Wyeth got to Fort Vancouver, McLoughlin entertained him with the same gracious hospitality he showed to everyone. Wyeth found, however, that the Indians would not trade with him because they felt too much loyalty to the Hudson's Bay Company. Moreover, at Fort Vancouver Wyeth learned that his ship had sunk near the Society Islands. This represented not only a big financial loss, but meant that he would not have trade goods to exchange for furs even if he could find any for sale.

McLoughlin and Wyeth seem to have made some agreement whereby McLoughlin would not oppose Wyeth in a salmon-salting enterprise. Consequently, when Wyeth got back to Boston in the summer of 1833, he raised more capital and sent another ship to the Columbia, following overland himself with a second group of employees. On his way home the preceding year, he had arranged with Milton Sublette, brother of William, to bring out a load of trade goods that the Sublette brothers would buy from him at the 1834 rendezvous. However, when he got back to the rendezvous, Wyeth found that Milton was not there, and William refused to accept the goods.

Wyeth tried to offset this setback by building a hut on the Snake River as a warehouse for the goods, leaving a man to watch them. When he got to Fort Vancouver again in 1834, he found that his second ship had been struck by lightning and had had to spend three months in a South American port for repairs. As a result, it had reached the Columbia "too late for fish and too early for furs." Wyeth built a fort on Sauvies Island at the mouth of the Willamette River and tried trading for a year, but he could not survive losing the use of his second ship. To retrieve some of his losses, Wyeth arranged with McLoughlin for the Hudson's Bay Company to buy his storehouse. The Hudson's Bay Company men went with him as far as the 1836 rendezvous, taking possession of his warehouse on the way. The company named it Fort Hall, and it remained as one of the Hudson's Bay Company posts.

Fort Vancouver, Washington Territory.

Hall Kelley

Wyeth had originally been associated in his plans for the Oregon enterprise with Hall Kelley, a man who had an actual mania on the subject of Oregon. Kelley, a Boston schoolteacher, had heard the reports of Lewis and Clark and the fur traders and had been fired with a tremendous zeal to colonize Oregon for the United States. To undertake this task, he tried to organize the Oregon Colonization Society, whose members were to go with Wyeth in 1832; but he was late in completing the details, and Wyeth went on without him.

Kelley then set out alone for Oregon via the Southwest in 1833. He reached Mexico and started north through California where he joined a few Americans who had managed to engage in trade there. Among them was Ewing Young, who had been trapping in New Mexico and California. He and Kelley worked their way north until they met a Hudson's Bay Company brigade which took them on to Fort Vancouver. Kelley was very ill with malaria when the brigade met them, and they took care of him as best they could.

Before they reached Fort Vancouver, the Spanish governor had sent word by ship to McLoughlin that the Americans who were on their way were horse thieves. Consequently, McLoughlin refused to entertain them inside the fort, although he had the company doctor attend to Kelley in an outside building. This was particularly galling to Kelley because Wyeth, the man with whom he had planned to go to Oregon, was being royally entertained inside the fort. McLoughlin sent Kelley home via a ship in the spring. Kelley's frustration was so great that he spent the rest of his life writing pamphlets about the glories of Oregon and the duty of the United States government to seize it from England and the vicious monopoly, the Hudson's Bay Company, which, he felt, was getting all of the benefits of the great land. Although his writings had a decided influence on the subsequent migrations, Kelley died embittered and practically a hermit.

With Wyeth on his second trip in 1834 had come the first missionaries to Oregon, Jason and Daniel Lee. The fur traders thus were the guides for the missionaries who, as our first settlers, claimed the land for agriculture and spelled the doom of the fur trade. In the next chapter, we shall see how these various forces in our history dovetailed to bring in settlement.

Missionary Period

5

EARLY INDIAN CONTACTS WITH CHRISTIANITY

In our discussion of Indian culture, we noted that the Indians believed that whatever a person possessed resulted from his persuading the spirits to give it to him. Therefore, when the Indians saw the ships, guns, metal, and other amazing possessions of the whites, they took it for granted that these strange people had some powerful means of controlling the spirits in order to secure such miraculous things.

When the early maritime fur-trading ships reached our coast in the eighteenth century, the Indians observed the religious services that both Catholic and Protestant officers conducted on shore as well as on board. The songs, prayers, communion services, sign of the cross, robes of Catholic priests, and other religious observances were, in the Indians' eyes, the "medicine" (magic) by which the white newcomers persuaded the spirits to give them what they wanted.

The inland tribes also saw white religious services early in the nineteenth century when the North West Company traders began to reach the northern Plateau Indians. The southern Plateau tribes witnessed both Catholic and Protestant rituals when Lewis and Clark and the Astorians were in their country. Too, between 1812 and 1821, a group of Christian Iroquois Indians had settled among the Flatheads.

In 1824 when George Simpson, the governor for the Hudson's Bay Company, escorted John McLoughlin to the Columbia, they looked around for promising Indian boys who were to be educated in white schools. One of those chosen was young Garry, the son of the Spokane chief. Simpson took Garry back to the Red River settlement near present Winnipeg, Ontario, where he attended a mission school for several years. Garry returned in 1827 and persuaded more Indian boys to go east to school. Then in 1831 Garry came home to stay. His accounts of life with the whites may have added to the Indians' desire to acquire for themselves the remarkable possessions of the whites.

1831 Delegation

From these or other contacts, in 1831 a number of Flatheads and Nez Perces (and possibly others) decided to go to St. Louis to find William Clark, whom the Nez Perces regarded as their friend because of his visit to them in 1805. They evidently hoped to induce Clark to send them teachers who could show them how to use the proper magic to secure material things. They probably had no notion of wanting missionaries in the Christian sense to convert them to a new life or to save their souls for a life after death.

Four of this delegation of approximately ten men did reach St. Louis in 1831 and found Clark, who referred them to Catholic priests. Records of their baptism and the deaths of two of them have been found in St. Louis Catholic church archives. The remaining two started home the next summer, going up the Missouri River on a boat that also carried an artist, George Catlin, who painted their pictures and mentioned them in writing. It is not certain that they got back to their tribes, although there is a story among the Nez Perces that one of the tribe did return.

Clark told the details of the visit to William Walker, an Indian agent who was moving the Wyandotte Indians west of the Mississippi. He wrote an article for an eastern Protestant religious magazine, emphasizing the eagerness of the western Indians for Christianity as shown by their dangerous journey made to get the "white man's book," since teachers had not been sent to them.

The article aroused immediate interest among eastern church members who felt that they had committed a great wrong in not having realized earlier that the far western Indians wanted missionaries. They were therefore anxious to atone for their negligence by sending out religious teachers as soon as possible. They thought, of course, as did Walker, that the Indians were concerned about their spiritual condition and wanted missionaries to bring them the doctrine of Christian salvation instead, as later events indicated, of desiring stronger magic to add to their Indian culture the mechanical advantages of the whites.

PROTESTANT MISSIONS
Methodist Group

The Methodist Church answered this call first, sending out in 1834 Jason and Daniel Lee (uncle and nephew) as missionaries to the Indians of the Oregon Country. Cyrus Shepard, a teacher, accompanied them. They joined Nathaniel Wyeth, the independent fur trader, in order to have a guide from Independence, Missouri, to the coast. Heavy supplies for the missionaries were sent around South America by sea.

Although the Flatheads and Nez Perces who had asked for missionaries lived east of the Cascades, the Lees went on to Fort Vancouver with Wyeth, since it was the only place where they could get supplies. Since McLoughlin and Simpson had chosen the site for the fort partly because it was north of the Columbia in the region England hoped to secure for herself, McLoughlin was opposed to having Americans settle among the Flatheads to the north, and even among the Nez Perces since they were in the richest beaver country still existing. Consequently, he persuaded the Lees that they would do better to go down into the Willamette Valley, south of present Portland, an area which England had no hope of retaining. McLoughlin argued that if the Lees were going to teach Indians to farm, they should start in a good agricultural area, such as the Willamette Valley. The interior country of the Nez Perces and Flatheads was considered much too dry for any type of farming.

The Lees built their mission first on the east bank of the Willamette, about ten miles north of present Salem in an area where there were already white settlers, largely ex-employees of the Hudson's Bay Company who were too old for the rigorous occupation of fur trading and had settled down with their Indian wives to farm in the fertile Willamette Valley. The white people were delighted to have Christian ministers near them, and the Lees naturally paid attention to their needs. Moreover, the Coast Indians had been in contact with the white traders so long that they had become weakened by the diseases which were new to them, particularly smallpox and measles. As white goods became more plentiful, they had also dropped more of their native customs than had the inland Indians, but the coast tribes had not adopted the accompanying white social system. This left them somewhat between the Indian and white cultures and confused and apathetic about what they wanted. They were thus not in a condition to respond to the type of education that Jason Lee intended to provide.

It happened that three Indian orphans needed a home, and the Lees took them in as wards. As soon as the missionaries could build a cabin for shelter, Shepard started a school. The following year, there were nineteen pupils. Shepard proved to be an excellent teacher, who liked the Indians and enjoyed his work with them. The boys learned not only to read and write English, but to farm, and the girls, in addition, were taught white methods of cooking. The missionaries wrote letters lamenting the lack of white women at the mission which forced the men to do the cooking and other housework. Jason Lee complained in one letter that he had had to interrupt his writing a number of times to attend to the bread which he was baking.

The requests of the Lees for young women seemed sensible to the Methodist Mission Board because it took for granted that white civilization should accompany Christianity. In 1836, therefore, Dr. Elijah White and his family escorted three young women, plus a carpenter and a blacksmith and family, to Oregon by ship, arriving in May, 1837. The young women soon married the three missionaries, and, in the fall of 1837, another group of ministers and teachers arrived.

In 1838, Jason Lee went east to secure still more reinforcements, and he brought back fifty-two people by ship in 1840. The mission was moved in 1841 to the site of present Salem, and some settlers bought the Indian school, whose pupils had dwindled away, and converted it into Oregon Institute, a boarding school having separate sections for boys and girls. At first, it provided training only for primary grades, but courses corresponding to the current high-school level were added as fast as pupils and teachers were found for them. Later, Oregon Institute became the present Willamette University.

As the population of the mission increased, it began to take on the aspect of an American town whose residents felt the need of a civil government. In the next chapter, we shall note the missionaries' part in the formation of local government even before the United States had title to the area. Such activities soon occupied so

much of the missionaries' time that the Mission Board decided that
Jason Lee was more interested in building an American community
than in ministering to the Indians. The Board therefore replaced
Lee with George Gary, who was instructed to confine his efforts
more completely to religious work with the Indians. In the meantime, substations had been opened at The Dalles and other places
where missionary work continued.

The difficulties in living under the primitive conditions meant a
heavy loss of life in these early communities. Jason Lee's first wife
died in childbirth a year after they were married while he was on
his way east. His second wife, whom he brought back in 1840, died
in 1842 a month after the birth of a daughter, who was reared in
Oregon. Lee himself lived only a short time after his dismissal from
the mission, dying in 1845 at the home of his sister in Canada.

American Board Group

The second group of Protestant missionaries to reach the Oregon
country were the Whitmans and Spaldings, better known than the
others because of the Whitman massacre in 1847 in which fourteen
people were killed by the Cayuse Indians, including Marcus Whitman and his wife Narcissa.

In 1834, at the age of thirty-two, Whitman was a physician,
practicing medicine in Wheeler, New York, when the Reverend Samuel Parker came to the town recruiting missionaries for the far-
western Indians. Whitman told him that he had previously offered
to go to some field as a medical missionary, but had been refused
because of ill health. Parker was convinced that Whitman was
sufficiently strong to be a successful missionary and recommended
him for the appointment. The American Board of Commissioners
for Foreign Missions, representing the Presbyterian, Congregational, and Dutch Reformed churches, accepted Whitman as a missionary to the Indians in the Oregon country.

In a neighboring village, Parker met a talented young woman,
Narcissa Prentiss, who likewise offered to go as a missionary to the
Indians. He was certain that she had the intelligence, the education
(unusual for a woman of her day), and the Christian devotion to
make an outstanding missionary. However, the board did not appoint unmarried women. In fact, it opposed sending even unmar-

ried men as missionaries since it was their purpose, like that of the Methodist group, to develop white settlements among the Indians. The solution, obviously, was for Marcus and Narcissa to get married, and Parker is thought to have suggested that Whitman visit Miss Prentiss to see if such an arrangement appealed to them. At any rate, Marcus did go to see Narcissa in Amity, New York, in 1835, and within a few days she had agreed to marry him and go to Oregon.

Whitman's 1835 Trip to the Rendezvous

Parker and Whitman then started out immediately to make a preliminary examination of the tribes west of the Rockies to decide if they were actually eager for missionaries as reported. From Liberty, Missouri, they arranged to go under the protection of Lucien Fontenelle, a fur trader belonging to the American Fur Company.

The fur traders were annoyed at having missionaries with them, for they knew that these men usually disapproved of traveling on Sunday and reproved people for using profanity, for gambling, and for many other activities of the average trader. They were very rude to Whitman and Parker at the beginning of their trip, even throwing rotten eggs at them. Whitman, however, was of a caliber to change their opinion. For one thing, he had great physical strength, and he made it a point to do more than his share of the heavy work involved in making rafts to take baggage across streams, lifting Fontenelle's supply wagons out of the mud, or standing guard at night. Then cholera struck the men, and Whitman's medical knowledge was of great benefit to them. Whitman himself was ill from the fatigue of the journey, but he spent most of each night doctoring the sick. Although the medical knowledge of that time was inadequate, Whitman showed unusual skill in his own practice. The men were so grateful to him for his devotion and care that they quickly lost their feeling of animosity and had respect and even an affectionate regard for him. When their attitude changed toward Whitman, the fur traders also accepted Parker, although not to the same degree since he did not have Whitman's ruggedness of body or spirit.

At the rendezvous on the Green River, Whitman astonished the traders and Indians by successfully removing from Jim Bridger's back an arrowhead which had been imbedded there for three years. Bridger, an American trapper, became a fast friend of Whitman and sent his daughter to Whitman's mission school after it was founded.

At the rendezvous, Whitman and Parker talked to some Flatheads and Nez Perces who, through an interpreter, asked the missionaries to send teachers and doctors to their tribes. Whitman was convinced that they really did want Christian teachers and saw no need to continue to the coast to investigate further. Moreover, Whitman learned that in previous years the fur traders had taken supply wagons through South Pass, although Fontenelle that year left his at Fort Laramie. He then inquired if wagons could go on to the coast and was assured that they could.

This meant that his vision of encouraging not only missionaries but white settlers to go on to Oregon could be realized. So he arranged that Parker would continue on to Fort Vancouver with the Hudson's Bay Company men who had come to the rendezvous. The trip would give Parker an opportunity to pick out sites for missions while Whitman returned east with the fur caravans, married Narcissa, and secured additional missionaries to come out the following year.

1836 Trip of Whitmans and Spaldings

To accompany the Whitmans the board chose Henry H. Spalding and his wife. Although thoroughly devoted to a life of missionary effort, Spalding had something of a persecution complex, so that he was suspicious of people's motives and thus difficult to get along with. In addition, he had wanted to marry Narcissa Prentiss, who had refused him. He felt that she continued to act in an arrogant and spiteful manner toward him, and Narcissa did indicate in her letters, even after they were in Oregon, that she disliked having Spalding around.

Narcissa was not only beautiful, with lovely blond hair, but vivacious and charming. She had a good voice and liked to sing. People regarded her as an entertaining conversationalist, and she enjoyed being the center of a lively group. In view of these qualities, it is not surprising that she was inclined to feel herself superior to and impatient with anybody of a slow or plodding temperament. Her strong convictions of right and wrong forced her to do whatever she regarded as her duty, but apparently often without graciousness. After she was dead, a friend expressed the feeling that she had been much better suited by temperament to the life of an intellectual group in an eastern city than to that of a missionary among natives whom she regarded as savages.

Eliza Hart Spalding, on the other hand, although less gifted in many ways than Narcissa, was of a gentler nature. When they reached Oregon, she loved the Indians and became an excellent teacher for them. Her health was poor when they left New York for Oregon, and it seems amazing that a semi-invalid would have considered the possibility of making a trip regarded even by fur traders as difficult. The missionaries sincerely believed that God had called them to this work and, therefore, no question of health or safety was to be considered.

The Whitmans and Spaldings went by steamship to St. Louis where a mechanic for the mission station, W. H. Gray, joined them. In addition, they were accompanied by two Nez Perce Indian boys whom Whitman had taken back East with him from the 1835 rendezvous, partly as publicity in his campaign for funds. At Liberty, Missouri, they bought cows, horses, and mules for their overland trip.

The American Fur Company's men accepted them in their caravan going to the rendezvous near present Daniel, Wyoming. At the rendezvous, Narcissa and Eliza were the first white women whom most of the Indians had ever seen and the first whom many of the fur traders had seen for a number of years. They were thus extremely popular and probably accounted for the large number of traders who came to the missionaries' religious services. The missionaries thought that a religious revival had occurred among the trappers.

At the rendezvous, they found that Parker had not come back to meet them. He had been unable to face the hardship of another overland journey and had gone home by ship from Fort Vancouver. Whitman and Spalding were disappointed and annoyed since they were left with no information on the sites best suited to their work.

John L. McLeod and Thomas McKay of the Hudson's Bay Company had brought Wyeth back to the rendezvous in 1836, as we saw in the last chapter, in order to purchase Fort Hall from him.

The Hudson's Bay Company men then escorted the missionaries back to Fort Vancouver.

On the trip, Narcissa kept a diary, an extremely appealing one because of her descriptions of various trials and of their daily life along the way. The two wagons, which Whitman stubbornly insisted on taking along in order to prove that settlers could go overland to Oregon, were a source of irritation to Narcissa. Because they were nearing the mountain pass at Fort Laramie, the missionaries left the heavy wagon there and bought pack horses to carry the extra baggage. However, Whitman insisted on proceeding with the light wagon, one in which the women sat on top of baggage when they were not riding sidesaddle on their horses. On the sixth day after leaving the rendezvous, Narcissa wrote in her journal:

> Husband has had a tedious time with the waggon today. Got set in the creek this morning while crossing, was obliged to wade considerably in geting it out. After that in going between two mountains, on the side of one so steep that it was difficult for horses to pass the waggon was upset twice. Did not wonder at this at all. It was a greater wonder that it was not turning a somerset continually. It is not very greatful to my feelings to see him wear out with such excessive fatigue as I am obliged too. He [is] not as fleshy as he was last winter. All the most difficult part of the way he has walked in his laborious attempt to take the waggon over.[1]

The wagon broke down shortly thereafter, but the men made a cart with the back wheels, tied on the front wheels, and went on with it as far as Fort Boise. There they left it because of the weakened condition of the mules.

Food, of course, was a constant problem. On the plains, the group lived mainly on fresh game. Narcissa said of this:

> I thought of Mothers bread & butter many times as any hungry child would, but did not find it on the way. I fancy pork & potatoes would relish extremely well. Have been living on fresh meat for two months exclusively. Am cloyed with it. I do not know how I shall endure this part of the journey.[2]

[1] T. C. Elliott (comp.), *The Coming of the White Women, 1836, as Told in Letters and Journals of Narcissa Prentiss Whitman* reprinted from the *Oregon Historical Quarterly*, 1936-37 (Portland, Ore.: Oregon Historical Society, 1937), p. 25.
[2] *Ibid.*, p. 23.

When they reached the dry Snake River area, they had to substitute dried meat for fresh. They did have milk, however. Narcissa wrote:

> Our cattle endure the journey remarkably well. They are a source of great comfort to us, in this land of scarcity. They supply us with sufficient milk for our tea & coffee which is indeed a luxury. We are obliged to shoe some of them on account of sore feet. Have seen no buffalo since we left Rendezvous. Had no game of any kind except a few messes of Antelope which John's Father gave us. [John was one of the Indian boys who had gone east with Whitman the year before.] We have plenty of dry Buffalo meat which we purchased of the Indians & dry it is for me. I can scarcely eat it, it appears so filthy, but it will keep us alive & we ought to be thankful for it. We have had a few meals of fresh fish also which relished well. Have the prospect of obtaining plenty in one or two weeks more. Found no berries. Neither have I found any of Ma's bread. (Girls do not waste the bread, if you know how well I should relish even the dryest morsel you would save every piece carefully.)[3]

When they reached Fort Walla Walla (Nez Perce), she was ecstatic at the sight of a vegetable garden and commented on the joy of having a variety of fresh food again. Fort Vancouver, with its elegant furnishings and food, was, of course, almost overwhelming. McLoughlin entertained them graciously, offered to sell them supplies for their station, and invited the women to stay at Fort Vancouver while the men chose mission sites and built cabins.

Whitman's and Spalding's Missions

Whitman chose for his station a spot the Indians called Waillatpu (Place of the Rye Grass) about nine miles west of present Walla Walla where Mill Creek joins the Walla Walla River. He went there partly because the Cayuses, the Walla Wallas, and the Umatillas all spoke the Nez Perce language and partly because it was on the main brigade route from Fort Vancouver to Hudson Bay and on the route over which Whitman had just come. He foresaw even then that the "Oregon Trail" would emerge, and he wanted to aid the

---

[3] *Ibid.*, pp. 25-26. Narcissa sent her diary home at the end of her journey as a travelogue for her family.

people who, he hoped, would come along it. He and Spalding did not want to settle at the same place, probably because of the friction between them. Therefore, Spalding went to Lapwai on the Clearwater River, about ten miles east of present Lewiston, Idaho. Waillatpu proved to be a poor choice for the main mission. For one thing, the Nez Perces, who had asked for missionaries, resented having Spalding, the assistant missionary, rather than Whitman, the chief minister, in their midst. They begged both families to come to their area. In addition, the Cayuses were regarded by the Nez Perces as difficult, and they proved to be so as far as the whites were concerned.

Spalding and Gray helped Whitman put up a lean-to made of split logs fitted into grooved posts, the spaces being filled with mud, and Narcissa came to Waillatpu early in December (1836). Then the Spaldings and Gray went on to Lapwai where they lived in an Indian lodge until their house could be built.

The Whitmans and Spaldings in their separate stations worked furiously to get buildings up and gardens planted in the spring. The Nez Perces were willing to help the Spaldings, even at manual labor, but the Cayuses refused to do work with their hands which, they felt, was degrading to a man. Whitman was constantly on call to treat their sick, and in this he competed with their medicine men. Narcissa tells of cases where an Indian would think Whitman's treatment was having no effect and would call in the native shaman. A chief threatened to kill Whitman if his wife died, and his family did later kill an Indian medicine man for the death of a relative.

We have noted that a shaman refused to take a case if he thought he could not cure the patient. Whitman, on the other hand, believed that it was un-Christian to refuse to give help under any circumstances. This practice, of course, gave the Indians opportunity for suspecting Whitman's motives or his skill as a doctor.

Another main concern of Whitman and Spalding was in teaching the Indians to farm. They hoped to enable the natives to have a more abundant and more regular food supply from raising crops than they had from hunting. They thought, too, that an agricultural life would keep the Indians in one place where schools could be provided for them. It was difficult to teach them to read and write, for example, while they were roaming over their country hunting.

The Cayuses responded quickly to the idea of raising crops. Whitman had brought a plow for his own use, but had only hoes for the Indians, to begin with. They used them so vigorously the first year that Whitman wrote to the Mission Board for fifty ploughs and three hundred hoes to be sent to Oregon by ship for the next year. He also showed the Indians how to dig ditches from the river to their gardens so that water could be used to irrigate them. When Jason Lee visited Waillatpu in 1838 on his way east, he was surprised at the extent of their farms, some of them having two or more acres of wheat, potatoes, and other vegetables. The Nez Perces, in addition to raising crops, became proficient at raising cattle.

As far as formal education was concerned, the Spaldings were more successful than the Whitmans. Both Henry and Eliza Spalding were adept at learning languages, and Eliza was an excellent teacher. Spalding worked out a Nez Perce alphabet and began to print books for the Nez Perces in their own language on an old printing press sent to him from a mission in the Hawaiian Islands. He printed eight books on the press—a primer and various religious texts.

Coming of the Walkers and the Eells

Gray proved to be domineering and unpleasant, thus making life more disagreeable for the other missionaries. In 1837, without discussing his plans with the others, he suddenly went east to try to get reinforcements for the Spokane Indians whom he had visited. He succeeded in persuading the American Board to send eight additional people: Mr. and Mrs. Elkanah Walker, Mr. and Mrs. Cushing Eells, Mr. and Mrs. A. B. Smith, Cornelius Rogers, and a young woman whom Gray had married while in the East.

The four couples making the trip to Oregon got married, like Marcus and Narcissa, in order to be accepted as missionaries by the board. The trip to Oregon was made overland by this group, following the same procedure of going by ship to Independence, Missouri, and proceeding on horseback from that point. They accompanied the American Fur Company's brigade as far as the rendezvous held that year east of the continental divide at the junction of the Wind and Popo Agie rivers. They, too, went on to Wail-

Tshimakain Mission in 1843 (?): A drawing by Charles A. Geyer. The house on the left was the Walkers'; that in the middle was the Eells's. The low building at the left of the Eells's home is thought to be the first building constructed by the two families. (The original drawing is in the Walker Manuscript Collection of the Washington State University Library, Pullman, and is used here by permisson of Eunice Karr, granddaughter of Elkanah and Mary Walker.)

latpu with the Hudson's Bay Company men who, as usual, had come to the rendezvous.

At Waillatpu, the entire group of missionaries decided that the Smiths should stay with the Whitmans and that the Walkers and Eells should go to the Spokane tribes. Since Gray was so unpopular, no one wanted him, but Spalding agreed that Gray and his wife might go back to Lapwai with them.

The Walkers and Eells built their mission station at Tshimakain, near present Ford, Washington, about twenty-five miles northwest of Spokane, but they spent most of the winter of 1838 at Waillatpu because the men were not able to complete houses before cold weather.

Whitman's home of handmade adobe bricks, consisting of a large kitchen, two bedrooms, and the lean-to, was very crowded with these additional people. When it was cold, everybody gathered in the kitchen where was a fireplace. Their tempers became short because of the discomfort and lack of privacy, and Narcissa Whitman thought the other women did not do their share of the work. Mary Walker inclined to agree with her. In December, a son was born to the Walkers, and in the spring they and the Eells moved to the half-completed houses at Tshimakain. The two families got along more congenially than the other missionary families, and the Spokanes were cordial to them.

Mary Walker found her husband Elkanah difficult, however. She was an extremely intelligent, strong-minded woman, unusually well trained in the sciences of her day, particularly botany. She was also physically vigorous, and of a hearty, out-going nature. Elkanah, on the other hand, was frail and timid, suspicious, and given to moody, irritable spells when he was cross and ill-tempered with Mary. He believed that a woman should not speak or pray in public, and he probably was somewhat annoyed by Mary's education.

She, also, believed that it was a wife's duty to obey her husband and try to please him in all things. Her independent spirit, however, was too much for her conscience, and she would reply sharply to Elkanah and then reproach herself in her diary for not being a good wife. One time on a visit to Lapwai, she urged Elkanah to take chickens back to Tshimakain with them. Her diary entry reads:

> Husband very much out of tune. Scarce spoke pleasant all day. Out of patience, because in accordance with my wish, he tried to bring some chickens, all of which except one died. . . . I am tempted to declare: better to have lived and died an old maid with none to share and thereby aggravate my misfortune! But such reflections are but a poor solace to a grieved and disappointed wife—disappointed not because he is not so good as I anticipated, but because I have not gained that place in his heart that I fondly expected and which I think a wife ought to possess.[4]

It pleased Mary to talk to the English botanists, or other educated men, who visited Fort Colville on trips for the Hudson's Bay Company. In 1838, the United States government sent Charles Wilkes on an exploring expedition to Oregon, and some members of that group visited the Walker mission in 1841. When Mary was told that they were approaching, she hurried out to try to milk the cows before the men arrived. She was too late, however, and was much embarrassed to greet them as a milkmaid. She mentioned in her diary that she felt better when one of the men told her the next

---

[4] Ruth Karr McKee, *Mary Richardson Walker: Her Book* (Caldwell, Ida.: Caxton Printers, 1945), p. 199.

Fort Colville, Washington: The remains of a Hudson's Bay Company fort in 1888. The original stockade is visible on the left. (Scamahorn's Studio, Colville, Washington)

day that "the most pleasant sight he had seen in Oregon was a lady milking her cows" and added, "It is a rare treat indeed to meet literary men in such a wilderness." Two of the group were botanists, and Mary remarked, "I had a pleasant time as I found they knew much more than I do on the subject and gained several items of intelligence." In their reports, the visitors remarked on the good food and gracious hospitality encountered at the mission.

She, like the other missionaries, worked at an unbelievable pace—washing, cooking, cleaning house, sewing, milking cows, tending garden, raising children (five more were born during the eight years they were at Tshimakain), and trying to teach the Indians. Housework was done under difficult conditions and often proved too much for Mrs. Eells. However, Mary Walker, after a good "bawl" when things got unbearable, had the buoyancy necessary to regain her gaiety and start again. The following are examples of the many entries in her diary on her daily chores:

> Felt quite out of patience this morning on account of the miserable old door and the cats and the Indians; first one and the other would knock out a piece and the wind came in without the least ceremony, so that I could not be comfortable in the room long enough to get my breakfast. I was tempted to fret, but concluded I would go to work and see if I could not fix it. I nailed it together as well as I could and then lined it with mats so that it is quite comfortable.[5]

[5] *Ibid.*, p. 210.

I spent the day cording my bed and setting our little room to rights. Got a boy to help me mend the chimney; put up mats, traded berries, boiled brine, picked over feathers, which nearly completed a lot of little jobs on hand. . . . Made a first attempt at teaching. I think I succeeded pretty well as the children seemed pleased and are telling over their new idea. . . . I went out to the lodge, took both my children and they were very quiet. I gave them a lesson in geography on an egg shell which I had painted for a globe.[6]

Start of American Immigration

Part of the good feeling between the Tshimakain missionaries and the Spokanes came from the fact that their post was not on the immigrant route from the east. In 1840 the first immigrant wagons reached Waillatpu with a small group of American settlers, largely ex-fur traders. In 1841, twenty-four people arrived, and in 1842 Dr. Elijah White returned from the East bringing 114 immigrants.

The Nez Perces and Cayuses who lived along the immigrant route (soon to be called the Oregon Trail) began to be uneasy at seeing this increasing number of incoming white settlers. It was obvious to the Indians that if it continued at such a rate, the whites would soon be able to drive the Indians off their land.

The missionaries were appalled to find out that Dr. White had brought with him a letter from the American Board ordering them to close Waillatpu and Lapwai and send the Spaldings, Smiths, and Grays back to the East. The Whitmans were then instructed to join the Walkers and Eells at Tshimakain. The board had reached its decision because letters from all of the group had contained accounts of their quarrels and bad feeling which were blamed largely on Spalding, Gray, and Smith. Before the missionaries received the board's order, however, Gray and Smith had decided to leave, and the Spaldings and Whitmans had agreed to settle their differences for the good of the mission. Because letters took six months or more by Hudson's Bay express or special messenger, the board did not know of the reconciliation.

Since Waillatpu made a rest stop for the immigrants, Whitman was almost frantic at the thought of closing the mission. Most of these people reached the mission without food and exhausted from

[6] *Ibid.*, p. 213.

the harrowing trip over the Blue Mountains. His farm produce and the shelter of his station were almost essential to them if they were to continue. Since he believed that white civilization had to be combined with Christianity for the Indian if he were to survive, working as a missionary at an isolated spot like Tshimakain seemed to him a waste of time by comparison.

Whitman's Ride

Whitman, therefore, sent messengers to call the other missionaries to an emergency conference in which it was decided that he should go to Boston to lay their case before the American Board to try to persuade them to leave Waillatpu and Lapwai open.

After traveling overland to Washington, D.C., Whitman talked to the secretary of war, James M. Porter, about the possibility of the federal government's setting up a chain of posts from the Missouri to the Columbia to aid the settlers, who, Whitman was certain, would soon be coming to Oregon. The secretary evidently asked Whitman to draw up a proposed bill on the subject because such a document, probably prepared by Whitman, was found in Porter's files years later. Apparently nothing was done with it. There is also evidence that Whitman talked to President Tyler about his interest in aiding the Oregon settlers.

The main purpose of Whitman's journey, however, was to persuade the American board not to close his two main mission stations. When he reached Boston, he convinced the board that the stations had great value to immigrants, who were vital to the project of bringing white civilization and Christianity to the Indians. The board, as a result, granted his request and allowed Gray to leave.

Whitman stopped briefly to visit relatives where he persuaded a nephew, Perrin Whitman, to accompany him and then hurried back to St. Louis with the boy. From there they went on to Westport, Missouri, where the 1843 migration was assembling.

1843 Migration

In later years, the statement was made that Whitman was responsible for gathering the group of around one thousand people who went to Oregon in 1843. He could not have organized the group since it took months for most people to arrange their affairs and assemble a wagon, livestock, and supplies; and we have seen that Whitman was east of the Mississippi only from March until May 22 when the westward trek began. During that time, in addition, Whitman was busy on his mission affairs.

It is likely that his enthusiastic comments about Oregon along the way east made some people who were considering the matter decide to go. It is also certain that Whitman's presence with the migrants was of enormous help to them. While they were assembled at Westport waiting for the grass to reach a stage to support their animals, Whitman was able to contradict statements made in St. Louis that wagons could not get through to the Columbia. Along the way, he showed them how to arrange their wagons at night; he advised about areas where grass and water were scarce; he doctored the sick; and at the Laramie River, he was the only one willing to swim across with a rope to make a guide line for the wagon beds that were floated across. His energy was endless, and he did not shirk any labor. With the arrival in the Willamette Valley of this large migration, the Oregon Trail was definitely opened, and settlers to Oregon continued to follow it each year.

After Whitman's death, some people who remembered his remarkable services began to think that Oregon would have remained in British hands permanently if he had not gone to Washington, D.C., and brought back the huge group of 1843 settlers. Regardless of how much responsibility he had for their coming, practically all of them settled in the Willamette Valley, south of the Columbia, and by that time England had given up her attempt to hold any area south of the river. The Hudson's Bay Company may have been somewhat more willing to get out of the Snake River country when its officials realized that the fur-bearing animals were being gradually driven back by the stream of immigrants arriving each year. Even before 1843, letters written by McLoughlin and other members of the Hudson's Bay Company indicated that their profits were dwindling to a dangerous point in the Snake country. One cannot demonstrate from the evidence that "Whitman saved Oregon for the United States." His services to the American settlers, however, were certainly of tremendous value to them.

While Whitman was away during the winter of 1842, things had

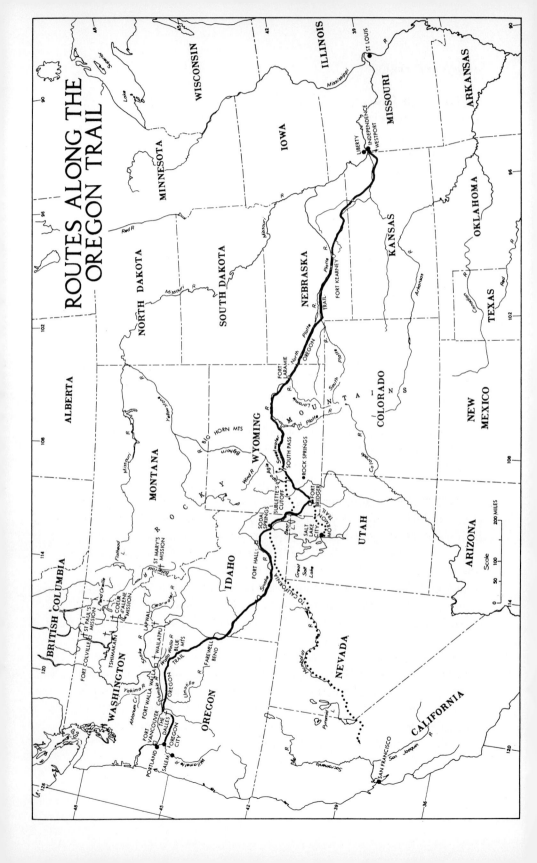

ROUTES ALONG THE OREGON TRAIL

not gone well at Waillatpu, and by the time he returned, indications of the final tragedy were becoming clear. Narcissa Whitman had intended to stay at Waillatpu while her husband was gone, but the Indians there became so hostile that Archibald McKinlay, the Hudson's Bay Company factor at Fort Walla Walla, became uneasy about her safety and sent a wagon to bring her to the fort. After staying there for awhile, she was invited to the Methodist mission at The Dalles where she was happy to spend the time with congenial white people.

Shortly after she left Waillatpu, an eastern Indian, Tom Hill, got the Cayuses excited over his claim that Whitman had gone east to get United States troops. Hill warned the Indians that they would lose their land to the whites just as Indians in the East had done. The Cayuses became so angry over this prospect that they burned the flour mill which Whitman had built.

Dr. Elijah White tried to pacify the Indians. When he arranged to return to Oregon in 1842, he persuaded the United States government to give him the title of Sub-Indian Agent. The Linn Bill, which was being considered by Congress at that time, provided that the President should appoint two Indian agents for the country west of the American states and territories. Although the bill had not passed, the President appointed White as one of these agents. The missionaries and Hudson's Bay Company men were surprised at this appointment since the United States did not have title to the Oregon country and therefore, presumably, could not send officials to govern the Indians.

White's powers were not clear, but he sought every occasion to show his authority. Therefore, when White heard of the destruction of the mill, he took nine men from the Willamette Valley to persuade the Indians to agree to laws drawn up by him. The Cayuse chiefs would not sign such an agreement, but the Nez Perces did. The laws required that punishment for murder or burning a home should be hanging; for burning an outbuilding, stealing, riding a horse without permission, or injuring crops, the penalty was to be flogging plus payment of damages. The chief of the tribe was to enforce the laws on its members, and White promised to enforce them on the white people. As we saw when we studied Indian culture, our tribes did not have a central authority capable of enforcing the laws. Even the chief had to depend on his degree of prestige and persuasive powers to make a tribal member do what he wanted. Therefore, when the Nez Perce chiefs began to try to enforce White's laws, as some of them did—even to the extent of flogging the Indians—they caused much bitterness within the tribe.

Although, when Whitman reached Waillatpu in 1843, he was not leading troops as the Indians feared, his bringing a thousand settlers was almost as serious a threat to the Indians' permanent control of their country. Distrust of Whitman continued to mount as around fifteen hundred people arrived the following year (1844) and three thousand in 1845.

Immediate Causes of Whitman Massacre

In 1844 another event occurred, closely connected with the coming tragedy. A group of Indians from the Waillatpu area went to California to drive cattle back to their tribes. One of the Indians was the son of Peu-peu-mox-mox, a Walla Walla chief, who had sent him as a boy to the Methodist mission school in the Willamette Valley, where he was given the name Elijah Hedding for a Methodist bishop. Elijah was killed by a white man while the party was in California. When the group returned, they asked Dr. White to punish the murderer in California in accordance with his promise that whites as well as Indians would be punished for wrongdoing.

White, of course, had neither means of pursuing the murderer, nor any authority to bring him to trial. When the Indians saw that he planned to do nothing, they organized a war party that started for California in the spring of 1846 to kill the murderer. On the way they contracted measles, which killed almost thirty of the party.

When the survivors returned in the summer of 1847, the Cayuses and neighboring tribes were grief-stricken and furious. Their native doctrine of blood satisfaction after a murder permitted a member of the aggressor tribe having the same rank as the victim to be killed as retribution. Since the war party had failed to avenge itself on the actual murderer, the Hudson's Bay Company men warned Whitman that the Indians might kill him as a substitute for Hedding inasmuch as both had the rank of chief in the eyes of the Indians, and Hedding had been educated at a white mission school.

Even if they did not follow that reasoning, they might also kill Whitman for encouraging whites to come into the area, bringing diseases like measles and smallpox against which the Indians lacked immunity. William McBean, the Hudson's Bay Company factor at Fort Walla Walla who had succeeded McKinlay, sent a messenger to Whitman warning him to leave Waillatpu and come to the fort for protection. Whitman refused to leave.

He had, however, considered leaving in 1844 because the Catholic church was contemplating sending missionaries into the Walla Walla area. At that time the Protestant missionaries, believing that the Indians were almost better off in their native state than converted to Catholicism, felt extreme animosity toward the Catholic church. Whitman told the Indians that he would leave if they preferred to have the Catholics come in, but the Indians did not ask Whitman to leave. He was then convinced that it was his duty to stay.

The final cause of the massacre was an unusually severe attack of measles which came with the 1847 migration. Even some of the white children who took measles died at the Whitman mission. The Whitmans had taken in a large number of orphans to rear a few years earlier, including seven Sager children whose parents had died on the trail. Some of these children had measles, but recovered.

When the Indians saw that most of the whites got well, whereas most of the Indians who had measles died, they suspected that Whitman was poisoning them. Joe Lewis, another eastern Indian who hated the whites, assured them that he had heard Whitman and his wife discussing the matter. They remembered McDougall's story (p. 109) about having a bottle containing the spirit of a disease which he could turn loose on the Indians by removing the cork. They concluded that this was what Whitman was doing.

Some of the Indians who did not believe Whitman was deliberately poisoning them felt that he was not a successful medicine man; for that reason, he deserved death. The Whitmans had had a daughter, born several months after they reached Waillatpu in 1837, who drowned in the creek near the mission when she was two years old. The Indians were shocked by the accident, saying that if Whitman had much skill as a doctor (shaman), he would have known how to keep the spirits from taking the life of his child. Some suspected after that time that he was an impostor.

The Hudson's Bay Company men warned Whitman repeatedly in

1846 and 1847 that his life was in danger, and two days before the massacre, Spalding, who had brought his daughter to the Whitman school, expressed his concern to Whitman over the situation. Whitman protested that his death would do as much for Oregon as his life. It was obvious that he believed the Indians would kill no one except himself.

On November 29, 1847, a large group of Indians gathered at the mission, presumably to watch beef being cut up. Dr. and Mrs. Whitman were in the dining room of the mission house taking care of a number of sick people, including children with measles. Two Indians came into the kitchen and asked for medicine. When Whitman got the medicine and returned to the kitchen, one of the Indians struck him from behind with a tomahawk, and the other shot him. They then ran outside where the Indians had begun a general attack at the signal of the shots.

Altogether, fourteen people were killed, including two of the Sager boys. This number was a smaller percentage of those present (seventy-four) than was often killed in an Indian attack. Because the Whitmans had, according to their viewpoint, been trying to help the Indians, their martyrdom made the massacre seem more tragic than others in which more persons were killed.

The Indians held their captives at Waillatpu for over two weeks until they were ransomed by Peter Skene Ogden, one of the Hudson's Bay Company men who brought goods from Fort Vancouver for that purpose.

Father Brouillet, one of the Catholic priests on the Umatilla River, heard of the tragedy from the Indians and hurried to the mission, where he helped bury the victims. He then warned Spalding, who was on his way to Waillatpu, to hide. Spalding was thus enabled to escape and get back to Lapwai. He did not know for some time, however, that his daughter was safe. The Nez Perces gave the Spaldings safe conduct to Fort Walla Walla, and from there they went to the Willamette Valley to settle.

A Spokane Indian brought word to the Walkers and Eells of the massacre on December 9. They were thrown into a state of dejection, of course, both because of grief over the death of their friends and fear for their own safety. The Spokanes assured them of their support, however. Since Mary Walker was expecting her sixth child within a few weeks, they stayed on until the baby was born on December 31. By that time, the Spokanes were urging them to stay, and they felt it their duty to remain for awhile. Late in May of the next year, however, volunteer troops escorted the two families to the Willamette Valley, where they settled for the rest of their lives.

Cayuse War

In the meantime, the Americans in the Willamette Valley, who had formed a local government in 1843, which they called the Oregon Provisional Government, had raised a military force of volunteers to find the murderers of the Whitman group and bring them to trial.

The Oregon Provisional Government put Colonel Cornelius Gilliam in command of the 537 volunteers who pursued the Cayuses in what is known as the Cayuse War, 1848-50. After a few skirmishes, the Indians fled to the mountains where the white soldiers could not fight successfully. Fifty men were therefore left in a camp near the mission, and the rest were discharged.

In 1850 five Cayuses surrendered as the murderers: Tomahas, Isaiachalakis, Klokamas, Tiloukaikt, and Kiamasumpkin. The first four were identified by survivors as ones who had killed one or more whites. The fifth seems to have had nothing to do with the murders, and it would be gratifying to be able to say that he was freed by the court held at Oregon City in May, 1850. Feeling, however, was too high to allow such a decision, and all five were hanged.

Results of Protestant Mission Effort

The mission stations of the American Board were abandoned permanently after the massacre. Spalding, however, who had been sent by the Presbyterian denomination, went back to Lapwai in 1871 where he organized a Presbyterian church that had many Nez Perce members. He also visited the Spokane tribe, baptizing over two hundred in 1873.

Differing assessments are made of the effect of the work of these Protestant missionaries. Some historians feel that the Indians were right in their belief that the missionaries were "softening them up" for the final attack on them by the settlers. The other view is that white settlement would have come only slightly later even if the missionaries had not preceded it and that the adjustment to the strange civilization was much easier for those Indians who had been prepared by the missionaries.

It is certainly true that Whitman had succeeded to a surprising degree in making farmers out of the Cayuses. In fact, during the eleven years of Whitman's mission, the local Indians had become so dependent on farming for food that when they fled to the mountains after the massacre, they were unable to support themselves there by hunting. It is thought that the murderers surrendered themselves for that reason—to save their tribe from starvation and to allow it to go back to the Walla Walla Valley. We have noted also that the Nez Perces had become adept at raising cattle and continued to be excellent cattle ranchers.

Although there is room for argument as to the effect of the Protestant missions on the Indians, there can be little doubt about Whitman's aid to the American immigrants. The coming of American settlers would presumably have been delayed for a number of years if he had not demonstrated that families could reach Oregon overland and if his mission had not provided an early rest stop.

CATHOLIC MISSIONS

The Catholic missionaries did not encourage white settlement and so were not feared by the Indians as were the Protestants. Moreover, the colorful ceremonies of the Catholics seemed to appeal more to the Indians than the simpler services of the Protestants. The first Catholic priests sent to the Oregon country were Father Francis N. Blanchet and Father Modeste Demers, who went to Fort Vancouver in 1838 and to the Willamette Valley in 1839. In the next chapter we shall discuss their connection with the Oregon Provisional Government.

Catholic Ladder

One religious achievement for which Father Blanchet was well known was the construction of the so-called Catholic ladder, a device used for teaching Catholic doctrine to the Indians. At first a drawing was made on wood, with forty marks representing the centuries before the birth of Christ and thirty-three dots the years of his life; the time afterward was shown by eighteen marks and thirty-nine dots. Accompanying pictures were drawn, showing Biblical scenes.

Under the dash representing the sixteenth century, a line labeled the "Reformation" left the ladder and ran downwards, indicating that the Protestant movement had led away from the true Christian faith. This implication made the Protestant missionaries so angry that they prepared their own ladder, showing the Reformation as the beginning of modern true Christianity. This evidence of conflict and bad feeling increased the Indians' distrust of white missionaries.

Father DeSmet

Probably the most famous Catholic missionary in the Oregon country was the Jesuit, Father Peter John DeSmet, who, with two other priests and three lay brothers, came overland to the Flathead tribe in 1841, using as a guide Thomas Fitzpatrick, a former member of the Rocky Mountain Fur Company. They built their first mission, St. Mary's, in the Bitterroot Valley, twenty-eight miles south of present Missoula, Montana.

DeSmet established many other missions in the northern part of the Inland Empire, including St. Paul's on the former site of Kettle Falls near Colville, Wahington. He was tireless in his travels from one tribe to another and also in returning to the East or to Europe to raise more money for the mission work. Like Whitman, he was large, extremely vigorous, and fearless.

One of his main contributions to the development of the West was his ability to bring about friendly feeling between Indians and whites. He was eager to persuade the Blackfeet to stop attacking whites and other Indian tribes. While at Rocky Mountain House, a Hudson's Bay Company post in the Canadian Rockies, he managed to get an invitation from a Blackfoot chief to visit his village. He then started out alone, since he could not find a guide, and had to spend the winter at Fort Edmonton. In March he fasted thirty days to reduce his weight to the point where he could make a trip on snowshoes over the dangerous sixty-mile stretch from Rocky Mountain House to the northern end of the Columbia River.

When he finally got to a Blackfoot camp on the Yellowstone, he found that the Blackfeet had been persuaded by the priests at St.

Mary's to make friends with some Nez Perces and Flatheads and camp with them; but the Blackfeet were uneasy about the intentions of the Flatheads, their traditional enemies. When a band of Crows attacked, the Flatheads, their women and children kneeling in prayer during the battle, aided the Blackfeet in driving off the Crows. The Blackfeet were so affected by this display of loyalty that DeSmet was able to get them to call a large council of many of the neighboring tribes where a policy of friendship was adopted.

He was so successful with the Indians that government agents later used him as a negotiator. At the close of the Yakima War, which we shall describe later, DeSmet was of great service both to the Indians and whites in bringing about a greater spirit of friendliness. After the Whitman massacre, Catholic priests set up a mission, which maintained friendly relations with the Indians, on Ahtanum Creek in the Yakima country.

THE OREGON TRAIL

Whitman's encouragement of white immigration over the Oregon Trail that he opened was the fundamental cause of Indian hostility to him, but his death did not halt the influx of white settlers over this route. However, even before 1847 some of the immigrants were by-passing the mission, taking what was known as the Umatilla Cutoff from a point just below the source of the Umatilla River to its junction with the Columbia. After the massacre, that line became the main route of the Oregon Trail until paths could be cleared through the Cascades north and south of the Columbia. From the east, the Oregon Trail went northwest from Independence, Missouri, to the Platte River; along its north fork through present Nebraska and Wyoming where it crossed the Rockies through South Pass near present Rock Springs, Wyoming; and from there west and northwest to the Snake River, which it hit just north of Bear Lake in southeastern Idaho. It followed the Snake, crossing it at various points, to a place called Farewell Bend near present Huntington, Oregon, where it headed northwest through the northern edge of the Blue Mountains to the Umatilla River.

Stories of the hardships and romance of the Oregon Trail are familiar to almost everybody who has lived in the Pacific Northwest.

Many of today's high-school and college students have heard grandparents or other relatives tell of their own hair-raising experiences along the way. Yet it is hard to analyze the reasons for the "Oregon fever" which was truly an obsession with Americans from the 1840's to the 1860's. Many writers have compared their mania to the overwhelming urge of the salmon to force their way back up a stream to spawning grounds, fighting against each new obstacle even though getting weaker each day with hunger and approaching death. The Oregon immigrants felt something of this same kind of unreasoning drive. Invalids came, thinking they would get well, and some did. Others died along the way. Poor people without sufficient livestock or suitable wagons came, and many of them were killed by Indians or disease. Fatal accidents in crossing rivers, mountains, or deserts occurred many times. People pushed on without food or water sometimes until their cattle died, or they drank from polluted ponds and died of cholera.

We have seen why the missionaries came, but what about the ordinary settlers? In trying to answer this question, historians have listed the following factors as a partial explanation. In the 1830's there was a severe depression in the East, and many people were badly in debt and eager to better their lot. The fur traders' and explorers' tales about the Oregon country made it sound like a place where free land and a mild climate would enable a person to live well without initial financial resources.

It has seemed strange to many people, however, that the immigrants did not gradually push west from the Missouri, occupying the uncultivated land as they came to it, instead of leaping from the Missouri to the Pacific and then working their way back, the process which they actually followed. One explanation for this is that the plains west of the Missouri frightened the eastern migrants who could not imagine farm land without trees and many rivers. They thought the treeless prairies were not suitable for agriculture, and the heavy forests and considerable rainfall on the Pacific coast, which they had heard about, sounded much more like home.

In addition, the eastern markets were overflowing with surplus food, and transportation was so poor even from the Missouri eastward that farms to the west of the river would be almost completely without access to a market. Easterners believed that the Orient represented a possible market for food and other commodities produced in Oregon, and this hope was another incentive for going there.

The tales of adventure appealed to some people, too. The dangers of the trip made it seem exciting. Some also were pleased at the thought of extending the hold of the United States to the Pacific. We saw how obsessed Hall Kelley was, for example, with the idea that the United States should take Oregon away from the British.

Manifest Destiny

The phrase "manifest destiny" was used in 1845 in a newspaper article to refer to the inevitability of the acquisition of Texas by the United States. The phrase then became popular in expressing the feeling that it was the obvious destiny of the United States to continue to expand, perhaps even beyond the limits of the North American continent.

From whatever combination of causes, "Oregon fever," as part of the drive to the Pacific, brought pioneers to the Pacific Northwest in the wake of the missionaries, who, in turn, had followed the fur traders, leaving the great plains for later settlement.

Evolution of Washington State from Oregon Country

6

Jason Lee's Methodist Mission, as we learned in the preceding chapter, became the nucleus of an American settlement in the Willamette Valley in the 1830's. In the same area there were groups of ex-Hudson's Bay Company employees living on farms with their Indian wives. The men were British subjects (largely French Canadians) loyal to John McLoughlin, the Hudson's Bay Company factor in charge of the Oregon country. It was inevitable that friction would develop between the English and American groups since both wanted to gain title to the region and to control it.

TREATY OF 1818

Since England was in physical possession of the area through the Hudson's Bay Company, she allowed the chief factor to administer the laws of Canada for British subjects. These laws could not be applied to the Americans, however, and they had no government of their own.

In 1818, England and the United States had signed a treaty, sometimes called the Treaty of Joint Occupation, in which they agreed that both countries could trade and settle in the Oregon country for a period of ten years. This arrangement was made because, after the War of 1812, the two countries could not agree on a boundary line west of the Rocky Mountains, and the treaty, in essence, postponed the making of that decision. By 1826, England and the United States were still not ready to settle on a boundary line; consequently, they extended the Treaty of 1818 for an indefinite period, with the provision that either country could end it by giving a year's notice. This agreement was still in effect when the missionaries started arriving in 1834. Therefore, McLoughlin hoped

153

that by keeping the Americans south of the Columbia he could at least hold the region north and west of the river for Great Britain, even if the United States should get present Oregon.

AMERICANS MOVE FOR GOVERNMENT

There was nothing in the Treaty of 1818 to keep the Americans from settling on whatever tracts of land they picked out, but there was no way for them to register their title to the land nor to settle disputes over ownership when two people claimed the same piece of land. Moreover, the American settlers could not be certain that the land they claimed would continue to belong to them if England should get title to the Oregon country.

The Americans felt countless other needs, too. They had come, mostly, from established towns in the United States where they had taken for granted the orderly existence and security which their government made possible. The early settlers missed the regulation of everyday affairs in the wilderness and felt the need of some type of government. They wanted roads and schools. They were afraid of Indian attacks and needed a military force strong enough to protect them.

The Oregon pioneers soon found that they needed a court system. One would expect them to want a court as a means of punishing the outlaws whom we think of as part of frontier life, but this was not their main concern. There was some crime, of course, but the settlers required a legal system chiefly to regulate liquor traffic, register marriages, regulate trading, settle (probate) the estates of persons who had died, register land titles, establish a money system (currency), and to do the many other routine tasks taken for granted today. The early Americans in Oregon had no agency to provide any of these services. Consequently, almost as soon as the first groups arrived, they began to ask the United States government to recognize Oregon as a part of its territory in spite of Great Britain's claim. For example, in 1838, when Jason Lee went east to get helpers for his mission, he took with him a petition from the American settlers asking that the United States set up a form of government in Oregon. After that, scarcely a year passed without some kind of similar plea being sent to Washington, D. C.

For awhile, the missionary in charge of each American mission acted as a head of the little community connected with it, but these settlements soon grew too large and the interests of the people too varied for this type of administration. As a result, the early settlers had to exercise legal functions on occasion without any formal governmental organization. For example, in 1835, while Nathaniel Wyeth, the American fur trader, was at his trading post on Sauvies Island at the mouth of the Willamette River, a Mr. Hubbard there was suspected of homicide, and some Americans made up a jury which heard the case and acquitted him. At McLoughlin's request, Jason Lee, the Methodist missionary, acted as guardian for orphaned French-Canadian children in his vicinity. In 1838, the Americans in the Willamette Valley elected David Leslie justice of the peace, and in 1841 he presided at the trial of an Indian woman accused of theft. In 1840 the settlers at Astoria hanged an Indian for murder.

Public Meetings

By 1841 the sentiment in favor of setting up some kind of formal government had reached the point of calling public meetings. Residents who in later years tried to remember the order of these meetings could not agree on the exact dates. However, if we follow the sequence as given in the *Oregon Archives,* which was based on research done for the Oregon Territorial Legislature in 1853, we find that a group connected with the Methodist Mission met early in 1841 and elected a committee to work on the problem of forming a local government. Shortly afterward, the death of Ewing Young, the American who had remained in the Oregon country after his overland trip with Hall Kelley, made it essential to have a probate court to settle his estate. The committee took advantage of this need to gather the inhabitants together for another meeting after his funeral on February 17, 1841.

The reason for the urgency was that Young had built up a large herd of cattle from groups which he had driven overland from the Spanish settlements in California, and, when he died, something had to be done about them. As far as people knew at that time, he had no heirs; therefore, at his funeral, the settlers arranged to meet the next day at the Methodist Mission to set up a court to dispose of his property.

Probate Court, 1841

At this meeting on February 18, 1841, a probate court was organized, with Dr. Ira L. Babcock, a lay member of the Lee Mission, as judge; George Le Breton as clerk of the court and public recorder; William Johnson as high sheriff; and Xavier Ladaroute, Pierre Billique, and William McCarty as constables. Since there happened to be a copy of the laws of the state of New York in the community, Dr. Babcock was instructed to follow them until a code of local laws could be drawn up. The court was expected to oversee the sale of Ewing Young's property and also to take care of any matters of probate in connection with other estates. The court settled the Young estate and held the money in trust; many years later, when it was found that Young had a son in the East, the money was turned over to him.

Committee of Organization

At the same meeting which set up the probate court, the Americans were anxious to organize a complete government. However, the Canadians and the Catholic priests, who were in sympathy with the Hudson's Bay Company, did not want to see a government formed, because they believed that the Americans would control it. They were able to prevent the immediate drafting of a code of laws, but they did agree to the appointment of a committee of organization, consisting of nine members. This committee was to work out a plan of government and report on it at a general meeting to be held on June 1, 1841. In order to get the support of the various groups living in the Willamette Valley, representatives from each one were included in the committee. For example, Father Blanchet, the Catholic priest, was made chairman. Members of the committee were Jason Lee and two others from the Methodist Mission, three French Canadians, one American settler, and one Englishman. Father Blanchet, however, did not call the committee together, and, when the settlers met on June 1, 1841, as they had agreed to do, Father Blanchet asked to be excused from the chairmanship of the committee. Dr. W. J. Bailey, one of the American settlers, was named to take his place, and this second committee was to report in October, 1841.

Wilkes's Attitude

During the summer, the committee met with Lieutenant Charles Wilkes, who was sent out by the United States government to make a report on conditions in Oregon. Wilkes told the committee that he was opposed to the creation of a local government by the Americans. He had been royally entertained by McLoughlin before he went into the Willamette Valley, and the obvious contrast between the power and wealth of the Hudson's Bay Company and the struggling condition of the American group probably influenced him. He stated that he did not think the Americans were strong enough to enforce the laws they might make. Moreover, he seems to have thought that the bar across the Columbia was so difficult that a settlement on the Fraser River would be much preferable for the main outpost of the American government. He felt that in the Willamette area the Canadians would be able to elect the officials for any government set up and that this fact might delay the incorporation of Oregon into the United States.

Since Lee had started on a trip to the Umpqua Valley, he was not able to entertain Wilkes at the Mission. Wilkes reported that he met Lee camping below Willamette Falls "with Mosquitoes and sandflies." His obvious dislike of the Methodist missionaries is apparent in many of his remarks. He complained of the food, of the fact that their harvesting tools were left out in the fields, and of many other things. This feeling may have made him more sympathetic with Father Blanchet's argument that the number of settlers was too small to support a government and that the Canadians were perfectly satisfied with the rule of the Hudson's Bay Company. Wilkes commented that since there was no crime in the valley, no government was needed. In this respect he overlooked the civil (noncriminal) needs of the people for a government, in connection with their land, roads, schools, and so forth, to which we have referred above.

At any rate, because of Wilkes's opposition, the matter of forming a government was dropped, and nothing more was done for two years. This did not mean, though, that people stopped thinking and talking about it. A men's debating club, called the Oregon Lyceum, was formed at Willamette Falls, and the members chose various aspects of the government question as subjects for their debates. Some of them were: "Should the new government be subject to that of some other country or should it be completely independent?" "Would peaceful relations between the United States and Great Britain be jeopardized by the establishment of such a government?" "How much authority could the new government assume?"

Wolf Meetings

It was the so-called Wolf Meetings that finally brought the matter of a local government to a head. People referred to bears, panthers, or any other type of predatory animals as wolves, and, on February 2, 1843, a group got together to arrange for bounties to be paid to people for killing such animals. At this meeting, a committee of six was set up to consider a bounty scale, and another committee was appointed to call a second wolf meeting and make a report. The second meeting was held on March 6, 1843, at which time a system and scale for bounties was recommended. The settlers then decided to go further and appointed a committee of twelve to form a civil government.

Champoeg Meeting

The committee met and is supposed to have called all the inhabitants together at Champoeg on May 2, 1843. Reports from Dr. McLoughlin to the Hudson's Bay Company and some other documents, however, suggest that several community meetings became lumped together in people's minds in later years when they tried to remember the sequence of events. It is therefore probable that the May 2 meeting actually occurred in March of 1843 and that there were no Canadians present.

The commonly accepted version of the Champoeg meeting is the following. The group was too large to use any of the buildings in the settlement, and, as a result, the settlers gathered on the river bank near a wheat storehouse of the Hudson's Bay Company. On the first vote, the motion to form a government lost because of the

French Canadians' opposition. At this point there was an argument between J. S. Griffin, one of the Methodist Mission group, and Father Blanchet. In the midst of the debate, Le Breton, a French Canadian, proposed a vote by division (those who favor a motion move to one side of the meeting place and those who oppose it move to the opposite side, then the two groups are counted to determine which has the majority; in pioneer groups, this was a favorite means of voting on questions).

Joe Meek, an American trapper, shouted, "Who's for a divide? All in favor of the report, follow me." His group formed on the right side of the clearing, the other on the left; and the count showed that the government party had won. Some accounts give the vote as fifty-two to fifty; others indicate sixty to fifty-five or fifty-four. The defeated French Canadians then left the meeting. The remaining Americans elected a new probate court and added four magistrates plus a militia.

At this meeting, the Americans also appointed a committee to draw up a code of laws for a temporary government and to make its report to the people on July 5, 1843. Whether the community meeting took place in March or in May and whether or not the French Canadians took part in it, this committee was probably the first lawmaking body in Oregon. In fact, the Champoeg meeting used to be regarded as the foundation of American government in the Oregon country. It is now generally considered, however, even by those who accept the story as given above, as merely one of the important steps leading up to the formation of such a government.

The legislative committee met May 16-19 and June 27-28 in an old granary of the Methodist Mission, drawing up the framework for the new government. A patriotic meeting was held on July 4 to stir up enthusiasm, and on July 5 the committee made its report to the people who adopted it under the title of the "Organic Act of the Provisional Government of Oregon."

The term "provisional" was used to indicate that this local government was considered merely a stopgap until the United States or Great Britain should be given control of the region. That the Americans were certain of the final success of the United States in securing possession of Oregon is indicated by the phrase in the Organic Act that the laws were to be adopted "until such time as the United States of America extend their jurisdiction over us." Since neither the French Canadians nor the Hudson's Bay Company took part in the government in the beginning, the wishes of the British subjects did not have to be taken into account.

Provisions of the 1843 Organic Act

If the Linn Bill, mentioned earlier, was passed by Congress, the court system of the territory of Iowa was to be extended to include the Oregon country, and, anticipating this step, probably some settler (perhaps Elijah White) brought a copy of the laws of Iowa with him.[1] These laws formed the basis for the Organic Act, which also incorporated the public land provisions of the Linn Bill—that every adult male settler could claim 640 acres of land not already occupied by another person by recording it at the office of the provisional government's land recorder and by making certain improvements on the land. He had to begin to live on it within a year. The Organic Act gave the Methodist Mission thirty-six square miles of land.

The Oregon region was divided into four parts, called districts, instead of counties. The Organic Act specified that their northern boundary was to be the northern boundary of the United States. This could be a line any place between 54° 40'—the limit agreed upon by Russia in 1824-25 as the southern boundary of her Alaskan possessions—and the Columbia River—the line desired by England at that time. For practical purposes, there was no need for the provisional government to talk of jurisdiction north of the Columbia since the Hudson's Bay Company had kept all American settlements to the south of the river up to that time. Dr. and Mrs. John P. Richmond, Methodist missionaries who had spent one year, 1840, at Nisqually, were the only Americans who had lived in the Puget Sound area up to 1843. The provisional government did list two of its four districts (counties) as extending north of the Columbia to 54° 40', but they existed only on paper.

The committee which wrote the Organic Act set up the conventional branches of government—legislative, judicial, and executive. The establishment of the office of governor aroused so much debate, however, that the committee compromised by putting the executive control of the provisional government in the hands of a

[1] The Linn Bill did pass, but not until 1850.

committee of three. The people seemed to have a fear of the office of governor, as such, and, in addition, the mission group and the nonmission American settlers apparently could not agree on one person. Each wanted the governor to be chosen from its members. The three who were selected as the first executive committee were among the less influential members of the community so that, presumably, people did not feel strongly about them, one way or the other. Two were settlers and the third was a lay member of the mission.

A committee could not work as efficiently as one person in administering the laws passed by the legislature of the provisional government, and the people became sufficiently dissatisfied with its operation that in 1845 they were willing to accept one man as governor even though he might not represent their own party. George Abernethy was elected as the first governor, and he served from 1845 until the end of the provisional government in 1849.

Since the committee was already familiar with the working of the successful probate court in the Willamette Valley, it had little difficulty in creating a similar probate court for the provisional government and adding a justice-of-the-peace court to hear minor civil and criminal cases. Because of the small population in Oregon country, it established a supreme court that not only heard appeals from the probate and justice court, but also acted as a trial court for serious crimes and certain civil cases.

The Organic Act set few restrictions on the powers of the legislature; therefore, it was able to adapt its operation to the changing needs of the community and functioned in a satisfactory manner. The committee did decide that slavery was forbidden by the Organic Act.

The most ticklish problem for the committee in writing the Organic Act was that of taxation. The members felt that the people would not accept a system of compulsory taxation and that the government would not be strong enough to collect taxes even if such a clause were contained in the Organic Act. Their solution was to ask for voluntary contributions for the support of the government. To us, today, this seems like a strange arrangement. If we were not required to pay taxes, our government would probably have little money. The Oregon settlers were anxious enough to have a system of government, however, that many of them were willing to pay for it by subscription as people do now for their churches or for charitable institutions. The system of voluntary contributions did not bring in enough money even then, though, to enable the government to function satisfactorily, and, in 1844, a small tax on personal property and a fifty-cent poll tax were levied by the legislature.

Since there was still very little money available, farm produce was accepted as payment for taxes. The government was not yet ready to try to seize property for nonpayment of taxes, but it ruled that anyone who refused to pay his taxes should not take advantage of any of the services of the government. Since these included, besides voting, the registering of land claims, the ruling was a strong lever for use in tax collecting. Joseph Meek, as sheriff, acted as the first tax collector and received $313.31 in 1844. He listed the names of the few who refused to pay the tax.

Dissatisfaction with Provisional Government

In the fall of 1843, the big migration of over one thousand Americans whom Whitman accompanied arrived in Oregon and settled in the Willamette Valley. Most of these Americans had rosy expectations of finding a land that would feed and clothe them without great exertion on their part. Instead, they arrived, worn out, at the beginning of the rainy season, to find much of the most desirable land taken and an enormous amount of work to do to erect a cabin. Materials were scarce and prices were high for those available. Even food was a problem, and, since most of the settlers had little cash, they were forced to take goods on credit either from local American merchants, who were all more or less identified with the Methodist Mission, or from the hated Hudson's Bay Company.

Since this group came out as ordinary settlers rather than as reinforcements for the mission, many of them were not sympathetic with the missionaries. Consequently, the disappointments of this large group of immigrants soon took on the form of complaints against the missionaries and the provisional government, in which the missionaries were the controlling group. The French Canadians, who felt that they were denied control of their own affairs and that there was too much governmental machinery, joined with the dissatisfied Americans in protesting against the provisional government. They took part in the voting in 1844, and the American mission group was defeated. In fact, six members of the 1844 legislative committee were new immigrants, and only two were from the older settlers. The ninth place on the legislative committee was not filled.

In the 1843 migration there were many southerners, particularly Missourians, who wanted only white settlers admitted. They recognized that Oregon was not suitable for plantations farmed by Negro slaves, and, as a result, they did not want slavery adopted in Oregon. On the other hand, they had not had enough money to own slaves in the South, and they had been afraid of competing for work with free Negroes. Consequently, they were able to change the law forbidding slavery to one which refused to allow any Negroes—slave or free—to live in Oregon. This law was in existence only one year, and after that slavery was again prohibited.

McLoughlin's Union with the Provisional Government

By 1845 McLoughlin had decided that it would be more to the advantage of the Hudson's Bay Company to join the provisional government than to stay out. The American settlers had become so numerous that the company needed more effective means of making them pay their debts and respect the land claims of the Hudson's Bay Company south of the river. If the company belonged to the provisional government, McLoughlin reasoned that it would make available courts through which the company's rights could be protected.

One difficulty was, however, that a British subject could not take the oath of office required of the provisional government officials since it included an expression of allegiance to the United States government. The oath of office was therefore changed to read, "I do solemnly swear that I will support the organic laws of the provisional government of Oregon, so far as they are consistent with my duties as a citizen of the United States or a subject of Great Britain . . ." so that either an American or an Englishman could hold office without being regarded as a traitor to his country.

With the cooperation of the Hudson's Bay Company officials, the provisional government was able to function effectively south of the

Columbia, and it also became a reality north of the river. In 1845 two groups of Americans defied McLoughlin and went into Puget Sound to settle. When the legislature of the Oregon Provisional Government met in August, it established Vancouver County to consist of the land north and west of the Columbia. At the next session in December, 1845, the name of the county was changed to Clark, and its western part was cut off to form Lewis County. James Douglas, the Hudson's Bay Company employee who succeeded McLoughlin in 1846 as chief factor, and Charles Forrest, another Hudson's Bay Company employee, plus Michael T. Simmons, one of the American settlers, had been selected as judges for Vancouver County with John Jackson, an American settler, sheriff. When Lewis County was created, these officials acted for it as well.

BOUNDARY SETTLEMENT

By 1846 England had decided that the Oregon country between the Columbia and Fraser rivers was not worth provoking a war with the United States. With the Snake River fur trade hampered by the thousands of immigrants coming over the Oregon Trail, the richest source of furs was giving out, and the Hudson's Bay Company was willing to move its western headquarters from Fort Vancouver to Vancouver Island. Moreover, a new tariff policy had been introduced by the United States which was favorable to English trade, and Britain's economic situation was none too good at the time. For these various reasons, England agreed to accept the forty-ninth parallel as the boundary between western Canada and the United States, and the United States Senate voted for that line rather than insisting on 54° 40′.

As soon as the boundary was settled in 1846, the people expected the United States to create a territory of Oregon, because now that the United States owned the region, there was no further legal obstacle to setting up a territorial government there. The residents had been encouraged by the debates in Congress over the Oregon question, and they knew, of course, that William Slacum, John Fremont, and Charles Wilkes had all been sent out by the United States government to report on the advisability of extending its au thority to Oregon.

Congress' Delay in Establishing Oregon Territory

After the boundary settlement in 1846, however, time elapsed, and Congress did not set up a government in Oregon. The provisional government had sent J. Quinn Thornton to Washington, D. C., to do what he could to persuade Congress to organize Oregon Territory, and he was influential in this respect. There were strong reasons, however, why Congress hesitated to make Oregon a United States territory. For one thing, Congress had its attention on the Mexican War, and, for another, the slavery issue was becoming a real problem. The South did not want to see any more free states or territories admitted, and, since slavery was prohibited by the local provisional government, Oregon would be expected to come in as a free territory. Until a satisfactory balance of free and slave territories could be worked out, the southern congressmen continued to block the admission of Oregon as a territory.

The Whitman massacre in 1847 was the main factor in breaking the deadlock in Congress over the creation of Oregon Territory. Joe Meek started for Washington, D. C., as soon as the worst of the winter was over, to report the murders and the fact that the provisional government was organizing a force to punish the Cayuse Indians. Meek was a cousin of President Polk's wife, so that he had access to the White House. In addition, his fur-hunter's costume and colorful personality made an impression wherever he went. People were, of course, profoundly shocked at the news of the tragedy, and they urged Congress to send immediate aid to the Oregon settlers.

OREGON TERRITORY

Even then there was a delay from May to August, 1848, until a favorable vote on admitting Oregon as a free territory could be secured in Congress. As soon as Congress passed the bill on August 13, 1848, President Polk signed it and selected territorial officials for Oregon. He appointed General Joseph Lane of Indiana as governor of the new Oregon Territory and Joe Meek as United States Marshal. These two men started for Oregon at once, going overland

Front Street, Portland, in 1852. (Oregon Historical Society)

to California and coming up the coast from there by ship. They arrived at Oregon City on March 2, 1849, and the next day Governor Lane proclaimed that the territory of Oregon was in existence. The territorial government automatically succeeded the provisional government of Oregon, which had been in existence as a local government since 1843. The federal Organic Act which created Oregon Territory, however, specified that all of the laws of the provisional government except those relating to land were to be kept in force until repealed or amended by the Oregon Territorial Legislature. This meant that Congress had given retroactive recognition to the provisional government's existence.

Oregon Territory's Boundaries

The boundaries of the territory of Oregon were set by Congress in 1848 as running from the Pacific Ocean along the forty-ninth parallel to the crest of the Rocky Mountains, down the crest to the forty-second parallel, and west again to the Pacific Ocean. This area consisted of what is now all of Oregon, Washington, and Idaho plus parts of Wyoming and Montana. It was much larger than the people had expected it would be, and the inland population was so small that no local government units existed in the eastern part of the territory for many years.

Congress' Treatment of McLoughlin

Shortly after McLoughlin joined the provisional government on behalf of the Hudson's Bay Company, he resigned as chief factor because Simpson and certain other officials of the company denounced him for having aided the American settlers and thus making it easier for the United States to make a successful claim to part of the Oregon country. McLoughlin replied that he could not allow people to starve even to advance the Company's interests, but that he had not encouraged the Americans in fur trading and that his loyalty to the Hudson's Bay Company had been sufficiently demonstrated over the years. He and Simpson had developed such ill feeling for each other, however, that no reconciliation seemed possible. After McLoughlin left the company, he applied for United States citizenship and retired to his land claim in Oregon City.

Samuel Thurston, who was the first delegate elected to Congress from Oregon Territory, denounced McLoughlin as the greedy foreign tyrant who had taken land away from the Americans and forced them to pay exorbitant prices for the materials which he had sold them. Therefore, the Donation Land Act, which Congress passed in 1850, specified that McLoughlin's land should be turned over to the territorial legislature, the proceeds to go to establishing a university. Many people in the territory objected strenuously to such treatment of McLoughlin, but he died in 1857 before sentiment in his favor reached the point where the legislature would try to make amends. It did so in 1862 by giving McLoughlin's heirs title to his Oregon City land claim for a nominal sum.

SETTLEMENT OF PUGET SOUND

Michael T. Simmons and John R. Jackson, the Americans who served as county officials for Clark and Lewis counties under the provisional government, had come to Oregon with the 1844 migration. In that group there was a mulatto, George W. Bush, who was of great aid to the other immigrants and highly respected by them. When they reached the Willamette Valley and found that the legislature of the Oregon Provisional Government had passed the law forbidding any Negro to live within its jurisdiction, the Simmons party crossed the Columbia River to present Washington with Bush, presumably to enable him to settle in the Oregon country, but to remain outside the area controlled by the local government.

During the winter of 1844-45, Simmons made exploring tours north from Fort Vancouver, and in October, 1845, he with his family settled at the edge of present Olympia, calling their village New Market (later Tumwater). Five familes plus two single men came north with Simmons and took up claims within a radius of six miles from Tumwater.

These Americans got supplies on credit from Fort Nisqually, the Hudson's Bay Company post on the Sound. In 1846 Simmons built a flour mill at Deschutes Falls, using stones chiseled out of granite slabs, and in 1847 he and some of the other settlers put up a saw-mill at Tumwater. The Hudson's Bay Company sold them some of its machinery which had been used at Fort Vancouver. It also bought much of the lumber sawed in the mill. A great deal was needed, also, by the settlers themselves for building their own homes.

The flow of settlers northward, begun after the boundary settlement in 1846, was interrupted in 1847 by the Whitman massacre. People were afraid for awhile to be isolated in small groups without protection from the Indians. Also, when gold was discovered in California in 1848, many of the Oregon immigrants turned south to the gold fields instead of north to Puget Sound. In the spring of 1849, Joseph Lane, the first governor of Oregon Territory, found through a census that there were only 304 white people north of the Columbia.

During 1849, however, unsuccessful prospectors from California began to return to Oregon. They told the settlers that the thousands of gold seekers in California needed lumber and food in immense quantities. The vast forests of Puget Sound could certainly supply the demand for the former, and, once the land was cleared, the soil was obviously suited to farming. Besides, fishing was clearly a potential industry. As a result, people began to hurry to the Sound region in such numbers that the census for 1850 showed 1,049 white inhabitants north of the Columbia.

In 1849 before the Cayuse War had ended with the surrender of the supposed leaders of the Whitman massacre, the Snoqualmie Indians became enraged at the influx of white settlers to the Sound, and a chief, Patkanim, evidently hoped to kill them. The Indians attacked Fort Nisqually, killing Leander Wallace, an American. Troops ordered into the area by Governor Lane chose a camp site where Fort Steilacoom was built a few months later. This ended the attempted Indian uprising. The first district court north of the Columbia held under the jurisdiction of the territory of Oregon met at Steilacoom in October, 1849, to try the alleged murderers of Wallace, and two of the six defendants were hanged.

The American settlers then felt more secure to venture farther north. Isaac Ebey and others took up claims on Whidbey Island in 1850, and in the following year Charles Bachelder and Alfred A. Plummer went as far as Port Townsend to settle. These two areas attracted other Americans at a steady rate.

In 1851 a group of immigrants waited in Portland until a few members could explore the area to the north for a suitable location to found a city. John N. Low and David T. Denny went to Olympia where they met Lee Terry and Robert C. Fay, and the four men went on by canoe up the east side of the Sound as far as Elliott Bay and then up the Duwamish River a few miles to a point where Luther M. Collins, Henry Van Asselt, and Jacob and Samuel Maple had arrived with their families just a few days earlier.

The Low party returned to a level area on Elliott Bay which seemed to offer a better site for a town than the steep bluffs which lined most of the shore. They began to cut trees to build a house, and on September 28, 1851, they had enough logs to lay a foundation. They decided to name their infant village New York.

Terry and Denny stayed to finish a house while Low and Fay returned to Portland to get the families. Arthur A. Denny, Carson D. Boren, William N. Bell, Charles C. Terry, Low, and their families traveled by ship as far as Elliott Bay, reaching there November 13. It was raining and cold, and the prospect of living in the unfinished cabin was evidently too much for the women, because, after they had worked for awhile getting their supplies off the ship, they sat down and cried.

During the first winter the Seattle settlers cut timber for a ship from San Francisco which came into the Sound looking for all kinds of produce. The men found, however, that it was too difficult to get the logs to the water. Therefore, in the spring they began to explore the inside shore line of Elliott Bay for a harbor, using horseshoes tied to a clothesline to take soundings. They found that the water was so deep right up to the land that ships could come in at any point.

All except Low and Terry then chose claims along what is now Seattle's waterfront. In March, Dr. D. S. Maynard decided to move north from Olympia where he had opened a store, and, in order to induce him to come to the new location instead of settling at "New York," the Denny party made room for Maynard by reducing their claims along the deep-water front. People in Olympia were beginning to call the new settlement "Duwamps," a name which did not appeal to the village's residents. Maynard therefore suggested that they name the new town for his friend Chief Sealth, a Duwamish chief. The settlers agreed to this choice of a name, but "Seattle" was as near the Indian pronunciation of the chief's name as they could get; consequently, the name has persisted in that form.

In an account of the experiences of the Seattle pioneers, *Pioneer Days on Puget Sound,* Arthur Denny tells of their difficulties in getting food during the winter of 1852. Unless ships came in, they had to make the difficult trip to Forts Nisqually or Steilacoom to get supplies. Often their pork and butter came around the Horn and their sugar from China. They paid $90.00 for two barrels of pork, one of which was washed away in high tide, and $20.00 for a barrel of flour. When the supply of flour on the Sound gave out completely, they had to exist on sugar, syrup, tea, coffee, fish, and venison until the arrival of the next ship.

During this winter, another famous Seattle settler arrived, Henry Yesler, who was a carpenter and millwright. He wanted to build a sawmill, and the settlers were so eager to have one that they rearranged their claims again to give him a site with the necessary waterfront. He put up a steam sawmill that had a capacity of fifteen thousand feet of lumber per day. A cookhouse near the mill was used for courthouse, jail, hotel, church, polling place, parties, and all other social activities and was the place where townspeople came to hear news of the world from the crews of visiting ships.

Since the New York of Terry and Low did not attract settlers as did Seattle, people facetiously began calling the smaller village New York Alki, meaning "New York bye and bye" in Chinook jargon.

The New York part was later dropped, leaving the name Alki Point as it is today.

AGITATION FOR SEPARATE TERRITORY

By 1851 the settlers in these various sections of Puget Sound felt the need for a government separate from that of the territory of Oregon, of which they were still a part. What is now the state of Washington was called northern Oregon. The chief objection of the northern residents was that the capital (then at Oregon City, and later at Salem) was too far away for them to reach without great hardship. In addition, in October, 1851, the district court was assigned to John R. Jackson's home on the Cowlitz River instead of to Judge Sidney Ford's place on the Chehalis River where the northern inhabitants wanted it. The jurors from the Port Townsend and Whidbey Island areas had to go about twenty miles farther, as a result, to get to court. With trails that could be traveled only on foot or on horseback where river travel was impossible, such a journey was more than a trivial inconvenience.

In fact, the northern residents felt that Oregon Territory was too large for its government to give the northern section adequate attention, and the Columbia River made an additional barrier between the two sections. As their interests became different, the northern settlers felt that the territorial officials paid no attention to their needs. They resented their "stepchild" situation. Nothing was done about roads in their region; the Surveyor-General had not surveyed any land north of the river; they had to make the difficult trip to the capital for much of their official business; and they were irritated by the control over the Indians which the Hudson's Bay Company still held while it wound up its business south of the Canadian boundary.

The northern section, including Clatsop County south of the Columbia, had only two representatives in the Oregon Territorial House of Representatives and one member in the Council, the upper house. Thus, it was impossible to focus the attention of the legislature on its needs, and this lack of interest caused the northern part of the territory to lose its fair share of federal or territorial appropriations.

During 1851-52 the northern part of the territory had even less legislative representation. In February, 1851, the legislature passed a law moving the territorial capital from Oregon City to Salem, but, when the next session convened, the northern legislators plus three other representatives refused to go to Salem and held their own minority legislature at Oregon City. When the one council member north of the river resigned in November, 1852, the Governor's proclamation calling a special election to choose his successor was published only in the Portland papers, and by the time the residents north of the Columbia learned of it and arranged for an election, the next session of the legislature was almost over. These incidents angered the inhabitants of northern Oregon even more.

On the other hand, the southern half of Oregon Territory did not like to have present Washington included because the two representatives from the north sometimes held the balance of power when the legislature was closely divided on some issue. Since the river made separate geographical units of the two parts, the southern half with its larger population found the northern half simply a nuisance.

Cowlitz Landing Convention

At Fourth of July celebrations in 1851 and 1852, the speakers north of the Columbia stressed the need for a separate territorial government, which one of them referred to as the "future state of Columbia." People were sufficiently concerned to call a convention at Cowlitz Landing in August, 1852, and they prepared a petition to Congress asking that northern Oregon be made into a separate territory. In the fall of 1852, a newspaper, the *Columbian,* was begun in Olympia, and it also took up the campaign.

Monticello Convention

As a result of this agitation, forty-four persons were elected as delegates to a second convention held at Monticello on November 25, 1852. They adopted another petition to Congress, requesting that it pass a law organizing the country north and west of the Columbia into the "Territory of Columbia." Before this petition could reach Washington, D. C., however, the question had already been presented to Congress. On December 6, 1852, former Governor Lane, who was the Oregon territorial representative in Congress at that time, introduced a resolution asking the Committee on Public Lands to report on the advisability of creating a separate territory in northern Oregon.

WASHINGTON TERRITORY

Two months later, on February 8, 1853, a bill to create the "Territory of Columbia" was introduced in Congress, and Representative Lane made a speech in favor of the bill. At the close of his remarks, the clerk of the House of Representatives read the memorial drawn up at the Monticello Convention, which had reached Congress by that time. During the debate on the bill, Representative Stanton of Kentucky inserted an amendment to substitute the name "Washington" for "Columbia" on the grounds that George Washington should be honored by having a future state named for him. The bill with this amendment was passed on February 10, 1853, and the President signed the bill creating the territory of Washington on March 2, 1853.

The territory of Washington consisted of more land than the residents had wanted, extending from the Pacific to the crest of the Rockies between the forty-ninth and forty-sixth parallels except where the Columbia formed the southern boundary. It included not only all of the present state of Washington, but the northern parts of Idaho and Montana as far east as the summit of the Rockies. In spite of this huge area, the population was extremely small, the first census showing 3,965 white persons.

Isaac I. Stevens

Major Isaac I. Stevens, the first governor of Washington Territory, was a man of such extraordinary energy and vigor that even the governorship of a large territory seemed to him too small a job to occupy his time. Therefore, when President Pierce offered the appointment to him, he asked for, and received, the title of Superintendent of Indian Affairs for the territory, also. In order not to waste his time getting from Washington, D. C., to the territory of Washington, he agreed to command an exploring expedition across the country to find the best northern route for a future railroad. This turned out to be the route used when the Northern Pacific Railroad was constructed years later (1870's and 1880's).

Stevens had graduated from West Point in 1839 at the head of his class and had served with distinction in the Mexican War. At the time he was named governor, he was chief assistant in the United States Survey Office in Washington, D. C.

In order to save time on the railroad survey, Stevens sent Captain George B. McClellan with one party across Panama and up the coast to explore from the Pacific eastward with the hope that McClellan's group would meet the party working its way west under the command of Stevens himself. Stevens, with 243 men—including surveyors, army officers, artists, and scientists—took wagons as far as Fort Benton on the Missouri River, which they reached by September, 1853. From that point, they crossed the Rockies on foot, using pack horses to carry their supplies. They examined nine different passes and reached Olympia on November 25, 1853, by way of the Columbia and Cowlitz rivers.

Tradition says that Governor Stevens rode into Olympia alone, ahead of the rest of his party, and arrived in the town during a rainstorm. He was dirty from the day's ride to begin with, and the rain had made him look so grimy that when he went into the dining room of the only hotel, he was told that it was reserved for a big party and that he would have to go someplace else to eat. When he protested that he was hungry, the cook took him out to the kitchen where he ate some scraps of food. Outside the hotel, shortly afterward, somebody complained to him that the new governor was late for the dinner prepared for him. When Stevens was able to convince the man that he was the new governor, a signal was given for people to come to the hotel for the banquet. They were embarrassed to find that the guest of honor was too full of his makeshift meal to enjoy the dinner prepared for him.

Whether or not this story is true, it is in keeping with Stevens' impatience with any delay or with ceremony if it took time. With this characteristic sense of haste, he set the date for the meeting of the first legislative assembly in Olympia for February 27, 1854, not quite a month after the first election. In the meantime, he sailed around Puget Sound and visited the Hudson's Bay Company post at

Victoria, British Columbia, to talk to the officials about negotiations for paying the company for its holding in the part of the old Oregon country which was now the territory of Washington.

Stevens had required that each person in his expedition keep careful notes on geography, geology, plants, animals, analyses of climate and natural resources of the country, as well as on customs of the various Indian tribes encountered. The accompanying artists drew pictures to illustrate these subjects, and this material was made into a report consisting of a large set of volumes, published by congressional order, which has been of great value to students of many aspects of the history of the Pacific Northwest: *Reports of Explorations and Surveys, to Ascertain the Most Practicable and Economical Route for a Railroad from the Mississippi River to the Pacific Ocean.*[2]

The other half of the expedition, George McClellan's group, had little success. Stevens had sent a letter to A. A. Denny in the summer of 1853, telling him that McClellan was coming ahead to open a road from Fort Walla Walla to Fort Steilacoom so that the immigrants of that year would be able to go directly across the Cascades from Fort Walla Walla without having to go down the Columbia to Fort Vancouver and then up the Cowlitz to Puget Sound. When McClellan reached Vancouver, he took a party to explore Naches Pass, but decided that such a route was too difficult for wagons. On his way to meet Stevens, he then went north from the Yakima country, examining the eastern ends of the various passes into the Okanogan country, and on east to the Colville country where he met Stevens on October 18, 1853. Stevens then proposed that McClellan try to penetrate the Cascades from that latitude, but McClellan persuaded the governor that it could not be done at that time of year. Later, from Olympia, Stevens sent McClellan to try to build a road through Snoqualmie Pass eastward, but he abandoned that as well.

In the meantime the coast settlers were disturbed because they knew that the 1853 immigrants would have been told in the East that the road would be ready for them. So a group of men cut a road as best they could from Fort Steilacoom through Naches Pass to Fort Walla Walla, and they succeeded sufficiently to let a small

[2] 33rd Cong., 2nd Sess., *Senate Exec. Doc.* No. 78 (Washington, D. C., 1855).

number of incoming settlers take their wagons over it in the fall of 1853. The worst place was a steep hill going down to the Puyallup River where the wagons had to be let down by ropes.

Indian Treaties and Wars

Stevens' first task as Superintendent of Indian Affairs for Washington Territory was to make treaties with the various tribes and remove them to reservations so that the remaining land could be legally acquired by white settlers. Even at that time, there were indications in the East that the reservation system was not working out to the advantage of either the Indians or whites. Since it was the accepted policy of the United States government, however, it is not surprising that Stevens accepted this method as the logical one for getting Indian lands into the possession of the whites.[3]

He threw himself into his treaty making with his usual energy and determination. Even on his way out to Washington, he conferred with as many Indian chiefs as possible west of the Rockies. He persuaded the Blackfeet chiefs whom he met to notify the other members of their tribe to meet him the following summer (1855) at Fort Benton for a council where Stevens hoped to make peace between them and the Flatheads. He believed that white settlement could not progress as long as hostilities continued.

Treaties with Coast Tribes

By the end of 1854, Stevens was ready to make treaties with the Coast tribes, and by the end of January, 1855, he had drawn up agreements with the main tribes west of the Cascades in the Medicine Creek, Point Elliott, Point-No-Point, and Neah Bay treaties. Although the details differed, in general, the Indians agreed to give up the title to their lands and to live in an area to be set aside for them, which might be changed by the President of the United States. Their rights to fish and hunt at certain places were to be protected, and they were to be paid for the land which they gave up. In

[3] In accordance with the Oregon Donation Land Act of 1850, Congress allowed 320 acres of land to be claimed by a single person and 640 acres by a married couple. The claimant could not receive final title to the land until he had lived on it for four years and had made certain improvements.

addition, the United States government was to furnish schools, doctors, and other services to them. The Indians, in turn, were not to trade in Canada; and they were to free their slaves, to maintain order on their reservations, and to keep liquor out. Only one group of Coast tribes refused to sign—those immediately north of Grays Harbor, and even they entered into a treaty after a few months.

Treaties with Inland Tribes

Stevens was pleased by the ease with which treaties had been made with the tribes west of the Cascades and so confidently turned his attention to the inland Indians. A council was called for May, 1855, near present Walla Walla to which the Yakimas, Walla Wallas, Cayuses, and Nez Perces were invited, and about five thousand Indians came. This conference did not proceed as smoothly as those on the coast, however, and some of the leading chiefs—such as Kamiakin of the Yakimas and Peu-peu-mox-mox of the Walla Wallas—refused to sign the treaties at first, and signed later only with great reluctance.

It was natural that the Plateau Indians would object more than the Coast Indians to giving up their freedom and going on reservations. For one thing, the Coast tribes required less room for fishing than the inland Indians did for hunting, and, if fishing rights were protected, the Coast Indians would not be greatly restricted by reservation life. The Plateau Indians, on the other hand, were used to traveling long distances on horseback to hunt, and, in fact, since they did no farming, it was often necessary to cover large areas to secure sufficient food for the winter. In addition, because they were hunters, they were more warlike in their habits than many of the Coast tribes south of Vancouver Island whose sedentary fishing life and state of transitional culture had made them more peaceful. The Coast Indians, who had been in contact with white traders much longer than the Plateau tribes, were more accustomed to white ways, but they had been weakened by the exposure to new diseases and vices.

When the Walla Walla Council met, Governor Stevens, with his remarkable energy, was perhaps too impatient with the Indians. The Indians did not value time and liked to deliberate at length and with much ceremony over any important question. At another time,

Stevens acknowledged that although the Indians put on all of their finery for parleys, he was too busy to change from his work clothes, and the Indians protested about his lack of formality. At any rate, the Indians at the Walla Walla Council asked to have a second conference before they signed a treaty, and Stevens refused to give them more time.

Historians who approve of Stevens' actions state that he took pains to see that the treaties were explained fully to the tribes through interpreters and to make certain that they understood them. Such students believe that the Indians asked for another council only as a ruse to put off signing treaties which they did not like. Many years later, however, some of the Indians told white friends, such as A. J. Splawn, that they lost faith in Stevens and believed that he was trying to trick them when he insisted that they sign the treaties immediately.

Even with every good intention of making the treaties clear to the Indians, the whites could still easily have failed, because the background of the two races was so different that certain ideas of one could not be expressed exactly in the other's language. The inland Indian's conception of land ownership is a good example. He believed that the Great Spirit had lent the earth to human beings for their use, but that no one owned it in the sense of being able to sell it to another. The place where he grew up, moreover, was his home, a place to which he could always return. Consequently, when a chief signed a treaty selling the land of his tribe, that did not necessarily mean to him that his tribe could no longer use it.

The lack of a central government in an Indian tribe was another feature that made a treaty system with Indians unworkable. Even if the chief who signed a treaty understood it and accepted the white interpretation of its clauses, he had no means of forcing other members of his tribe, or even of his own village, to follow it. Even in battles between Indian tribes, if a particular Indian did not approve, he refused to fight and was not censured for his failure to do

Chief Kamiakin. (W. Park Winans identified this as young Kamiakin. However, the identification has been disputed by some others. In the Winans Manuscript Collection, Washington State University Library, Pullman. Used by permission of Mrs. George L. Converse)

so. The whites did not understand this and expected a chief who signed a treaty to make certain that it was obeyed by all members of his tribe.

In spite of their objections, the chiefs finally signed the treaties, mainly on the advice of Lawyer, a Christian Nez Perce chief. During the heat of the discussion, Lawyer one night moved his tent close to that of Stevens, giving as his reason his desire to protect Stevens from an attack planned by some of the other Indians. Many years later, some of the Indians who had attended the council insisted that just the reverse was true—that Lawyer was afraid of being killed by members of some of the other tribes, particularly the Cayuses, because of his championship of the white cause.

As soon as the treaties were signed, Stevens went overland to Fort Benton to meet the Blackfeet as planned the previous year. Just at this time, gold was discovered at Fort Colville, and prospectors began crossing the Yakima country to get to Colville. Stevens had promised that the whites would stay out of the areas set aside as reservations. Therefore, the Indians thought that the whites had no intention of keeping their part of the bargain, and Kamiakin and several other Yakima chiefs decided to kill all whites found on Yakima lands. Qualchan and several of his relatives found six white men camping on the Yakima River and killed them. A. J. Bolon, one of Stevens' Indian agents whom the Indians liked because of his sincere interest in their problems, heard of the murders and went to investigate. He, too, was killed by some young Indians.

When C. H. Mason, who was acting as governor while Stevens was on his treaty-making expedition, heard of the murders, he asked Major Gabriel Rains, the commander of federal troops at Vancouver, to send some of his men into the Yakima country. Rains sent Major Granville Haller with eighty-four men from The Dalles and Lieutenant W. A. Slaughter with fifty men through Naches Pass.

Yakima War

Kamiakin and his warriors met Haller in the Yakima country. Both sides claimed that the other fired first in the initial engagement of what developed into the Yakima War. On the third day of the battle, Haller found himself surrounded by Indians on a hill with no water. The Indians' manner of fighting was to withdraw from a bat-

Spokane ferry on the military road from Colville to Walla Walla. (Water-color sketch by James M. Alden, 1810-77. Original in the National Archives; courtesy of the University of Washington Library)

tle at sunset and return the following morning to renew the fight. The white troops took advantage of this custom to slip away during the night and return to The Dalles. A few days later, one of Slaughter's scouts met an Indian who told him of Haller's defeat, and Slaughter was thus able to hurry back through Naches Pass to the Sound ahead of the pursuing Indians. Rains then took troops into the Yakima country in October, but he, too, was unable to adapt his strategy to Indian warfare and had to retreat again to The Dalles.

By this time the residents of Washington Territory were concerned about Stevens' safety on his return from the conference with the Blackfeet, and they raised a company of volunteers to try to find him and bring him back unharmed. Because the territory had little money, the territorial officials wanted to have the volunteers mustered into the regular United States Army so that they would be paid from federal funds; therefore, the volunteers went to Vancouver for induction. General John E. Wool was the commander of all United

States troops on the Pacific coast with headquarters at San Francis-co. He came to Vancouver, however, because of the hostilities and disbanded the company of volunteers there. He had great scorn for volunteer troops as opposed to regular army units, for one thing, and, for another, he is thought to have carried personal animosity toward Stevens.

When Stevens had been in San Francisco the preceding year, he and Wool had been a part of the same group at a social function where Wool began to brag about his exploits in a particular battle of the Mexican War. Stevens, with his usual brusqueness, reminded Wool that General Taylor was in command at the time of the battle and should be given credit for the victory. This could not have helped offending Wool, and it might have influenced his later atti-tudes.

Some scholars, however, point out that Wool's objection to vol-unteer troops came from his firm conviction that the white settlers were ordinarily to blame for troubles with the Indians. He felt that the white men saw enlistment in the territorial units as a means of getting a cash payment, and he accused the Washington territorial settlers of having this motive. Moreover, he wanted white people to stay out of the area east of the Cascades until the Indians gradually became more anxious to have white goods and, in return for them, would be willing to accept white settlement. In line with that idea, Wool did issue a proclamation in 1856 closing the eastern section to white settlement. Some miners, however, were not willing to stay out.

Since this was the case, the hostility of the Yakimas and neigh-boring tribes continued, and the Yakima War dragged on with oc-casional skirmishes and raids by the Indians on individuals or small groups of settlers. A messenger got to Fort Benton in the fall of 1855 and gave Stevens messages from the federal officers advising him to return to New York by way of the Missouri River and then take a ship back to Washington Territory. Of course, a person of Stev-ens' impetuous nature would refuse to do anything by a slow, safe means if there was a challenge to be met. So he turned back with the messenger and some friendly Nez Perces who had accompanied him and rode to the Spokane country where he was able to per-suade the Coeur d'Alenes and the Spokanes to refuse Kamiakin's

plea to join the warring tribes. Stevens then hurried on toward the
Snake River where he met a large group of Nez Perces. Looking
Glass was supposedly trying to stir up the Nez Perces to attack
Stevens, but if that was the case, he was overruled by the ones who
followed Lawyer's plea to remain loyal to the whites. Stevens
reached Olympia in January, 1856, and found that General Wool
had assigned Colonel George Wright to the command of federal
troops in the Columbia district.

The War West of the Cascades

Wright at that time was in sympathy with Wool's views of the
war and started for the Fort Walla Walla area to choose a site for
an additional fort. At the same time, Wool removed all but one
company of regular troops from Vancouver and left only nine men
in the blockhouse at the Cascades on the Columbia River. Kamiakin therefore decided to attack the Cascades. The Yakima,
Klickitat, and Cascade Indians planned to wait until both of the
small steamboats which ran between the Cascades and The Dalles
were at the Cascades and then sink them so that they could not go
for help. The Indians would then have little difficulty in destroying
the blockhouse and the few dwellings near the river.

Fortunately for the whites, when the steamboats were attacked,
a crewman of the *Mary* lay down on the floor of the pilot house to
avoid the gunfire and backed the ship out into the river from that
position. The *Wasco* also escaped, and the two ships went for aid.

In the meantime, the Indians killed the members of one family,
and many of the remaining settlers took refuge in a store, a two-
story log house. The Indians tried to set it on fire by throwing burning pitch on the roof, but the men on the upper floor managed to
push it off with poles and to pour brine from pork onto the fires
that did ignite. There was no water inside, but at night an Indian
boy who lived with one of the white families managed to creep
down to the wharf and return with buckets of water.

Farther down the river at the blockhouse, the men were able to
hold off the Indians with a cannon, and toward night they sent the
women and children in boats to Vancouver for safety. When they
arrived and reported the attack, Lieutenant Phil Sheridan started

immediately up the river on a steamship with the remaining skeleton force (forty men). When they neared the blockhouse, Sheridan saw that the Indians were stationed on a narrow strip of land that he could not attack with so few men, but he managed to move his men part way across the river to an island along which they pulled the boat and then rowed to the back of the blockhouse without the Indians' knowledge.

He intended to make a surprise attack on the Indians. Just at that moment, however, the relief party which had come from up the river to aid the besieged whites in the store reached the blockhouse with Colonel Edward J. Steptoe in command, and the bugler made the mistake of blowing his bugle to let the whites know rescue was at hand. This warned the Indians too, and they fled. Steptoe had been with Colonel Wright on the way to Walla Walla when the crews of the *Mary* and the *Wasco* reached The Dalles. A messenger hurried after them to inform them of the attack, and they returned as quickly as possible on the two steamboats. The Indians around the store disappeared, also, when the ships appeared. A group of Cascade Indians who had taken refuge on the island were all that could be found. Nine of them were hanged because their guns had recently been fired, and it appeared that they had taken part in the attack.

During this same period (the winter of 1855-56), there were also sporadic attacks by Indians on Puget Sound settlements, but those villages were fortunate in having United States naval vessels stationed at various points on the Sound. The naval officers took the viewpoint of the settlers rather than that of Wool and kept their ships in readiness for battle. In spite of the presence of the ship *Decatur* in the Seattle harbor, the Indians did attempt to attack Seattle. The settlers, however, learned of the attempt[4] and the ship's crew broke up the attack by firing shells into the woods where the Indians were gathering.

The settlers along the Strait of Juan de Fuca were more afraid of the British Columbia tribes than of the local Indians; therefore, for their protection forts were built at Port Townsend and Bellingham. In 1857 a war party from Kake killed Colonel Isaac N. Ebey at his

[4] Angeline, the daughter of Chief Seattle, is supposed to have made a stealthy trip by canoe one night to warn the settlers of the plan. Another version is that Jim, a friendly Indian, kept the *Decatur*'s captain informed of the Indians' plan for attack.

Block house on Whidbey Island. The "tongue and groove" corners illus-
trate the crude methods of construction necessary before nails were easily
available. (Courtesy of the University of Washington Library)

home on Whidbey Island and carried off his head to avenge the murder of a chief. This gruesome act outraged the whites, although the previous year, when Peu-peu-mox-mox was killed while attempting to escape from his white captors, some of the soldiers scalped him and cut off his ears. Atrocities were thus committed on both sides.

In 1857 the criticism of Wool's policy of resisting the use of volunteer troops and his lukewarm response to the requests of the settlers for aid from the regular army reached the point where he was recalled, and General Newman S. Clarke was appointed in his place.

Battle of Rosalia

Until 1858, however, the United States Army officers in the interior continued to believe that a decisive battle with the Indians was not necessary. That attitude, however, was changed suddenly in May of that year by the defeat of Colonel Steptoe in the neighborhood of present Rosalia, Washington. Steptoe left Fort Walla Walla with 158 men on May 6, 1858, intending to seek some Indian cattle thieves, confer with the Spokane Indians, and go on to Colville to investigate reports that the Indians there were becoming hostile. Since he regarded his expedition as an investigative one and something in the nature of a peace mission, he evidently felt no necessity for seeing that his men had a normal supply of ammunition. In fact, the quantity taken amounted only to forty rounds for each soldier. Some of the soldiers said later that the packer loaded liquor in preference to ammunition, but that was denied.

Near present Rosalia, Steptoe's party met more than six hundred Spokane Indians on horses, who warned the whites that they would not help them cross the Spokane River because they feared that Steptoe intended to attack them. Steptoe camped there that night and the following day the Indians began to fire on the whites after they had turned back toward Fort Walla Walla. Because of Steptoe's lack of ammunition, he had to get his troops to a protected spot, and after several skirmishes, they reached the hill just east of what is now Rosalia, where a monument now commemorates the battle. They were able to defend themselves there, but the surrounding Indians cut them off from any drinking water. Consequently, Steptoe decided to attempt to get his men away after dark when the Indians left the battlefield for the night.

After they had buried their dead and strapped the wounded men onto their horses, they rode away as silently as possible, until they were out of earshot of the Indians. Then they sped to the Snake River. The next morning the Nez Perces used their boats to take Steptoe's party across the Snake, and the group continued to Fort Walla Walla without further trouble. In later years, because Steptoe Butte, not far from Rosalia, was named for Colonel Steptoe, people began to think that the battle was fought on it. That was not the case, however, and historians now usually refer to Steptoe's encounter as the Battle of Rosalia in order to place it properly in its geographical setting.

Some controversial points about the campaign may never be settled definitely. There were reports that Timothy, a friendly Nez Perce who lived at the Alpowa village (known as Red Wolf's Crossing), stayed with Steptoe after he ferried the soldiers across the Snake on their way to the Spokane country and helped get them back through a short cut on their flight to the Snake after the battle. Some of the officers with the expedition later insisted, however, that Timothy was not with the troops and gave no help except with ferrying them across the river. Kamiakin is said by some writers to have been present at the battle, urging the Indians to fight. Others have evidence that he was miles away and had nothing to do with it.

Another puzzling point has been the ease with which the white soldiers got away in the night without making enough noise to arouse the Indians camping nearby. Judge William C. Brown, in *The Indian Side of the Story,* suggests that the Nez Perces who were with Steptoe made an agreement with the Coeur d'Alenes whereby the Steptoe party was allowed to escape in return for the horses and supplies that they left behind. The Palouses, Spokanes, and other Indians, presumably, knew nothing of this arrangement.

Wright Expedition

The outcome of the Steptoe fiasco was that the regular army officers changed their attitude toward the Yakima War. They were convinced that a vigorous attack had to be made, and Colonel Wright left Fort Walla Walla on August 6, 1858, with seven hundred men. They marched toward the Spokane country and met a large number of Indians on hills overlooking Four Lakes near present Spokane. This time, the white troops were not only well supplied with ammunition, but they had a new type of rifle that could shoot farther than the Hudson's Bay guns used by the Indians. Consequently, after another unsuccessful Indian attack, Chief Garry came to talk to Wright and offer peace. Wright insisted on unconditional surrender. The next day (September 8, 1858), the white soldiers managed to capture all of the Indians' horses (more than eight hundred). Wright, believing correctly that the Indians would be helpless without their horses, had them all killed except for those which his men could use. The various Indian tribes surrendered, giving up certain of their men as the murderers or instigators of the fighting. Wright hanged a number of them in each instance, except the Coeur d'Alenes.

Trial of Leschi

During the war, some of the Coast chiefs who had fought the whites went into the Yakima country for protection, and Colonel Wright refused to deliver them to Governor Stevens. The most famous of the chiefs was Leschi, who was accused of participating in many of the attacks west of the Cascades. Stevens was determined to arrest him because he symbolized the spirit of Indian resistance to white settlement. He also appeared to be under the protection of Wright, who was at that time the most prominent representative of the regular army which had been constantly opposed to Stevens. He offered a reward for the capture of Leschi, and one of the chief's relatives succumbed to this temptation and turned him over to the whites in November, 1856.

At his trial, many white people became convinced that Leschi had killed white people as an act of war rather than as one of murder and that he was being tried as a symbol. Feeling ran so high that the first jury could not agree on a verdict at all. A second trial in 1857 resulted in a death sentence that was appealed to the Territorial Supreme Court on a writ of error. A stay of execution was issued until the Supreme Court could rule on the question. When it did, the decision was in favor of the prosecution, and Leschi was again ordered to be executed on January 22, 1858. On that day, a deputy United States marshal stationed at Fort Steilacoom arrested the sheriff who was to carry out the death sentence on a federal warrant for selling whisky to Indians. The marshal held the sheriff in custody until the time set for the execution had passed. Even people who were sympathetic with Leschi were angry at having federal officers interfere with the orders of a territorial court. The feeling was strong enough that the legislature, which was then in session, passed a law requiring the Supreme Court judges to meet to consider the new developments. The Supreme Court ordered the district court judge to resentence Leschi, who was then hanged.

CIVIL WAR

During the Washington territorial period, the most important happening in the United States as a whole was the Civil War. In spite of their great distance from the battle area, the people of Washington Territory took a keen interest in the war. The sympathies of our residents were largely in favor of the northern side. This would have been true, undoubtedly, simply because there had been almost no support for slavery north of the Columbia.

There were other reasons, however, which brought the Union cause vividly to mind. For one thing, many of the leading military figures had been territorial officials here before the Civil War. General Grant, for example, had been stationed as an army officer at Fort Vancouver in 1853, and Governor Stevens, who had served as territorial delegate to Congress after his period of governorship, was killed in the battle of Chantilly in 1862, fighting on the northern side. (The effect of the national political situation on the local politics in Washington Territory will be discussed in the next chapter.)

An incident which further turned the minds of the Washington residents against the Confederate cause was the performance of the *Shenandoah,* a Confederate ship under the command of Captain James I. Waddell. He toured the northern Pacific during the war, capturing thirty-eight merchant ships, eight of which he released loaded with the crews from all of them. He burned or scuttled the others. When a captain of an English ship finally convinced him that the northern armies had won and the war was over, Waddell went to England where he surrendered his ship. The English government then turned it over to one of our consuls.

The fervor created by these various factors showed itself in the work which the women of Washington Territory did to try to relieve the suffering of the wounded Civil War soldiers. At that time, groups like the Red Cross were not sufficiently well organized for adequate medical attention. To help remedy such a situation, the women here, even though they were far away from the battle area, prepared clothing and hospital supplies for the Sanitary Commission, which had charge of that work. In fact, the women of Washington Territory are supposed to have done more work of this kind than women in any other of our states or territories.

Since the United States government was anxious to move as many as possible of its regular troops from this section of the country to the Civil War battlefields, volunteer groups had to be organized to take their places. Consequently, the War Department authorized the forming of the First Washington Territory Volunteer Infantry, which was stationed partly at Fort Vancouver and partly at Fort Steilacoom. These troops guarded the posts and were present to protect our citizens from possible attacks by Indians.

Sale of Port Angeles Townsite

One interesting result of the Civil War to this region was the sale of the Port Angeles townsite. In trying to raise money to carry on the war, the northern officials decided to sell land belonging to the United States. In 1862, President Lincoln had set aside a reserve consisting of 3,520 acres at Port Angeles, to be used for lighthouse and military purposes. In 1863, part of this was kept for lighthouses, but the rest was thrown open to sale under the new law providing for sale of federal land. Since the plan did not bring in the amount of money that was anticipated, in 1894 the officers of the United States Land Office in Seattle were authorized by new acts of Congress to sell the townsite lots to the highest bidders.

SAN JUAN BOUNDARY DISPUTE

During the territorial period, a boundary dispute occurred between the United States and Great Britain. When the Treaty of 1846 was written, the northern boundary of the United States was set along the forty-ninth parallel "to the middle of the channel which separates the continent from Vancouver's Island; and thence southerly through the middle of said channel, and Fuca's Strait, to the Pacific Ocean." It was thought at that time that there was only one channel between Vancouver Island and the mainland, but it developed that there were at least two.

The use of an additional channel was probably brought about by the change from sailing to steamships. The earlier sailing vessels preferred Rosario Strait, but the later steamships could use Haro Strait more easily. At any rate, the title to several of the San Juan islands was disputed. If the Rosario Strait had been considered the "middle of the channel," all of the islands in our present San Juan County would have belonged to England. If, on the other hand, the Haro Strait were taken as the dividing line, we would be in posses-

Port Angeles, 1898: "The caissons go rolling along" in a parade probably in celebration of the Fourth of July. The sign "Cyclery" in the background advertises a bicycle shop—cycling being the favorite sport of young people in the Gay Nineties. (Seattle Historical Society)

sion of this group.

Both Americans and British settled in the islands, and the fact that both countries claimed the region naturally caused many disputes to arise. For example, in 1855 the sheriff of Whatcom County went to San Juan Island to collect taxes for the Washington territorial government. When the English residents refused to pay taxes to the American government, the sheriff took some sheep away with him as payment. The governor of Vancouver Island, James Douglas, then wrote to Governor Stevens, demanding back the sheep or their equivalent in money. Governor Stevens insisted that the island was part of the United States and that taxes for this country would be collected on possessions there.

Although each official threatened to take the matter to the governing body of his own country, nothing was actually done about this particular incident. Under such circumstances, however, there were bound to be repeated instances of friction between the United States and British officials, and the action which finally caused trouble was the killing of a pig.

In 1859 an American, Lyman Cutler, planted a patch of potatoes. Since supplies had to be brought a long way in a rowboat, the Americans were extremely anxious to dig a plentiful crop of potatoes from Cutler's garden. However, a pig which belonged to Charles Griffin, the representative of the Hudson's Bay Company, insisted on getting into the potato patch and digging up the potatoes. When Griffin refused to keep the pig penned up, Cutler shot it. Although Cutler offered to pay for it, Griffin threatened to have Cutler arrested and tried in a British court. Cutler and the other Americans defied Griffin's authority, and he left the island, although he said he would take further action.

When President Buchanan heard of the incident in September, 1859, he did not want to provoke a war with Great Britain over the ownership of San Juan Island since the much more important dispute over title to the Oregon country had been settled peaceably not many years previously. Therefore, he sent General Winfield Scott out to San Juan at once with instructions to make an agreement on his own responsibility, if possible. Scott arrived in October and soon arranged to cut down the number of American troops and to allow the British to station an equal number at the other end of the island. This proved to be a satisfactory arrangement, and the British and American troops entertained each other and were very friendly.

In 1871, a Joint High Commission was meeting to settle various disputes between England and the United States. Our government decided to allow that commission to refer the San Juan dispute to an arbitrator, and the commission chose William I, the German emperor, to decide the question. After hearing the arguments presented by a representative of both the British and United States governments as to why each should have the islands in question, Emperor William ruled that the claims of the United States were stronger. Therefore, he named Haro Strait as the dividing line between the British and United States possessions. As a result, since that time we have been in undisputed possession of the islands comprising the present San Juan County.

NEZ PERCE WAR OF 1877

The Indian treaties were the cause of the only major Indian war, the Nez Perce War of 1877, to affect the Pacific Northwest after the Yakima War. In the 1855 treaty, the Nez Perces were given the area extending from the Clearwater River south through the Wallowa and Imnaha regions of present Oregon and Idaho. The Upper Nez Perces, with Lawyer as one of their prominent chiefs, lived around Lapwai, and the Lower Nez Perces, with Old Joseph and Looking Glass as two of their leading chiefs, lived farther south around the Wallowa and Imnaha valleys. In 1860 gold was discovered in the Clearwater-Salmon region, and, as prospectors began to cross from Walla Walla to the gold fields, they traversed the beautiful and fertile Wallowa region and wanted it for themselves as farming land. The Lower Nez Perces protested, of course, when the whites began to settle there because one of the stipulations of the treaty was that no white person could take a land claim on a reservation.

By 1863 so many white people had settled on Nez Perce land that the federal officials decided that they could not be ousted. Therefore, the United States government ordered that a new treaty be made with the Nez Perces, limiting them to the area around Lapwai. Old Joseph, the most influential chief of the Lower Nez Perces, refused to sign the new agreement, but Chief Lawyer and other Upper Nez Perces signed it. The whites accepted the latter's signatures as binding all of the Nez Perces, although as we have seen, according to Indian custom, they did not have authority to enforce it even on the Upper Nez Perces, along the Clearwater, let alone on the Lower Nez Perces from the Wallowa country.

Since the Lower Nez Perces had not signed the treaty, they paid no attention to it and attempted to prevent white people from claiming land in that part. By 1877, however, the friction between the settlers and the Wallowa Nez Perces had reached the point where some agreement had to be made. The federal government, therefore, ordered General O. O. Howard to remove all of the Nez Perces to the Lapwai area, the area set aside in the 1863 treaty as their reservation.

General Howard tried to persuade the Nez Perces to move to Lapwai. By this time Old Joseph was dead, and his son Joseph, Looking Glass, and White Bird were among the influential young chiefs. They finally decided that their people must leave their beloved valleys, and if General Howard had allowed them a reasonable time to move, they might have done so without violence. Instead, Howard ordered them to be out of their homeland in a month. It was spring when the rivers were high, and the Nez Perces should have been allowed to wait until the water was lower in order to move their thousands of horses and cattle. Instead, they had to force them into the rushing streams, where several hundred drowned.

Resentment over this unnecessary loss plus personal grievances on the part of some of the young Nez Perces whose relatives had been killed or mistreated by whites drove a group to kill four white men. The Nez Perce leaders knew then that Howard would attack them in retaliation; consequently, they decided to flee across the Rockies and get completely away—perhaps to Canada where Sitting Bull was in exile. They came close to making good their escape in one of the most thrilling chases in all history. The story has all the elements of a good western drama, but it does not affect our own area sufficiently to warrant telling it in detail. In the reading list on pp. 337-38, however, books on the battles are suggested as outside reading.

In *Hear Me, My Chiefs,* L. V. McWhorter, who spent many years studying the subject, says that the Nez Perces who were young men at the time of the war told him many years later that Joseph was not the sole leader of the Nez Perces as he has long been considered. McWhorter maintains that he was simply one of the many able Nez Perce chiefs who planned the strategy that enabled them to take their women and children, in addition to the fighting men (seven hundred people altogether along with fifteen hundred horses), over the Lolo Pass, a route so difficult that the white soldiers fell far behind in trying to follow them.

Chief Joseph. (Photo in the McWhorter Manuscript Collection, Washington State University Library, Pullman. Used by permission of Mrs. V. O. McWhorter)

In fact, the Nez Perces outwitted Howard's troops time after time in their trek up the Bitterroot Valley, through Yellowstone Park, and north to the Bear Paw Mountains. Here the Indians stopped to get some rest, believing that they were safe since their scouts reported that Howard's troops were too far behind to molest them.

They did not know, however, that Howard had sent a telegraph message to General Miles, stationed at a fort on the Yellowstone River, to intercept Joseph. Miles hurried northward and surprised the Nez Perces in their camp. They were thus forced to surrender, and Joseph made one of the great speeches of all time. He said:

> Tell General Howard I know his heart. What he told me before I have in my heart. I am tired of fighting. Our chiefs are killed. Looking Glass is dead. Too-hul-hul-sote is dead. It is the young men who say yes or no. He who led on the young men is dead. It is cold and we have no blankets. The little children are freezing to death. My people, some of them, have run away to the hills, and have no blankets, no food; no one knows where they are—perhaps freezing to death. I want to have time to look for my children and see how many of them I can find. Maybe I shall find them among the dead. Hear me, my chiefs. I am tired; my heart is sick and sad. From where the sun now stands I will fight no more forever.[5]

Miles promised Joseph that the Nez Perces would be allowed to go back to Idaho in the spring, but he was overruled by his superior officers, and the Indians were moved from one place to another, part of the time in box cars, until they finally reached Oklahoma. They contracted diseases in the hot country, and half of them died. In 1885, public opinion had been aroused to such a point in favor of making some amends to the Nez Perces for their treatment that the federal government ordered that they be returned to the Pacific Northwest. However, those whose home had been in the Wallowa Valley were sent to the Colville Reservation instead of to Lapwai where they wanted to go. Joseph remained at Nespelem until his death in 1904.

[5] *Report of the Secretary of War; Being Part of the Message and Documents Communicated to the Two Houses of Congress at the Beginning of the Second Session of the Forty-Fifth Congress* (Washington, D.C.: Government Printing Office, 1877), I, 630.

SETTLEMENT OF EASTERN PART
OF WASHINGTON TERRITORY

During the period from 1855 to 1877, white settlement east of the Cascades increased to the point where it touched off the Yakima and Nez Perce wars. The expanded population also caused agitation for shifts in political boundaries, some of which were changed.

The first move was toward creating a new territory out of parts of eastern Oregon and Washington. The first Washington territorial legislature in 1854 created Walla Walla County to consist of all land between the Rockies and the Cascades north of the Washington-Oregon boundary and south of 49°. The number of settlers around The Dalles in 1855 was sufficient to cause them to call a convention to meet there to consider creating a new territory out of Walla Walla County and eastern Oregon. The convention was not held, but the discussion continued.

At the close of the Wright campaign in 1858, mining interest in the Colville area increased, and the territorial legislature of 1858-59 evidently thought that there were enough people in the region to support a county government, because it created Spokane County during that session. It consisted of all land between the Columbia River and the Rocky Mountains north of the Snake River.

Congress made Oregon a state in 1859 with its present boundaries and added the eastern part of the former Oregon Territory to Washington Territory, throwing into it present southern Idaho and the northwestern tip of present Wyoming.

In 1860 the influx of miners to the Orofino gold fields increased the population of what was then the southeastern corner of the territory of Washington to such an extent that those residents began to feel the need for a separate territory to comprise approximately the area now called the Inland Empire. The miners were particularly eager to have a territorial capital nearer to them than Olympia. Their mining camp regulations often forbade a prospector to leave his claim for more than seventy-two hours during the summer, and it was impossible for the miners in much of present Idaho to get to Olympia and back in that length of time. A large group was thus inconvenienced. Moreover, even the residents around Walla Walla felt that the territorial legislature did not pay enough attention to their needs. They thought that the legislature was almost entirely concerned with the problems of the people on the west side of the Cascades.

Move for Creation of Walla Walla Territory

As a result, the earlier agitation for creating a new territory out of parts of eastern Oregon and Washington was revived. By 1861 the feeling was strong enough that one of the members of the Washington territorial legislature introduced a bill in the form of a petition to the United States Congress, asking it to create the territory of Walla Walla. The bill was defeated in the Olympia legislature because the majority of the members from the west side of the territory did not want to lose control of the section east of the Cascades. The eastern residents did not give up, however. They drew up petitions asking the territorial legislature to draft a constitution for a new state of Idaho. The upper house (Council) passed such a bill, but in the House of Representatives the word "Washington" was substituted for "Idaho," and the bill was tabled (that is, it was set aside for future consideration).

Move for Creation of Pacific Republic

There was even a movement, which had begun many years before, to create a separate republic out of the Pacific coast region. Before the Union Pacific Railroad was completed to California in 1869, transportation to any part of the Pacific coast was so slow and difficult that many people sincerely believed that the area from the Atlantic to the Pacific coast was too large to make one nation successfully. In the late 1830's and early 1840's when the Willamette Valley residents were discussing the formation of a local government, John McLoughlin, the Hudson's Bay Company factor, had favored forming a separate nation out of the present Oregon and California region. Then when the boundary was settled in favor of the United States, as we have seen, the Americans in Oregon expected Congress to set up the territory of Oregon at once. They also assumed that the United States would extend its government to California when American troops took possession in 1846. When

Congress delayed such action for both Oregon and California, there was more reason for thinking that the two areas might be better off as an independent country. After Congress made Oregon a territory in 1848 and California a state in 1850, however, agitation for a separate republic died down until the transportation difficulties of the mining period again raised the question for Oregon.

The question of a separate republic was therefore in people's minds again at the beginning of the Civil War. Those on the West Coast who favored the southern cause again proposed the creation of a northwest republic which would be separate from the United States government as the Confederate states proposed to be. However, there was only a small proporation of southern sympathizers in Washington and not a sufficient number in Oregon to make such a move successful. On January 30, 1860, the Washington territorial legislature passed a resolution against the Pacific Confederacy, and the following year, as we have seen, it refused to ask Congress to create a separate Walla Walla Territory.

Creation of Idaho Territory

The eastern miners decided then to appeal directly to Congress for a separation from Washington Territory, and in 1863 Congress complied with their request by creating the territory of Idaho, with first Lewiston and then Boise as its capital. At that time Idaho was given its present boundaries, thus reducing the territory of Washington to its present size as far as its eastern and southern boundaries were concerned. The settlers in that area were satisfied, but the people left in the Walla Walla region were disappointed that they were still in Washington Territory with the capital at Olympia on the other side of the Cascade Mountains. Walla Walla, at first called Steptoe City, was growing at an astonishing rate. By 1870 it had 5,300 inhabitants, whereas King County, the Seattle area, had only 2,210.

Move to Annex Walla Walla and Columbia Counties to Oregon

Because people in the Walla Walla region felt neglected by the Washington territorial legislature, a bill to annex Walla Walla and Columbia counties to Oregon was introduced in Congress in 1876.

The bill was defeated, but the people in the western part of Washington Territory, who did not wish to see eastern Washington cut off, were frightened at the thought that such a bill might eventually pass. Consequently, as a substitute measure the territorial legislature decided to work for statehood. The legislators provided for an election of territorial delegates who were to meet in Walla Walla and draw up a state consitution.

Walla Walla Constitutional Convention

Fifteen delegates were elected, and northern Idaho was permitted to send one representative who could join in the debate but who could not vote. At that time, many people in the northern part of Idaho Territory wished to have that area annexed to Washington. They found it difficult to get to their capital, Boise, because the impassable Salmon River cuts directly across Idaho. Consequently, they were glad to be able to take part in the Walla Walla Constitutional Convention. Even at the present time, there is occasional agitation for changing our state boundaries to coincide with geographical units. Proposals have been made for the creation of a "State of Lincoln" to consist of the Inland Empire. Recently some interested persons have suggested that a new state be made from North Idaho alone. In 1963 a group named "North Idaho, Inc." filed articles of incorporation in the office of Idaho's secretary of state as an organization to investigate the feasibility of the establishment of a new state from the ten northern counties of Idaho.

The delegates who began work on the proposed constitution on June 11, 1878, had finished it by July 27. At the next election, the people were asked to vote on whether they wished to accept this constitution, and they voted to approve it. The congressional delegate from Washington Territory, Thomas Brents, then asked Congress to grant statehood to Washington, using the Walla Walla constitution as the new state constitution. Congress refused to do so, however, and the people of Washington Territory had to continue their agitation until 1889, when Congress finally allowed Washington to be admitted as a state.

By 1878 the telegraph was in use, the Union Pacific Railroad had been in operation to the California coast for nine years, and the

Northern Pacific Railroad was being constructed. These developments in the ease of communication made the distance from Washington Territory to Washington, D. C., seem small enough that the people of Washington stopped thinking of the Pacific Northwest as a possible separate country. They were merely anxious to become a state of the union.

Congress' Delay in Creating Washington State

Several times between 1882 and 1889 bills were introduced into Congress for the admission of Washington as a state. In 1886, for example, such a bill passed the Senate, but was defeated in the House. The other bills, for the most part, were never reported back to Congress by the committees to which they were assigned for consideration.

The reasons for Congress' delay were various. There were other territories at that time which were also anxious for statehood—Dakota, Montana, Idaho, and Wyoming. Both the Republican and Democratic parties in Congress hesitated to bring that many new states into the union for fear their congressional representatives might upset the balance of power existing between the two political parties.

Washington Territory at that time was predominantly Republican, and from 1881 to 1883 both houses in our national Congress were Republican. Consequently, one would think that Congress would have admitted Washington as a state during that period. There were other factors, however, that made Congress hesitate. For one thing, it was not until 1883 that the Columbia River branch of the Northern Pacific Railroad was completed to Tacoma and not until 1887 that the main line of the Northern Pacific across the Cascades to Tacoma was finished. Until then, the incoming settlers had to come overland by wagon, or by the longer sea route, or by railroad to California and up the coast by ship. Any of these routes was long or difficult enough that the number of immigrants was still comparatively small. In 1880 the population of the territory was only 75,116. There was also no assurance that the population would increase in the near future to a point where a state government could be easily supported. For another thing, one of the counties in the territory of Dakota had repudiated its bonds, and this fact made Congress suspicious of the credit standing of the other territories seeking statehood.

From 1883 to 1888 the Democratic party was in control of Congress, but it was not favorable to the creation of the new state. There had been anti-Chinese riots in both Washington and Wyoming, making Congress hesitant to admit those areas as states. Many eastern congressmen, too, were afraid to admit a territory where woman suffrage was permitted, as it was in Washington Territory from 1883 to 1887.

CREATION OF THE STATE OF WASHINGTON

During these years, also, the Republican group in Congress was almost as strong as the Democratic one, and the two parties made political footballs of the territories. The Republicans made a clean sweep in the election of 1888, and the "Lame Duck" Congress of 1888-89 was willing to admit four states—Washington, Montana, North Dakota, and South Dakota—before it went out of power. The bill admitting these territories was approved on February 22, 1889, an appropriate date for the authorization of the new state of Washington since it was George Washington's birthday.

In the Enabling Act written by Congress to outline the steps that the territory would have to take in order to become a state, it was stipulated that the voters of the territory would have to elect delegates to a constitutional convention to write the constitution for the new state. The people would then have to decide whether they wanted to accept the constitution in the form in which the convention delegates had written it. Once the voters approved (ratified) it, the President of the United States, acting for Congress, would examine a copy of the constitution, and, if it seemed to him to have followed the provisions of the Enabling Act, he would declare the new state of Washington to be in existence. The residents of Washington Territory fulfilled their part of this assignment, and, on November 11, 1889, President Harrison proclaimed that the state of Washington was admitted to the union.

Political Life

7

WASHINGTON TERRITORIAL PERIOD

Although Washington Territory was cut off by distance and lack of easy communication from the East and Middle West during most of our territorial period, the territorial residents were vitally concerned with national politics, and national rather than local issues often determined their party allegiance. The most obvious reminder of the party in power in the federal government was the territorial officials appointed by the President of the United States with the consent of the United States Senate. These officials, unless extremely unpopular, influenced the residents toward their own political beliefs and tried to find local issues to align with the national platform of their political party.

Congress passed the bill creating Washington Territory at the end of the term of a Whig President, Millard Fillmore, who signed the bill two days before he was succeeded in office by President Franklin Pierce, a Democrat, who also had a Democratic Congress. President Pierce therefore appointed Democrats as our first territorial officials—Isaac Stevens, as we have seen, being the first governor.

At the first election in the new territory on January 30, 1854, the voters had to elect their territorial representative in Congress as well as a number of territorial officials. Columbia Lancaster ran for the office of territorial representative on the Democratic ticket and William Henson Wallace on the Whig ticket. Colonel Wallace had a more flamboyant personality than Lancaster and was eager to enter politics. In fact, the Olympia *Pioneer and Democrat* later said that before he got off the boat at Cowlitz Landing, Wallace was "electioneering" for the office of congressional delegate. The Democratic sentiment was strong enough, however, to elect Lancaster, who got 698 votes as compared with Wallace's 500. Michael T.

Simmons, who had lost to Lancaster for the Democratic nomination, ran as an independent, but received only eighteen votes.

In 1854 Congress passed the Kansas-Nebraska Bill, allowing territories in the nonslave-holding areas to adopt slavery if the voters favored it. Some Democrats in Washington Territory who objected strongly to this possible spread of slavery into the formerly free areas of Kansas and Nebraska left the Democratic party, which supported the extension of slavery wherever a territory wanted it. The people who were opposed to slavery formed the Free-Soil Party in Washington Territory. The party nominated candidates for the 1855 election, but at that time it had comparatively little support. We saw in an earlier chapter how this party had advocated the exclusion of all Negroes from Oregon during the period of the Oregon Provisional Government. The national organization, however, supported only the abolition of slavery.

Before the election of 1856, the Democratic party under Stevens' leadership suffered a further setback because of Stevens' declaration of martial law in the spring of that year. During the Indian attacks on the Sound, ex-Hudson's Bay Company employees living with Indian wives near Steilacoom had not been molested by the attacking Indians. Therefore, Governor Stevens concluded that the white men were conniving with the Indians and spying for them.

He had the "squaw men" taken into custody and then prevented the territorial courts from trying them by proclaiming a state of martial law which allowed military courts (courts-martial) to hear the case. This act led to a feud between Stevens and the district judges (also Democrats) that became farcical, with Stevens arresting one of the judges who insisted on holding court despite Stevens' order, and the judge trying to arrest Stevens because he would not allow the men to stand trial in the civil courts. Many of the residents were so incensed by Stevens' highhanded tactics that they were inclined to support the Whigs and the new Republican party, which was emerging as a national political party, against the Democratic party, which Stevens represented.

Isaac L. Stevens: First Governor of Washington Territory. (Photo in Stevens Manuscript Collection, Washington State University Library, Pullman)

The Democrats hoped to win back their former supporters by securing approval of Stevens' action from the federal government, but, instead, President Pierce condemned his declaration of martial law and appointed Joseph Lane to take Stevens' place as governor. However, the Senate did not confirm the change in appointment, and Stevens retained his governorship. In the 1856 summer election, however, his opponents won a majority in both houses of the territorial legislature.

In 1857 Stevens let the Democrats know that he would like them to nominate him for the office of territorial delegate to Congress. Some of his fellow Democrats, like the judge whom he had arrested, opposed him bitterly, but he won the nomination because most of the members of the Democratic Convention thought he would be a great aid to the territory as its congressional delegate.

Although by 1856 the Whig party was defunct nationally, several county organizations in Washington Territory continued to nominate candidates on the Whig ticket. Most of the Whigs, however, joined the Free-Soil Democrats in the 1856 territorial election, and the Free-Soil party elected nine out of thirty-one members in the territorial House of Representatives. The following year this group accepted the new Republican party as its mouthpiece, taking for their national principles the platform which the Republicans had used for their campaign in 1856. One of these planks had been a strong statement of opposition to the Dred Scott decision of the United States Supreme Court, which had ruled that the owner of a slave could move his slave from a slave state into a free territory and still hold him there as a slave. The Republicans in Washington Territory had trouble persuading anybody to run against Stevens, but finally on the third attempt, Alexander Abernethy accepted the nomination. The Olympia *Pioneer and Democrat*, which supported Stevens, of course, jibed at the Republicans on May 22, 1857: "the prospective crown, (?) after having been at least thrice gently laid aside, was at length firmly planted upon the *hard,* gigantic thinking apparatus of Hon. A. S. Abernethy . . . who meekly yielded up himself a subject to be placed upon the sacrificial altar."

On local issues the new Republican party in Washington Territory differed little from the Democratic group, since they both wanted the same things—a railroad, settlement of the Hudson's Bay Company claims so that it could no longer operate in the territory, unquestioned possession of the San Juan Islands, and the power to elect their own territorial officials. Even though many of the successful Whig candidates had been elected to the legislature in 1856 on their opposition to Stevens, the Republican party did not make an open criticism of him in their 1857 platform. They were afraid that if they denounced his declaration of martial law as part of his conduct of the Indian battles, Congress would refuse to accept the debt which Stevens was incurring in prosecuting the war. It was mentioned earlier that Stevens had to raise money to pay the volunteers who fought in the Indian wars because General Wool refused to muster them into units of the federal troops.

Stevens was easily elected in 1857 as the territorial delegate, defeating Abernethy by 987 to 542 votes. Clallam, Cowlitz, King, and Pierce counties gave Abernethy a majority, but the margin was only a few votes, except in Pierce County where the residents had been most infuriated at the declaration of martial law. Three Democrats and one Republican were elected to the Council, the upper house of the Washington territorial legislature, and twenty Democrats and five Republicans were elected to the lower house, the House of Representatives.

In 1859, Stevens was again elected as the Washington territorial delegate to Congress, and the Democrats had a majority, as before, in both houses of the territorial legislature. During his second term as delegate, Stevens succeeded in getting Congress to appropriate money for the Indian war debt, and the Democratic party in the territory was hopeful that he could be elected for a third term. Even when Abraham Lincoln was elected President in 1860 on the Republican ticket, Stevens' supporters in Washington Territory assured him that the change in the national political picture would not seriously affect his popularity in the territory. However, when South Carolina seceded from the Union in December of 1860, a large percentage of the Democrats in Washington Territory were horrified at the prospect of a breakup of the United States government. They turned to the Republican party since it was the one advocating the preservation of the union at all costs. Stevens came west in the spring of 1861 to campaign for re-election, but, when the territorial Democratic Convention met, he withdrew his name as a candidate and returned to the East where he joined the northern army in the Civil War and was killed at the Battle of Chantilly in 1862.

After the Civil War, the Republican party remained the dominant one for many years nationally and also in the Pacific Northwest, although a number of territorial and local contests were won by Democrats and many were very heated. The charges made by candidates against their opponents in those days would be considered violent personal abuse at the present time. In 1873 a financial collapse in the East was so severe that it was labeled a "panic," and the ensuing depression caused much bitterness to be directed against both major political parties, particularly the Republican because its representatives were the dominant figures.

Construction of the Northern Pacific Railroad, which was under way at the time, was halted at present Bismarck, North Dakota, as a result of the financial depression, and the residents of the Pacific Northwest were distressed by the news that the railroad might not reach them for many years, Before long, business in Washington Territory suffered, too, when eastern orders for lumber, wheat and other commodities fell off sharply as a result of the depression.

Even after prosperity returned and work on the railroad was resumed in the early 1880's, the farmers and laborers in most parts of the country saw prices rising faster than their income, and, in the West, people were conscious that fortunes were being made by eastern capitalists from western lands in the very areas where the westerners were having difficulty making a living. The farmers began to meet to discuss their grievances in communities all over the country and to organize local groups which eventually merged into the National Grange and other influential farmers' organizations.

In Washington Territory people began to feel strongly that much of their trouble came from the fact that Congress had given huge grants of public land to the railroads (in our case the Northern Pacific, which received forty-seven million acres altogether). The purpose of the land grants had been to supply the railroad companies with capital for building railroads which were needed to extend settlement as well as to link the country in a transportation network. The arrangement was that the railroad company might have a certain amount of land on either side of tracks that it actually completed. In many instances in the East, however, the companies would claim the land on a proposed route, but not complete the railroad. Lawsuits would then be necessary either to reclaim the land or to force the company to finish the road.

This situation threatened to be true for the Cascade division of the Northern Pacific, which was to have been completed in 1884. When the company did not fulfill its agreement in this respect, both political parties demanded that Congress force the railroad to return the lands given to it along the proposed route. The Democratic candidate for territorial delegate to Congress who won the 1884 election agitated so forcefully for forfeiture of the land grant that the railroad company was fearful of losing it and hurried to complete the line.

The railroad companies naturally chose the best land for their grants whenever possible. In some eastern areas, there had been scandals in which congressmen and state legislators came under the control of railroad officials and framed laws giving the railroads extremely valuable timber lands. People in Washington Territory were afraid that such things would happen here. After 1883 when a line was usable across the territory via Pasco, the farmers made the definite complaint that they were forced to pay what seemed to them exorbitant freight charges for shipping their produce across land which might well belong to them if it had not been given to the railroad, and which was bringing income to the railroad company.

Because a great many of the immigrants to the Far West traveled on trains as soon as they were available, the railroad companies wanted to increase the flow of settlers. They were not only potential passengers, but also prospective purchasers of goods to be shipped from the East, perhaps by rail. The railroad companies might also be able to sell their western lands to the incoming settlers. For these reasons, the railroads advertised widely in the East and Middle West concerning the advantages of moving west to take up a homestead on the "free" land offered to settlers by the federal government, and immigrants to Washington Territory jumped from 66,979 in 1880 to 239,544 in 1889. Thousands of these settlers came by the Union Pacific, Northern Pacific, or Canadian Pacific railroads.

A few of the immigrants were prosperous and came expressly to use their capital in a frontier region where there were countless opportunities for investment. Some were single men who had no money and worked their way to the coast by doing logging or seasonal farm labor along the route. The greatest percentage, however, were families who were having difficulty making a good living in the East or Middle West and hoped to better themselves on the Pacific coast. Very few were desperately poor. That group could not finance the trip west. Many, however, had little more money than was required for the trip. If, when they arrived in the territory, they found that most of the good land was gone and were told that large sections of valuable timberland were held by eastern capitalists, they naturally resented it.

Many of them were already familiar with the dissatisfaction expressed by farmers and laborers over similar situations in eastern areas where they had lived. They were easily in a position, therefore, to encourage like protests here. In Seattle in the 1880's, an organization called the Knights of Labor was gaining strength, and in 1886 that group plus other residents in the city who were disgruntled over their condition held a mass meeting at which they declared that the existing mayor and city council represented a group overly conservative and too much concerned with protecting the interest of the "old" families—those who had come first to Seattle.

The dissatisfied group adopted the name "People's party" and nominated W. H. Shoudy for mayor. The conservative voters then held a mass meeting and chose the name Loyal League for their party, giving A. A. Denny, one of the early pioneers, the nomination for mayor. The *Post-Intelligencer* supported the Loyal League and the Seattle *Press* upheld the People's party. In the city election, to the dismay of the conservative element, the slate of the People's party won by forty-one votes.

In some instances during this period, violence occurred when groups were unable to persuade governmental agencies, including the territorial legislature, to follow their wishes. One such occasion was the anti-Chinese riots of 1885-86. As we shall see in chapter 9, many Chinese laborers had been brought into the Pacific Northwest to work in the gold mines in the 1860's and 1870's. Then when the mining boom ended, the Chinese turned to hop picking, coal mining, fish canning, laundry work, and other menial tasks which many white people refused to take in prosperous times.

In the mid-eighties when the Canadian and Northern Pacific

Chinese coolies working on railway switchback near the summit of the Cascades in 1886. (Courtesy of the University of Washington Library)

railroads were completed, enough men were thrown out of work to make a serious unemployment problem. Therefore, white laborers wanted even the disagreeable jobs; the three thousand Chinese who had the jobs were easily identified, and they seemed to represent a threat of cheap foreign labor.

Some Chinese coal miners in Wyoming were killed by a mob in September, 1885. The agitators in Washington were encouraged by this action, and in the Squak Valley five white men and two Indians fired into the tents where Chinese hop pickers were sleeping. Three were killed and three wounded. Four days later, Chinese coal miners at Coal Creek near Seattle were beaten and their barracks burned down.

By September 28, feeling was so high in Seattle that the labor organizations and agitators were able to call an Anti-Chinese Congress of which one author later said, "Every socialist and anarchist who could walk or steal a ride to Seattle was a self-elected but none the less welcome delegate."[1] R. Jacob Weisbach, mayor of Tacoma, was chosen president of the congress, which drew up a resolution calling for the expulsion of all Chinese residents by November 15. Committees were appointed to drive them out of both Seattle and Tacoma.

Although the labor organizations took the lead in demanding action against the Chinese, many businessmen and professional people also favored their expulsion. The question was largely whether it was to be done legally or by force, and later there were accusations on all sides as to who had urged violence. Both the governor of Washington Territory and the President of the United States asked if troops were necessary to protect the lives and property of the Chinese, but the Sheriff of Pierce County replied that he had deputized a sufficient number of men to maintain order. It later developed that the Sheriff and the deputies were in sympathy with the anti-Chinese element. On November 3, a mob ousted the Chinese from Tacoma. Loading the belongings of the Chinese on wagons, the crowd drove them outside the city and dumped the contents there. The next day their vacated homes were burned by the mob.

In Seattle, the same kind of agitation was going on, but the sheriff there was not in sympathy with the mob, and a number of civic leaders organized what they called the Citizens' party to see that the Chinese were not molested and that their property would be protected when they left the city, as they were willing to do. Governor Watson C. Squire issued a proclamation calling for support of law and order and telegraphed to Washington, D.C., for aid from federal troops. The President ordered them sent to Seattle from Vancouver, Washington, and 350 soldiers reached Seattle on November 8. These were joined by a local home guard, and the presence of the troops was enough to discourage the anti-Chinese committees from taking action. Employers dismissed Chinese who worked for them, and many Chinese left of their own accord. The crisis seemed to be over, and the federal troops were withdrawn.

In December, 1885, people who wanted to get rid of the remain-

[1] Clarence B. Bagley, *History of Seattle from the Earliest Settlement to the Present Time* (Chicago: S. J. Clarke Publishing Company, 1916), II, 458.

ing Chinese peacefully persuaded a representative in the territorial legislature to introduce bills to forbid aliens ineligible for citizenship (as the Chinese were at that time) to hold land; to allow cities to license laundries and refuse licenses to such aliens; and to forbid cities and private industries to hire them. A memorial was also introduced, asking Congress to enact any necessary federal laws to support the territorial legislation. The bills passed the House, but only the first was accepted by the Council, largely because of the opposition of Orange Jacobs, who argued that such laws were probably unconstitutional and that, since the United States was declared to be a free country, it should act like one and welcome anyone wanting to come.

When the legislature failed to pass the bills which would have made it impossible for the Chinese to earn a living, the anti-Chinese committees took the opportunity in early February, 1886, to force the Chinese from their homes and try to put them on a ship ready to sail for San Francisco, but there were one hundred too many for the size of the ship. The home guard was summoned to protect this group, and, after members of the guard were able to get the Chinese in their custody, they formed a circle around them and ordered the mob to let them through. Instead, certain members of the crowd charged the soldiers, who fired, injuring several rioters, one fatally. The home guard then marched the Chinese safely back to their homes and guarded them. In the meantime Governor Squire proclaimed martial law, with federal approval, telegraphed the President again for aid, and ten companies of United States troops were sent to Seattle where they stayed for several months until the agitation died out.

STATEHOOD

Populist Movement

The various dissatisfied groups who tried to take political action to secure relief from what they regarded as oppression by big corporations, foreign cheap labor, or other agencies began to realize that similar groups were making themselves heard all over the country. In all of them a feeling of common opposition to the Republican and Democratic parties made the formation of a third national political organization seem a logical move, and it emerged in 1892 as the People's party, whose members were called Populists.

In their platform, they called for government ownership of railroads and telephone and telegraph systems, with a civil service system to see to it that the additional employees in these areas were not political appointees. They favored national labor organizations, the donation of public land to actual settlers only, and a graduated income tax. They also supported the policy of free silver, which meant that the Populists wanted the federal government to buy as much silver ore as was mined in the country and make silver dollars out of it to be put back into circulation. This money was to be accepted on a par with gold coins, to redeem notes issued by the United States Treasury Department. At that time, the federal government was buying a limited amount of silver which the Populists felt was insufficient. People in the West were particularly interested in a greater use of silver because of the many silver mines which had opened west of the Rockies. Besides the many people who worked in the mines or sold produce to the miners, there were some who owned shares in the mining companies and profited in that way. Moreover, in the West there were a great many people not connected in any way with the silver mines who owed money to banks or other creditors, and, if the federal government bought silver in great quantities, much of the money paid for it would be put into circulation in their region. Easier money would mean more jobs, better wages, and a greater chance for the ordinary person to make money with which to pay off his debts—an inflationary trend.

Even in 1889 when our state constitution was written, many of these ideas were popular, although no active political party in the Pacific Northwest had adopted them. The candidates for election as constitutional delegates campaigned for or against some or all of the proposals later associated with the People's party, and a sufficient number of persons with Populist beliefs were elected to have an effect on the tone of the state constitution. A number of Populist clauses were included in it, such as the one to prohibit any state official from accepting a pass on the railroad; exemption of a certain amount of property from seizure for debts; and permission for the legislature to create a Railroad Commission to regulate rates and services of common carriers. The constitutional convention was predominantly Republican, however, and the first governor of the state, Elisha P. Ferry, the other state executive officials, and a majority of both houses of the 1889-90 legislature were Republicans.

As soon as the Populist party was officially organized in 1892 it became influential in the new state of Washington. In 1893, for example, eight Populists were elected to the state House of Representatives and in 1895 twenty Populist representatives and three senators were elected. The marked increase in that year was largely due to the results of the panic of 1893 throughout the country, another serious depression in which fourteen out of twenty-one banks in Tacoma closed. Other areas of the state were similarly affected.

In fact, the depression of 1893 was so severe all over the United States that thousands of people, regardless of their political beliefs, tried to get governmental aid. In 1894, the famous Coxey Army marched on Washington, D.C., to demand relief for the unemployed. It was led by Jacob S. Coxey of Ohio who proposed that Congress issue large amounts of paper money with which to pay for large public works. In our state, "General" Jumbo Cantwell demanded free railroad transportation to the East to join Coxey's Army, and he gathered together between two thousand and thirty-five hundred unemployed men and moved as many as possible into a Puyallup hotel which was in the process of construction. Each morning, certain of the men went to designated areas in the city and ordered the housewives to prepare dinner. They complied for fear of reprisals if they refused. When Governor John H. McGraw threatened to call for aid from federal troops stationed on the coast, most of the hotel's inhabitants scattered, but Cantwell, his wife, and a number of others rode freight cars to Chicago and joined Coxey's Army on its march to the capital.

In the 1896 state campaign, George Turner, a former Territorial Supreme Court justice from Spokane, became an effective advocate of free silver even though he did not accept many other planks of the Populist platform. The residents of the present Inland Empire were, of course, eager to sell as much as possible of the area's silver; thus Spokane became the center of the free silver forces. Turner, a Republican, was able to unite the silver Republicans with the silver Democrats and persuade them to support the Populist party because of its stand for free silver. The candidate for governor on this fusion ticket was John R. Rogers, a Populist, who was elected easily along with a majority of Populists in both houses of the legislature.

Rogers was a strong, well-liked governor whose administration increased the strength of Populist principles here. In 1895 as a member of the state House of Representatives, he had sponsored the Barefoot Schoolboy Law, as it came to be called, which provided that a certain minimum allowance for the education of each child in the state should be made available by the legislature. In effect, this was the beginning of the principle of *equalization* in education between counties, the procedure by which wealthier counties contribute more to state educational funds than poorer counties, the difference being used to increase the amount of money available in the latter. This concept is accepted now in many areas of government, but at that time it was startling to many people because until then a county that could afford money for schools and most other services provided them; a county that could not afford them did without.

When Rogers ran for governor in 1896, he campaigned for free schoolbooks and for other Populist tenets, such as reduction of railroad, telephone, electricity, and other public utility rates, lower salaries for public officials, women's suffrage, large exemptions for personal and real property taxation, prohibition of railway passes for state officials, and procedures to reduce foreclosures for debt.

In the presidential election of 1896, William Jennings Bryan, aided by his famous "Cross of Gold" speech pleading for free silver at the Democratic Convention, gained the Democratic nomination for President. The Populist party then decided to support him for President instead of nominating a presidential candidate. When Bryan was defeated by the Republican candidate, William McKinley, in the general election, the People's party disintegrated as a national organization.

In 1897 the first cargo of gold dust and nuggets reached Seattle from Alaska, and the resulting stampede brought such prosperity to the Pacific Northwest that there were more jobs than there were people needing work. Therefore, many of the people who had formerly been poor and who had supported the Populist party because of its appeal to the underprivileged lost interest in it. In the

1898 election, the voters in the Pacific Northwest followed the national trend toward a more conservative government. In this state, the remaining Populists combined with the Democrats and managed to retain control of the state Senate. The Republicans carried the House of Representatives easily. In 1900 the Populists again joined the Silver Republicans and Democrats under the name of the Democratic party with Rogers as its candidate for a second term as governor. He was so popular that he won the election even though all of the other state offices and a majority in both houses of the legislature went to the Republicans.

Even though the Populists did not again nominate officials on a separate ticket, they continued to work through the Washington State Grange and labor organizations to counteract what they regarded as the attachment of both the Republican and Democratic parties to financiers who were trying to exploit the resources of the Pacific Northwest for the benefit of railroads and other big corporations. It seemed to the former Populists that additional control by the voters over public officials and legislation was the best answer and they were able to make significant progress in this direction by reforms, such as a direct primary system for the nomination of state and local officials and an advisory primary vote for United States senators in 1907; women's suffrage in 1910; the adoption of the initiative, referendum, and recall in 1912. In a *direct primary* election, the voters choose nominees to run for public office on behalf of political parties instead of having party leaders select candidates at political party conventions. The *initiative* is a system whereby the voters themselves can pass laws by a petition and election; the *referendum* is a similar procedure whereby the voters repeal or accept a law passed by a legislature; and the *recall* is a device by which the voters remove an elected official during his term of office.

Until the 1914 election, United States senators were chosen by the legislatures of the various states, but in the state of Washington, the agitation for greater power by the voters to select public officials extended to the office of United States senator. Therefore, the state legislature included in the primary law of 1907 a provision that persons wishing to run for the office of national senator could declare themselves candidates. At the primary election when the people voted to nominate one person from each political party for a

Ladies of the Washington Equal Suffrage Association, 1910. Although women were allowed to vote in Washington by a state constitutional amendment approved in 1910, national women's suffrage was not passed until 1920. (Original photo belongs to the Washington State Historical Society; courtesy of the University of Washington Library)

particular local or state office, they also voted for a candidate for the office of United States senator.

The candidates for representative or senator in our state legislature could, if they wished, make a statement that when it came time for the legislature to choose a United States senator from our state they would vote for the candidate in their party who received the largest vote in the primary election. The legislature did confirm, by a big majority, the voters' choice. Therefore, beginning with the 1908 election, the state of Washington, in effect, had a type of direct election of United States senators. The only choice of the legislature was between the political parties. If there were more Democrats than Republicans elected to the legislature, that group would, of course, choose for United States senator the Democratic candidate receiving the largest number of votes in the primary election.

If more Republicans than Democrats were elected to the state legislature, the reverse would be true. Beginning with the 1914 election, voters throughout the country were allowed to elect United States senators directly because of the Seventeenth Amendment to the United States Constitution, ratified in 1913.

In 1907 and 1909 bills for initiative, referendum and recall did not receive the necessary vote in the state legislature to bring them before the voters as proposed constitutional amendments. The State Grange and State Federation of Labor campaigned vigorously for their passage however, and by 1911 the legislators were convinced that they were desirable procedures and referred the question to the voters who approved their adoption as constitutional amendments. These measures represent a greater direct control over state and local government by the people themselves, which was one of the remedies proposed by the Populists for tyrannical or corrupt government.

Even before the general recall amendment was ratified in 1912, first-class cities had the privilege of choosing their own type of municipal government (the system of *home rule*), and Seattle and Tacoma both had the power of recall. In 1911 the Seattle voters used the device to recall their mayor. Hiram Gill, who had run for office the previous year on a slate of making Seattle a "wide-open" town, prepared to condone various types of activities ordinarily forbidden by law. At that time, however, the First Presbyterian Church of Seattle had a very forceful minister, the Reverend Mark A. Matthews, who was shocked at the obvious support which vice operators had from members of the city government. He decided that Gill was largely responsible for the situation and gathered sufficient evidence against him to provide the basis for the recall petition and the election at which Gill was ousted and a reform mayor, George W. Dilling, elected. Women voted for the first time since territorial days, and they were credited by many people with defeating Gill. He evidently was convinced that, with public opinion demanding the suppression of gambling and prostitution, he should campaign for re-election on that platform and did so. Ironically enough, although he did not succeed in becoming mayor in 1912, he was elected in 1914 again, and, whether or not he had actually had a change of heart, he did not encourage vice as he had done in 1910.

Eastern papers made many sarcastic remarks about the caliber of the Seattle voters in first ousting its mayor and then re-electing him. For example, the Indianapolis *News* said, "The next thing in the regular order of business, presumably, is his recall." Direct government of the people in the initiative, referendum, and recall was regarded as extremely radical in the East, and a number of editors saw in the re-election of Gill proof that the voters could not act sensibly as legislators or judges. The Newark *News* said,

> If Gill deserved to be "recalled" four years ago, it would seem that he should not have been reelected to the same office. If he did not deserve "recall," he was the victim of a monstrous injustice inspired by popular clamor. On the face of things, neither alternative argues in favor of the "recall" as an effective weapon in the hands of the public to compel honesty and decency in office.

In 1911, Tacoma also recalled its mayor, A. V. Fawcett, on charges that his administration was lax in its handling of the city's services to the residents. When the criticism became heated Fawcett persuaded the city council to pass an "antitreating" ordinance which forbade anybody to buy a drink for another person in any establishment where liquor was sold. His opponents insisted that this was an attempt on Fawcett's part to divert attention from the charges brought against him. At any rate, newspapers in other parts of the country seized on this ordinance as a matter for ridicule, and the recall election was successful, in some people's opinion, partly because of the joking done at Tacoma's expense.

Progressive Movement

Between 1908 and 1912 many persons interested in political reform were content to remain in the Republican or Democratic parties since Theodore Roosevelt dominated the former party and the Bryan element was strong in the latter. We have seen that Bryan was regarded as a radical by the conservative Democrats, and conservative Republicans were uneasy about Theodore Roosevelt's political and economic ideas after he became President of the United States in 1901 on the death of William McKinley.

For one thing, Roosevelt requested the Attorney-General to prosecute big corporations under the Sherman Anti-Trust Act if they appeared to have a monopoly in a particular field. In 1902 he

Yakima Avenue, Yakima, in 1908. (Original photo belongs to the Washington State Historical Society; courtesy of the University of Washington Library)

threatened to seize the anthracite coal mines of Pennsylvania and have them operated by the United States Army if the operators did not make a settlement with the miners, who were on strike. He also spoke out in favor of federal reclamation projects, federal regulation of corporations dealing in interstate commerce, and a lower tariff.

Roosevelt was nominated as the Republican candidate for the presidency in 1904 and was elected. In 1908, he was willing for William Howard Taft to be his successor since Roosevelt was convinced that Taft supported his liberal views, particularly in regard to favoring a low tariff. Taft was nominated by the Republican party as its presidential candidate and elected, and he then began to appear conservative. He signed into law the Payne-Aldrich Tariff Bill, which raised instead of lowered tariffs. Liberal Republicans and Democrats thought, too, that Taft was antagonistic to their plans for conservation of natural resources, as we shall see in a later section.

During this period (1908-10), one of the United States senators from our state, Wesley L. Jones of Yakima, became a prominent supporter of Taft, and one of the United States representatives from Washington, Miles Poindexter of Spokane, emerged as one of his most vigorous opponents. In the first primary election in which our voters could indicate their choice of persons running for the office of United States senator (1908), Jones had the largest number of votes among the Republican candidates. Since the 1909 legislature had a Republican majority, it confirmed him in that office. In that same primary election, Poindexter was nominated as a Republican candidate for the United States House of Representatives and won in the general election in November of that year.

In the House, Poindexter soon became known as an insurgent, one who did not follow the party line. For example, he voted against the high tariff bill supported by President Taft. He joined a group of Republicans who were trying to curb the powers of the Speaker of the House of Representatives, Joseph Cannon, a strong conservative, who had become extremely dictatorial. Poindexter also supported a move to strengthen the Interstate Commerce Commission in setting maximum rates to be charged by railroads, something the conservative Republicans opposed vigorously.

Poindexter's voting record in these respects appealed to large groups in Washington; consequently, in 1910 he ran for the United States Senate, and he won the Republican nomination in the state primary election. Wesley Jones, whose senatorial term did not end until 1914, campaigned for another Republican candidate from this state, but Jones's antagonism did not prevent Poindexter from winning the subsequent election.

By 1912, Theodore Roosevelt's opposition to Taft had become so strong that he returned to active politics and sought the nomination for President of the United States at the Republican National Convention. When Roosevelt failed to get the nomination, his group withdrew from the Republican party and formed a third party, the Progressive or Bull Moose party, with Roosevelt as presidential nominee. Poindexter then joined the Progressive party, and, since his senatorial term did not end until 1916, he did not have to campaign for re-election, but gave his time to supporting Roosevelt. Jones campaigned for Taft, again the Republican nominee for President.

In the state of Washington, many former Populists joined the newly established Progressive party state organization. The 1912 election returns indicated that many others turned to the Socialist party in voting for state offices. Ernest Lister of Tacoma, the Democratic nominee, won the governorship. The Democrats also won eight out of the forty-two seats in the state Senate and nineteen seats out of sixty in the House election. Progressive party candidates won the two seats of congressmen at large, six places in the state Senate, and twenty-nine seats in the state House of Representatives. The Socialist party secured one state representative and one senator; and the remaining successful candidates in the congressional and state offices were Republicans. Theodore Roosevelt won a substantial victory in the popular vote in Washington (113,000 votes), and Eugene V. Debs, the Socialist candidate for President, won almost 40,000 votes. Taft, the Republican candidate, polled 70,000 votes, and Woodrow Wilson, the Democratic candidate, victorious in the national election, 86,000.

In 1914, Jones was re-elected senator by a large majority. By 1916 when Poindexter was running for re-election to the Senate, the Progressive party was no longer an effective national party. He returned to the Republican party, although continuing to support the progressive principles that he had endorsed both before and during his adherence to the Progressive party. Poindexter was elected by the biggest majority of any senatorial candidate in the state up to that time—202,287 to 135,339 votes for George Turner, his Democratic opponent.

In the 1916 election, even though Woodrow Wilson carried the state in the presidential election and Lister again won the governorship on the Democratic ticket, nearly all of the other state and national offices went to Republican candidates. C. C. Dill from Spokane, running for a second term, was the only Democrat to win a place in the United States House of Representatives from the state of Washington. A few months later (January, 1917), when Germany in a determined effort to defeat England in World War I announced that her submarines would attack merchant vessels, President Wilson asked Congress to approve the arming of American ships. Wesley Jones was one of the senators who prevented the passage of such a provision by a filibuster. Later that year, after United States ships had been sunk by German submarines, C. C.

Dill was among the small group in the House of Representatives who vóted against our declaring war on Germany in April, 1917.

In the election of 1918, Dill won an easy nomination to run for a third term in the United States House of Representatives on the Democratic ticket in his congressional district. Therefore, it would appear that his opposition to our entering the war was not objectionable enough to be a major issue. In the general election, however, he lost to his opponent in the Republican landslide of that year.

In the 1922 election, Dill ran for Congress as the Democratic senatorial candidate. To the surprise of many people, he defeated Miles Poindexter, running for re-election on the Republican ticket, in the November general election. By that date, Poindexter was regarded as a conservative Republican.

Except for Dill, all of the other Congressmen elected from our state were Republicans. Dill's victory was considered all the more amazing since the Farmer-Labor, the Socialist Labor, and the Workers' party[2] candidates polled comparatively heavy votes which would otherwise undoubtedly have gone to Dill rather than to Poindexter. The explanation generally accepted was that the farmers wanted help so badly that they voted for the major protest party, the Democratic party, rather than one of the smaller groups more specifically aimed at the agricultural population. Moreover, farmers had opposed our entrance into World War I, and by 1922 many other people were doubting that the United States had been right in participating. Dill's stand against our entering the war probably counted in his favor. Dill was again the only Democrat elected to Congress from Washington in 1928.

Conservative Reaction

During the remainder of the 1920's, the Republicans were overwhelmingly successful in both state and national contests. On the

[2] The Socialist Labor party is an old national organization, having been formed in 1877. The Socialist party split off from it in 1901. In the summer of 1920 the Farmer-Labor party was organized by former members of the Progressive party and others who wished to unite farm and labor opposition to the two major political parties. It became popular so quickly in the state of Washington that, by the November election, candidates for state as well as national offices were on the ballot for that party. In 1921 the United Communist party changed its name to the Workers' party.

state level in 1924, Roland H. Hartley, who had tried several times previously without success to win the nomination for governor on the Republican ticket, was nominated and elected to the governorship. He believed that during and after World War I, government regulations and agencies had multiplied without justification. He advocated reducing the number of state governmental agencies and services both to reduce taxes and to remove what he regarded as harmful governmental regulations on business. In this connection he persuaded the legislature not to ratify the Twentieth Amendment to the United States Constitution, which was designed to regulate hours and conditions of the employment of minors (Child Labor Amendment), since it represented another attempt—this time on the part of the federal government—to control business practices. He disapproved of increasing the state's contribution to public education in Washington and was considered extremely conservative or reactionary, depending on one's point of view, in almost every area. He was re-elected in 1928.

The New Deal

When the stock market crash occurred in 1929, the economy of the region was hit not only by the collapse of small businesses, but also of eastern holding companies that had subsidiary companies in the state. Seattle soon had over thirty thousand unemployed. Lumber and mining towns—such as North Bend, Cle Elum, Hoquiam, and Aberdeen—were in the worst condition. Sometimes almost every member of a small town would be completely without income.

In this situation, it was to be expected that the political party which could offer the people governmental aid in a convincing manner would win the election. The Democratic party, led by Franklin D. Roosevelt in 1932, succeeded in doing so to a remarkable degree. For the Pacific Northwest, Roosevelt advocated governmental ownership and operation of public utilities, including the sale of electricity. For the nation as a whole, he recommended that the federal and state governments hire as many of the unemployed as possible to construct huge public works and to perform "white collar" tasks in the public interest until private business revived.

In the election of 1932 our state was typical of the Democratic landslide. All of the Democratic nominees to Congress were elected, including Homer T. Bone who joined C. C. Dill as United States senator. All of the state executive offices went to Democrats with the exception of the office of State Superintendent of Public Instruction, which was at that time a partisan office, and the Republican incumbent, Noah Showalter, had no Democratic opponent in the election. The governorship went to Clarence D. Martin who had campaigned for the establishment of old-age insurance aid to farmers, public works, and other items of social legislation later embodied in the term "New Deal." After two terms as governor, he was defeated in 1940 by the Seattle mayor, Arthur B. Langlie, a Republican, who served as governor for three terms, although not consecutively.

In the election of 1934, C. C. Dill declined to run again for the office of United States senator and was succeeded by Lewis B. Schwellenbach, considered a conservative Democrat whom President Roosevelt later appointed judge of the United States District Court in 1939. In the primary election in 1940, Mon C. Wallgren, formerly a congressional representative, won the Democratic nomination for senator and defeated his Republican opponent in the general election. Henry M. Jackson and Warren G. Magnuson were elected to the United States House of Representatives on the Democratic ticket.

During the 1930's, there were groups of a semipolitical nature that advocated various depression remedies, some of which were considered sensible and some ridiculous. Since Washington had the tradition of being receptive to new ideas, it was accused at the time by other parts of the country of sponsoring more than its share of harebrained schemes. However, certain elements in most of them were later incorporated into the platforms of the major political parties.

The first of the depression organizations in our state was the Unemployed Citizens' League, which was formed as a political mouthpiece to inform the public of the plight of its members and as a means to ferret out available jobs for its members. Members of the League mended shoes and clothing, picked fruit and vegetables for distribution among the members, cut wood, and aided each other in similar ways.

Another idea that had enthusiastic support in Washington during the depression was the Townsend plan. Francis E. Townsend, a California doctor, conceived the idea that if a 2-per-cent tax were placed on all money transactions (a kind of sales tax), the proceeds would be sufficient to provide a pension of $200 per month for every person in the country sixty years of age or older. Each recipient would then be required to spend all of that money within thirty days to keep it in circulation and so provide the continuing taxation necessary to maintain the revolving fund. The idea swept the entire country, and the pressure exerted by the Townsend clubs on our political parties hastened the passing of federal and state laws providing the types of old age pensions in existence today. The Old Age Pension Union was formed in this state to work actively for state and federal pensions.

Technocracy was another proposal of great interest in the state. It was based on a study made by reputable scientists of the changes occurring in the methods of producing all kinds of commodities. They found that increased mechanization was making fewer and fewer man-hours necessary in all fields of industry from agriculture through manufacturing. From this study certain economists concluded that, with machines rapidly displacing human labor, unemployment would become so great that our social structure would collapse. In view of this change from man to machine power, they believed that our present system of measuring production by prices and money had lost its meaning. The future basis for setting prices of merchandise or services then should be in terms of the units of energy expended to produce the commodity or service.

In contrast to plans like these, which were considered more or less left-wing politically, there was some support for reactionary groups of a Fascist nature, such as William Dudley Pelley's Silver Shirts. Their following was never large, however, and none of the left-wing groups developed sufficient momentum to become an actual third political party.

In the Pacific Northwest, a third-party movement may have been sidetracked by Franklin D. Roosevelt's speech in Portland, Oregon, during his first campaign for the presidency in 1932. He stressed the importance of hydroelectric power production as a coming development that would provide employment during the construction of the necessary dams and power plants and would encourage industrial and agricultural development as a means of overcoming the depression. This hope drew many votes, which would otherwise have gone to a third party, to the Democratic party and helped increase the large Democratic majority in the state of Washington. Under Roosevelt's leadership, our biggest dams, including Bonneville and Grand Coulee, were undertaken, as we have seen, partly from Public Works Administration (PWA) funds to provide employment in this region.

Before these work projects and other aids could get under way, the unemployment problem became worse, and many families literally did not have enough to eat. The Communist party took advantage of this distress and urged people to join the party; many did, but they were to be disillusioned later about its promises. The Communist party also managed to get control of the Unemployed Citizens League at its convention in February, 1933. On March 1, 1933, when banks were closing all over the country and panic was rising, a group from the League marched on Olympia, but vigilantes, organized the week before, broke up the demonstration.

Before grievances built up to more violent action, direct financial aid through the new social security system was instituted by Congress and state legislatures, and employment on PWA, WPA (Works Projects Administration, which handled white-collar work programs), CCC (Civilian Conservation Corps, which employed young men in roadside beautification and national forest jobs), and other government projects eased the plight of the unemployed until there was no further need for the Unemployed Citizens League. It also suffered from lack of capital on which to base its cooperative undertakings and from opposition of private businessmen in the fields entered by the League.

In 1935 the Washington Commonwealth Federation was formed by a number of labor unions (both AFL and CIO), the Old Age Pension Union, and many individuals from other depression organizations. Although the leaders of this group tried to exclude Communist party participation and endorse Democratic candidates instead of nominating its own, individual Communists did attempt to dominate the organization. This group, too, gradually dwindled as prosperity returned and as the Communist affiliations of some of its leaders were brought to light in legislative investigations.

Olympia, the state capital, as it appears today. (Photo by Washington State Department of Commerce and Economic Development)

Recent Political Affiliations

During World War II, the Democratic party continued to win the majority of our state offices, but at its close Republican victories increased. For example, in 1944 Magnuson ran for the office of United States senator and won the election, as he did again in 1950. In the by-election of 1946, the congressional seats were won by Republicans with the exception of Henry Jackson, who retained his place in the House of Representatives.

In the state, Senator Wallgren defeated Langlie for the governorship in 1944; in 1948, Langlie defeated Wallgren for the governorship, but all of the other state executive posts were won by Democrats. In 1952 Langlie was re-elected governor and became the first person to be elected governor for a third term in this state. In 1956 Langlie ran for the senatorship and was defeated by Magnuson. The governorship was won by Albert Rosellini, a Democrat.

During the 1950's, the earlier inconsistency of the Washington

voters continued. State executive officials were usually divided between parties, and both houses of the state legislature seldom had a
majority from one party. The 1959 and 1961 legislatures were examples, however, of the exception, both houses being heavily Democratic. In 1963 there was still a Democratic majority but it was
smaller. Moreover, conservative Democrats united with the Republican minority in the House of Representatives to form an "opposition" block.

EFFECT OF PROTEST GROUPS IN SPECIFIC FIELDS

In certain phases of the state's development, the effect of
influential protest groups in the form of either third parties (such as
the Populists and Progressives) or less well-organized bodies of voters dissatisfied with one or both of the major parties, can best be
seen by tracing the history of specific movements. Two of the most
clearly defined areas are conservation of natural resources and
labor organizations.

Political Struggle over Conservation of Natural Resources

The effects of the campaign of the Populists, and later the Progressives, to achieve governmental control of our national resources
were felt in the struggle to establish national forests and other restricted areas where plant and animal life would be protected from
any human encroachment or, at least, used under strict regulations.
The purpose was to keep the forests and the wild life from being
depleted to the point where a continuing stand of timber and a supply of game animals could not be maintained. In our region, the
critical resource was timber. Forests in the Middle West and East
were already beginning to disappear; consequently, lumber companies in those areas bought much of the timberland in the Pacific
Northwest, largely from the railroads that had timberland in the
grants made by the federal government. This fact added to the local
resentment against the railroads since more of our resources were to
be used for the benefit of people outside our region. Also, it meant
that this land was acquired by corporations instead of individual
settlers.

Gifford Pinchot, a wealthy easterner, became alarmed by the fact

that toward the end of the last century most people considered that
our forests would last forever, even without care. They did not expect lumber companies to use any conservation practices. In fact,
the idea that an individual or business firm had any responsibility to
try to provide resources for future generations was virtually unknown. The lumber companies ordinarily cut all of the trees within
a given area and left the slashings, which prevented seedlings from
taking root. In 1891 Pinchot and certain other conservation pioneers who regarded this type of lumbering as harmful to society
persuaded Congress to pass a law allowing the President to create
forest reserves from federal land.

In 1896, during Bryan's election campaign, Pinchot accompanied a National Forest Commission to the Pacific Northwest to
make a survey of the public lands. As the commission reached the
Pacific Northwest, the Populists supported it vehemently. The
Spokesman-Review, normally a Republican paper, supported Bryan
because of his stand for free silver and for use of natural resources
by individuals rather than corporations. After the election when it
was known that McKinley had won the presidency but that Populists had been successful in the state of Washington, the *Spokesman-
Review* attributed their victories to a protest of the voters against
"the shameful and wholesale control of legislation, corporate
influences, and the frittering away of the public domain" under previous administrations, both Republican and Democratic.

When the National Forest Commission returned to Washington,
D.C., with its report, President Grover Cleveland established thirteen forest reserves totaling twenty-one million acres before he went
out of office in March, 1897. Lumber financiers fought this move to
keep timberland out of private hands, and in 1907 they were able
to persuade Congress to pass a law prohibiting the President from
creating any more forest reserves from federal land. Hereafter, they
were to be established only by Congress. Theodore Roosevelt, the
President at that time, was tremendously concerned over conservation problems. He called together Gifford Pinchot, who had been
made chief of the new Division of Forestry, and officials of the Department of the Interior, and they hurriedly established twenty-one
additional reserves before President Roosevelt signed the bill taking
such power away from him.

From 1897, when the Alaskan gold rush made Seattle a boomtown, to the First World War, times were so prosperous all over the Pacific Northwest that there was little apparent hostility to eastern exploitation of our natural resources. Nearly everyone had good wages and was optimistic about his future economic position. The conservationists had had considerable effect, too, in causing many people to expect more care on the part of lumbermen, commercial fishermen, farmers, and other persons whose occupations depended on using our natural resources. Some of the lumbermen realized that their business would be gone before too many years when the forests were used up. In 1900 when Frederick Weyerhaeuser bought nine hundred thousand acres of timber owned by the Northern Pacific Railroad in the state of Washington, he said that he was going to retain much of it uncut, "Not for us, nor for our children, but for our grandchildren."

Agitation over certain specific grants of federal land to corporations did continue, however, and one of these during Taft's administration (1908-12) involved Richard Ballinger from the state of Washington. He had been mayor of Seattle, Commissioner of the General Land Office under President Theodore Roosevelt, and finally Secretary of the Interior under Taft. He released waterpower sites in Montana and Wyoming on federal lands to companies for commercial development, and Gifford Pinchot, the conservationist mentioned earlier, who was at that time one of Ballinger's subordinates in the Department of the Interior, was so outraged at his superior official's action that he protested to Congress. Taft supported Ballinger and dismissed Pinchot. This was one more incident which helped to convince Theodore Roosevelt that he should leave the Republican party, when he failed to get its nomination for President in 1912, in order to form a third party that would fight for conservation of natural resources and other reforms which he advocated. As we have seen, he did organize the Progressive party and was nominated for President on its ticket.

Even with improved methods of logging, by the time of the Second World War some types of softwood (particularly Douglas fir) were so nearly gone that the public demanded governmental restrictions not only on methods of cutting trees on land owned by the state and federal government, but also on private land. Lumber companies accepted the fact that a greater degree of conservation was necessary, both to preserve their industry and to maintain friendly public relations. Consequently, in 1947 our state legislature passed the Forest Practices Act, which stipulates conditions for lumbering on private land.

Political Struggle in Labor-Management Relations

Labor-management relations was another social problem which had political implications. Although in times of prosperity the supply of laborers in the state was seldom great enough to meet the demand, jobs were seasonal in lumbering, mining, and fishing. Washington therefore had a greater percentage of transient laborers than was found in the East. Because there were not as many women as men on the frontier, there existed a large group of unmarried men who could move more easily from one place to another in search of work.

Since it was difficult for temporary workers to demand satisfactory living conditions in company-owned towns, the beds in company barracks were often infested with vermin and the food extremely bad. At that time neither the companies nor a governmental agency took responsibility for injuries to the workmen, and, in logging camps particularly, men were often mangled in accidents and were then usually without money to pay for medical care. The aftermath of such tragedies was often worse than the disaster itself. However, when jobs were plentiful enough that able-bodied workers could move on to another town to look for better conditions, the employers had to meet some of the demands for improvement of working conditions to retain their workers.

Moreover, in the 1880's, labor unions were formed in Seattle, partly to protect the permanent residents from the influx of these migratory workers. By 1900 waitresses and retail clerks had a union and in 1906 farmer delegates were admitted to the Seattle Central Labor Council. The salespeople were able to force the stores to close on Sunday and at six o'clock on weekdays. In later years, under the leadership of David Beck, the teamster boss, the city unions were absorbed largely into the American Federation of Labor (AFL) whereas the transient loggers, fishermen, and dock workers preferred the Congress of Industrial Organizations (CIO).

Toward the end of the last century, the demands of laborers found much sympathy in the Populist party because of its fear of big corporations. As the Populist party disintegrated, many of its labor adherents joined the Socialist party. In 1894, while the depression of the previous year still gripped the country, a Baptist minister in Seattle—Dr. H. F. Titus—advocated that the wealth of the country should be distributed equally. Forced to resign by his congregation, Dr. Titus became the leader of the Socialist party in Seattle; under him, the subscription list for the party paper grew to five thousand.

By 1905 the most radical of the labor leaders all over the country had become dissatisfied with the American Federation of Labor, and even with the Socialist party, as being, in their opinion, too conservative and too slow in forcing better working conditions and higher pay. Therefore they met in Chicago to found a labor organization that would be one inclusive union rather than a federation of separate unions based on particular crafts, like the AFL. The leaders hoped that the new industrial union would be powerful enough because of its unity to achieve its ends. The organization which emerged from the Chicago meeting was the Industrial Workers of the World, or "Wobblies," as they came to be called.

Branches of the IWW sprang up during the fall of 1905 in Seattle and in other lumbering towns, such as Hoquiam, Aberdeen, Tacoma and Port Townsend. The IWW leaders realized that they would have little success with the settled members of the AFL unions who were satisfied with their status. The Wobblies therefore had to appeal to the large mass of transient workers in our coast region for the main support of the organization. When delegates from the state of Washington went to the national IWW convention in 1908 in Chicago, they succeeded in getting control of the convention, and the westerners dominated the organization from that time. In fact, the Seattle Skid Road became, in effect, their national headquarters. The Pacific Northwest leaders changed the policy of the IWW from one of political action to that of force, since our transient laborers were seldom in one place long enough to vote and consequently had no conception of the power which could be exercised through a political organization.

In 1914, although the Puget Sound area still seemed prosperous, over ten thousand men were unemployed in Seattle alone. This tremendous oversupply of labor made the unions anxious about their bargaining ability and made the IWW members more determined to bring about a workers' revolution of some kind. Labor groups were still more alarmed in 1916 when the state legislature passed antilabor laws that were just barely defeated in a referendum. By this time, however, the First World War had been going on in Europe for two years, and orders were coming into the Pacific Northwest from Russia for munitions, locomotives, and other war supplies. This war boom put the coast industries into such high production that unemployment decreased to the point where a union of shingle weavers in Everett felt strong enough to call a strike. The mill owners hired substitute workers and a number of the Everett IWW group began to agitate on behalf of the strikers. The intrusion of the IWW infuriated the Everett industrialists, and they were able to run about forty Wobblies out of Everett, forcing them through a gauntlet where they were beaten as they left the city.

The Seattle IWW could not let this move go unchallenged and publicized its intention of going to Everett en masse on the following Sunday, November 5, 1916. Two hundred and fifty members chartered a steamboat for the trip. When they reached the Everett harbor, they saw that it was lined with spectators and with a large group of deputized policemen carrying rifles. The Seattle Wobblies refused to turn back, and, as the ship docked, the deputies fired on them. The men on board were said to have fired also, perhaps first. Five men on board were killed along with some bystanders on the dock.

The ship hurried back to Seattle where the city police arrested seventy-four of the passengers on a charge of murder. In the ship, however, the police found no firearms, only packages of red pepper and clubs. At that time, as we have seen, there was much opposition in the Pacific Northwest to the United States' entering the war. Both farm and labor groups vehemently denounced any proposal that this country take part. The lumber operators, on the other hand, favored our participation. Thus the IWW excursion to Everett became identified in the public mind, to a certain extent, with the organization's crusade against this country's declaring war. The defendants in the murder trial (represented by one of their number, Thomas H. Tracy) thus had considerable public support on issues not connected with the murders when the trial opened in March, 1917.

During the trial, the conditions under which migratory laborers worked were brought to the attention of the public through the testimony of Tracy, and much sympathy for the laborers resulted. Tracy was acquitted and the remaining seventy-three were released from jail. None of the Everett deputies was brought to trial.

In April, 1917, the United States entered the war and immediately the demand for lumber skyrocketed. The idea of a general strike, previously advocated only by the IWW, now seemed to most of the unions to be a good idea. They decided to stage a general strike in order to secure an eight-hour day; the time was ripe to show management and the general public that the economy of the area would be paralyzed without the aid of labor groups. Lumber operators were determined to maintain the ten-hour day since they could sell at high prices all the lumber which could be cut. They therefore refused offers from the federal government for mediation, and practically all of the loggers in the Pacific Northwest struck; however, a general strike did not materialize since at the last minute other unions failed to join the loggers.

In the fall when the loggers were in dire financial straits, many of them went back to work, but, at the end of eight hours, they would wander away and refuse to work the remaining two hours. The foreman would then fire them and hire another group which would repeat the performance the following day. By this time the federal government was so desperate for lumber (particularly spruce) for war needs that the War Department assigned Colonel Brice Disque to the task of sending soldiers into the woods to cut timber. Since most of them had never touched a saw, their attempts as loggers were farcical. Colonel Disque was forced in March, 1918, to instruct the lumber companies to hire the striking skilled loggers on an eight-hour-day basis with the additional stipulations that the companies would have to furnish clean bedding and burn the bunks that were too heavily infested with lice to be fumigated successfully. In return the loggers had to sign a pledge to stamp out acts of hostility against the United States government and to help win the war. With better working conditions, the IWW members were glad, for the most part, to sign the pledge and return to work.

Unions continued to gain in strength during the prosperous times. There were 11,523 wage earners in Seattle in 1914 and 40,843 in 1919. To many of the workers it appeared that American

This 1892 photograph suggests the overcrowded, inadequate facilities for housing loggers which finally helped spark the strike in 1917. (Courtesy of the University of Washington Library)

labor was obtaining its aims by the use of strikes instead of having recourse to a violent revolution as the Russian workers had done two years earlier in 1917. The state legislature, fearing violence in connection with the increasing number of strikes, passed a criminal syndicalism bill over the governor's veto in January, 1919. This bill made it a serious crime to advocate or practice violence or terrorism in working for social or political reforms. The Seattle shipyard workers called a strike immediately and those in Tacoma followed suit. The metal-trades unions then asked the Central Labor Council to call a general strike in Seattle. Many people were afraid that it might be the beginning of a revolution in this country.

Delegates from 110 unions formed the General Strike Committee, representing workers in all fields from carpentry to newsboys, and they set February 6, 1919, for the beginning of the strike. The experienced members of the committee wanted to set a limit of a certain number of hours or days for the strike, but they were voted down. The committee agreed to allow hospitals to be serviced, drugs to be sold, and food to be brought into the city. No other activities involving union labor were to continue. On February 6, 1919, sixty thousand workers stayed home. The next day the mayor, Ole Hanson, threatened martial law and the use of troops but nothing happened and the strike continued. Since no ending date had been set for the strike, the committee was then faced with the problem of ending it without appearing to be giving in to management's demands. The result was that strikers began going back to work gradually, and the strike died out.

Since a general strike is a terrific hardship on the public, many people who had been sympathetic with the workers' demands were so angered by their action that antilabor feeling increased rapidly. To make matters worse for the union members, the war boom was over by that time and unemployment was steadily rising. The newly formed American Legion decided that it would help rid the coast of the IWW members, who were still associated in people's minds with pacifism.

Rumors went around that the American Legionnaires were going to make some move against the IWW on Armistice Day (November 11, 1919) when there was to be a Legion parade in Centralia; therefore, the Wobblies armed themselves and stationed guards in their town headquarters, which the parade passed twice. The second time, the Legionnaires stopped at the hall and the firing began, with each group accusing the other of opening the attack.

Of the Legionnaires, the commander and three others were killed, one of them a bootblack. Two IWW members were killed and that night, after the police had rounded up and put in jail all of the Wobblies they could find, a crowd broke into the jail and lynched Wesley Everest, an IWW organizer. A mob burned the IWW hall.

Ten IWW members were charged with first-degree murder, and eight of these were later convicted of second-degree murder. One was sent to an institution for the criminally insane where he was held until 1930. One died in prison; five were pardoned by the governor in 1933; and the sentence of the eighth was commuted in 1939 by the governor. The trial gained nation-wide publicity, and feeling ran high between those who blamed the IWW for the violence and those who felt that the Wobblies were simply protecting

Slums of Seattle, June 10, 1937. This "little city" was an outgrowth of the depression. It was still in existence, although drastically smaller in size, as late as 1948. (Courtesy of the University of Washington Library)

their property and even their lives. In any case, the power of the IWW dwindled away after the trial.

Labor unions also were vitally interested in political support during the depression inasmuch as both skilled and unskilled laborers found it extremely difficult to find work. Since the relief measures, listed above, were sponsored and put into effect by a Democratic administration, labor, for the most part, supported that party.

Within the labor unions themselves, however, there was a constant struggle by various groups for control, and each leader tried to ally the local governmental agencies with his faction. This friction led in 1936 to the establishment of the CIO under John L. Lewis. We noted earlier that the IWW wanted to organize one large union in which each member would belong directly to the national organization. The AFL, on the other hand, maintained separate craft unions, which, in turn, were held together in a somewhat loose federation on the national level. Although many AFL spokesmen argued that the unions would never be strong enough under that system to force their demands on management successfully and that strength lay in one national union with a strong central government, this proposal was never given serious consideration in the AFL conventions.

In 1936 when the CIO was organized on this basis, the leader of the West Coast longshoremen, Harry Bridges, became the West Coast representative of the CIO, and the Seattle longshoremen joined him. Other Pacific Northwest unions, such as the lumber workers, the fur workers, and the Newspaper Guild, began to affiliate with the new organization. The unions which remained with the AFL under David Beck's leadership were determined that the CIO should not become a serious rival to the older organization, and a period of violence was the result.

The term "goon squad"—meaning a group of men hired to beat up or otherwise mistreat members of the rival faction—came into existence. In Seattle, the public became so disgusted with the violence that opposition to all labor unions resulted, and the voters refused to re-elect John Dore, the Seattle mayor, who had supported the AFL. Instead, a mayor and council considered by the unions to be antilabor were elected in 1938, and initiatives that would severely curb labor's rights began to appear on the ballot. At that point the AFL and the CIO unions had to cooperate sufficiently to defeat the initiatives, as they were able to do by a small margin. The same kind of necessity, on a national scale, led to the actual merger of the two labor groups into the AFL-CIO organization after the Second World War. For a time, the AFL in our state insisted that it would not combine with the CIO locally, even though the national merger had taken place, but it finally yielded.

During World War II labor's position was good because the demand for workers far exceeded the supply. When the postwar recessions caused some unemployment, agitation for curbs on labor's bargaining power revived. The agitation increased in 1958 when congressional investigating committees disclosed alleged misuse of labor funds by some of the labor leaders all over the country, including David Beck of Seattle, head of the teamsters' union.

In the 1958 election in this state, an initiative was presented to the voters proposing that it be made illegal to require membership or nonmembership in a union as a condition of employment. This would mean that neither unions nor nonunion groups could make an agreement with a company requiring it to hire all union or nonunion personnel. The initiative was defeated in the election.

In *Progress,* the quarterly publication of the State Department of Commerce and Economic Development (spring and summer issues, 1963), the state's labor force is listed for February, 1963, as 1,008,300 jobholders, and the following summaries are made:

> Total employment, which took a sharp drop at the end of World War II, quickly leveled off and regained momentum. The steady climb since then set new yearly records except for the three national recession years of 1954, 1958, and 1961. . . . Washington unemployment in 1962 at 5.4% of the civilian labor force was lower than the national rate for the first time in a number of years.

Social Life

8

EARLY HOMES

It is hard for a student who has grown up with central heating, plumbing, and electricity in the home to visualize the daily life of the pioneers. If one does manage to re-create a picture of a house without windows, floor, heat, or light (other than from a fireplace and candles), and bathroom, he may make the mistake of thinking that life in such circumstances could only be dreary. In spite of the primitive living conditions, the early settlers were so busy improving them that many of their diaries and letters show an enthusiastic zest for their daily life. Moreover, since they were largely dependent on their families or a few neighbors for companionship, they had to be resourceful in providing their own entertainment. Contemporary accounts of frontier social life show that they enjoyed the same basic types of parties and programs which people in eastern towns did at that time.

Circumstances varied, of course, in the homes of the first settlers. Those who came overland ordinarily had to continue to live in their wagon or a tent until they could build a cabin. One family actually lived in the hollow stump of one of the enormous trees on Puget Sound for several months. The men chopped trees to make the log walls of a house and split shakes for the roof. If a floor was put down to begin with, it, too, consisted of split logs laid with the rounded side down, called a *puncheon* floor. A frame for a bed, a table, and stools were also made from split planks.

Sometimes the builders did not cut windows at first since there was no glass to put in them. Mrs. Phoebe Judson, a pioneer on Puget Sound who wrote a delightful autobiography, *A Pioneer's Search for an Ideal Home,* said that in their first cabin her husband sawed holes for windows which she covered with muslin to let in as much light as possible. Some pioneers used deer skins for window coverings.

242

In the Judson cabin, the fireplace was made of blue clay mixed with sand, and the chimney was made from sticks and mortar. The crevices between the logs were filled with moss. Along the Oregon Trail, in order to make a lighter load, Mrs. Judson had had to throw out most of the furniture that her family had packed into the covered wagon when they started for the West. She kept three china plates, three cups and saucers, and a glass tumbler, however, and these she put on shelves built by her husband in one corner of their cabin. They also had their camping outfit of kettles, a long-handled frying pan, and a Dutch oven.

During their first winter, the Judsons lived largely on deer meat since they had used up most of their flour, dried fruit, and other provisions along the overland trail. In Olympia, the nearest town, flour sold for $20.00 a barrel, a price which they could not afford. Besides, the trip to and from the town by ox team or Indian canoe was a difficult venture. Mrs. Judson cried with pleasure when a neighbor gave her some potatoes that had been raised the previous summer.

Familes who could afford it brought books with them or had them shipped around Cape Horn. The number and types of books in the pioneer homes are surprising and show that the majority of the early settlers enjoyed reading and were willing to make a real sacrifice to be able to provide themselves with good reading material. It happened, however, that the Judsons brought only the family Bible and Webster's Dictionary. When the oxen were struggling to pull the heavy wagon over the mountains, Mrs. Judson said that she would have thrown out the Bible, too, because of its weight, except for her reverent feeling for it. During the long evenings of their first winter, in addition to reading the Bible by the light of the fireplace, Mrs. Judson entertained the family by giving her husband words to spell from the dictionary. Other pioneers mention that the family played all kinds of guessing games, and ordinarily one member of the family was the favorite storyteller who would entertain the others with tales of adventure or summaries of books read before he came to the Pacific Northwest. The younger members roasted apples or popped corn as an accompaniment to the stories and games.

Each pioneer family raised as much food as possible during the first summer in the new land, and for that purpose everyone brought seeds or obtained them from older residents on arrival.

Therefore, unless weather conditions were unfavorable, the new settlers ordinarily had a greater variety of food after their first winter.

The pioneers agitated immediately for roads in order to be able to reach the homes of other settlers and to go to a town for supplies. They built makeshift roads themselves until their governmental agency could raise money for better ones. During the Washington territorial period, part of a person's taxes could be paid through labor on the roads since the population had not reached the point where road crews could be maintained.

As soon as roads were built between settlements, the pioneers could buy most of the articles used in the East. Trade flourished by way of ships coming round South America, and after 1869 by way of railroads, at least as far as San Francisco. Glass in windows soon became common; kerosene lamps replaced the fish-oil lamps and tallow candles; and elegant furniture, including pianos and rugs, was available for those who could afford it. Before the turn of the century, living conditions in the older towns were approximately like those in all but the largest eastern cities.

Dances and other types of parties were given frequently in towns during our pioneer period and as often as people could get together in the rural areas. Whenever a new barn was to be built, the neighbors came to "raise" the barn and then stayed for a dinner and usually a dance at night. The dances were largely what we now call square dances. In a community where there were more men than women (as was often the case, at first), the required number of men tied ribbons round their arms to indicate that they were taking the place of feminine partners. We have seen that there was usually a "fiddle" or guitar among the overland parties on the Oregon Trail, and these same instruments furnished the music for dances after the settlers arrived. There were many references to card games, such as poker, casino, and Old Maid, as well as checkers and chess.

East of the Cascades where there was more snow, the settlers enjoyed skating and sledding in the winter. Often a sleigh was improvised by placing a wagon bed on bobsleds, filling its bottom with straw and covering it with skin robes and blankets. As many people as possible would climb in for a ride, usually stopping at an occupant's home for a supper.

EDUCATION

In our study of the settlement of the Willamette Valley, we saw how eager the settlers were to establish schools for their children. In fact, even before the first American settlers arrived, a school was in operation at Fort Vancouver, the main Hudson's Bay Company post. The teacher, John Ball, came to the Oregon country in 1832 with Nathaniel Wyeth, the American fur trader who intended to set up a fur-trading post and fish-packing plant near the mouth of the Columbia. When Wyeth failed in his project, Ball stayed on at John McLoughlin's request to conduct a school for the children of the fur traders attached to the post. Ball taught for a few months sometime during the winter of 1832-33 and then went back east by way of the Hawaiian Islands. Solomon H. Smith succeeded him as teacher and operated the school for a year and a half. Smith had also come out with Wyeth.

In the 1830's when the missionaries set up their stations, first in the Willamette Valley and later east of the Cascades, they provided schools for the Indian children and for any white pupils living in the area. Cyrus Shepard, the teacher at the Methodist Mission school, first at present Oregon City and later at Salem, was an excellent teacher. Eliza Spalding and Mary Walker were also ingenious in devising ways of instructing the Indian children without the usual books and other teaching equipment. Mrs. Walker, as we saw earlier, used an egg shell for a globe in teaching geography and made use of the native vegetation for many subjects. The Spokanes were receptive to teaching from the whites since Spokane Garry, the son of a chief, had been taken by the Hudson's Bay Company officers in 1824 to the Red River School near present Winnipeg, Canada, where he studied for five or six years. When he returned to the Spokane tribe around 1830, he had conducted classes occasionally.

After the missionary period when the first settlers began moving north of the Columbia in 1844, each family was responsible for seeing to the education of its children. In many instances the mother would teach her children as much as possible during the winter months. In settlements where there were a number of families, one woman would often be chosen school teacher, and the other parents would pay her in produce for holding a village school in the largest cabin available. These were makeshift arrangements, and whatever training was available lasted, at the most, only a few weeks or months during the year.

From 1848 to 1853 while Washington was a part of Oregon Territory, school districts were organized north of the Columbia River, but until 1852 none of them seem to have actually operated a public school. In the winter of 1852-53, however, a public school was in operation in Washougal. When the territory of Washington was created in 1853, Congress set aside sections sixteen and thirty-six from each congressional township for the support of public schools in the territory. Then in 1854 the first territorial legislature established machinery for operating common schools in each county. The framework for the maintenance of schools has remained essentially the same to the present time.

The fact that schools were established in 1854 did not mean that they existed in every locality. Often the population was too small to pay for school buildings. In Walla Walla, for example, no tax had been levied for a schoolhouse in 1864, and the board of school-district directors tried to raise money for a schoolhouse by subscription. When this attempt failed, the residents agreed to a tax of two and a half mills.

Sometimes even when there were facilities for a school, no one could be found to teach. Most of the early teachers were wives of the settlers, without teaching experience except for the lesson periods held for their own children. Many of them, however, proved to be successful teachers in spite of having pupils ranging from six to forty years old in their classrooms and in spite of using as texts whatever books happened to be present in the community. Many men and women had grown up either on our frontier or in pioneer communities in the Middle West where they had had no chance to attend school. Consequently, when a public school opened near them in Washington Territory, they took advantage of it to learn to read, and this tremendous spread in ages made great difficulties for the teachers. Reminiscences of the early school teachers have been included in *Early Schools of Washington Territory* by Angie Burt Bowden.

Schools were often in session during part of the summer since

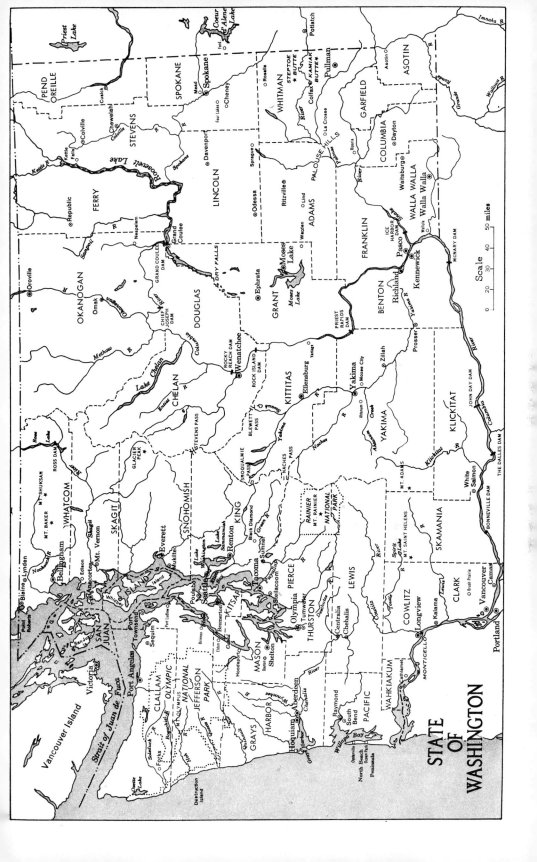

STATE
OF
WASHINGTON

roads were impassable in the winter. Moreover, whenever home or farm duties claimed the children, they were automatically kept at home to do the work since the family's winter sustenance depended largely on what could be stored during the summer. Throughout the territorial period, few schools managed to hold classes for more than three months out of the year,

The first high school in Washington Territory was a private academy opened in Seattle by George Whitworth, who later became president of the University of Washington. In 1877, the territorial legislature permitted graded public schools, and some of these offered beginning high school work. The first school to call itself a high school was one in Dayton in 1880, and in the same year a Catholic high school, Holy Names, was established. Seattle opened a public high school in 1883. After Washington became a state in 1889, the number of high schools increased rapidly, although in 1895 there was a question about the legality of using public funds for secondary schools. In that year the legislature specifically included high schools as a part of the public school system, resolving any doubt about their legality. In 1889-90, there were six high schools in the state; in 1900, forty-seven; and in 1910, 307. Long before statehood, the settlers were anxious to have institutions of higher learning available for their children.

Whitman College in Walla Walla was the first private college, of the ones still in existence today, to be established in Washington. We have noted that Elkanah Walker and Cushing Eells were serving as missionaries at Walker's Prairie north of Spokane when they were forced to leave in 1847 because of the Whitman massacre. They went to the Willamette Valley where they continued as teachers and ministers until the close of the Yakima War in 1858 when eastern Washington was again thrown open for settlement. Eells wanted to return to the areas east of the Cascades where he and the other missionaries had worked during the 1830's and 1840's. In 1859 he went on horseback to Waillatpu where he was so much affected by the sight of the Whitmans' grave and the rubble remaining from the burned mission buildings that he determined to found there a college to be named for the Whitmans.

He secured a charter for Whitman Seminary from the Washington territorial legislature in 1860, and, in that same year, the town of Walla Walla boomed as an outfitting town for the Clearwater-Salmon miners. Eells and the other trustees therefore decided to build the seminary in Walla Walla, and by 1865 the school was opened.

In 1878 the Colfax Academy and Business Institute was opened as a college preparatory school. In later years under the name of Colfax College, it gave a four-year course in liberal arts and teacher training until 1900 when it closed. The Catholic church established two institutions: Gonzaga University in Spokane in 1881, and Seattle University in 1892. In 1888 the Methodist Church opened the College of Puget Sound in Tacoma; and in 1890 the Presbyterian Church established Whitworth College in Sumner; in 1900 the school was moved to Tacoma, and in 1915 it was located permanently in Spokane. In 1890, also, Pacific Lutheran College was opened near Tacoma. The Seventh Day Adventist Church located Walla Walla College in a suburb of Walla Walla in 1892.

Before statehood, the territorial legislature had also begun to provide a government-supported system of higher education. In the Organic Act written by Congress to create the territory of Washington, the equivalent of two townships of land had been set aside for the use of a territorial university. At its second session, 1854-55, the legislature created the Territorial University, but its location was not definitely settled until the session of 1860-61 when the legislature chose Seattle as its home, on condition that the residents would give ten acres of land to the territory as a site. Arthur Denny donated more than eight acres, and four other people gave the remainder. In 1861 the University opened, with thirty-one pupils and with Asa Mercer as president.

At first the University served all ages, and the students paid tuition. With the advent of statehood, however, additional funds were allocated to the institution by both the federal and state governments, and it developed rapidly into a distinguished university. When the Alaskan gold rush brought a tremendous influx of population around the turn of the century, the ten acres in the heart of Seattle were much too small, and, therefore, the University was relocated in its present site. Edmond Meany, the noted Pacific Northwest history professor for many years at the University, was instrumental in persuading the legislature to give land for this purpose. In

Seattle in 1870. In the foreground is the Alida, *a side-wheeler, built in Olympia in 1869. On the crest of the hill is the Territorial University of Washington. (Courtesy of the University of Washington Library)*

addition to providing the basis for an extensive curriculum in arts and sciences, the legislature allocated to the University certain professional schools in which the training is too expensive to be offered in more than one state institution until the population of the area creates a need for additional schools. Those which may be maintained only by the University are medical, dental, and law schools; degrees in forest products, logging engineering, commerce, journalism, library economy, marine and aeronautic engineering, and fisheries.

The second institution of higher learning to be established was Washington State University, formerly the State College of Washington, at Pullman. In 1862 Congress passed the Morrill Act donating federal lands to each state and territory for the maintenance of colleges specializing in agriculture and mechanical arts. The territorial legislature passed a law in 1864 accepting the provisions of the federal act and creating a college that was to be located at Vancouver. The legislature did not implement the law, and by 1889 when Washington became a state, the college had not opened.

The first state legislature began again to establish an agricultural college, and this time Pullman was chosen as the site. Washington Agricultural College, as it was called at first, began operating in 1892 with an enrollment of 234. The Morrill Act and subsequent federal laws for land grant colleges placed emphasis on a liberal arts curriculum as well as training in the scientific and practical aspects of agriculture and mechanic arts, and the state legislature has continued to envisage a well-rounded higher education program as the aim of the school.

The first state legislature also established normal schools for the training of teachers at Cheney and Bellingham. A third at Ellensburg was created in 1893 and opened in 1899. At first these schools were designed to train teachers for elementary schools only, and the University of Washington and Washington State University had the task of training teachers for high schools. In 1933, however, the legislature permitted them to train teachers and administrators for elementary and secondary schools and junior colleges, and in 1961 the legislature made them four-year general colleges, with the names, respectively, of Eastern, Central, and Western State College.

In recent years (particularly since World War II), the percentage of our high school graduates desiring some college education has increased at such a rapid rate that our colleges cannot take care of all of them. Moreover, some high school graduates for one reason or another do not intend to take a four-year college course, but do want one or two years' education beyond high school. The legislature has, therefore, established two-year colleges (junior colleges), now called community colleges, to fill this need.

Even before the war, a few quasi-public junior colleges had come into existence, largely as private vocational schools using high school buildings and, sometimes, public school teachers for night classes. The first junior college was established in Centralia in 1925. In 1941 the legislature authorized junior colleges as a part of the public school system of the state under regulations to be adopted by the State Board of Education and administered by the local school district. In 1961 the legislature changed the general name for these institutions to community colleges, but left the term "junior college" in the title of specific ones already using it. The fifteen community colleges in existence in 1964 are: Big Bend Community College, Moses Lake; Centralia College, Centralia; Clark College, Vancouver; Columbia Basin Community College, Pasco; Everett Junior College, Everett; Grays Harbor College, Aberdeen; Highline College, Seattle; Lower Columbia College, Longview; Olympic College, Bremerton; Peninsula College, Port Angeles; Shoreline Community College, Seattle; Skagit Valley College, Mount Vernon; Spokane Community College, Spokane; Wenatchee Valley College, Wenatchee; Yakima Valley College, Yakima.

RELIGION

Since missionaries were our first settlers, they gave the basis for the development of churches within the area. In chapter 5 we have noted the Methodist Mission in the Willamette Valley, with substations at The Dalles and elsewhere, begun by Jason and Daniel Lee in 1834; the American Board of Missions at Waillatpu, Lapwai, and Tshimakain, begun by the Whitmans and Spaldings in 1836; the Catholic missions in the Willamette Valley, near Yakima, and in northern Idaho and Montana, begun in 1838 with Fathers Demers and Blanchet; and a number of independent missionary endeavors in the Pacific Northwest.

After the Whitman massacre in 1847, the missionaries withdrew from the area east of the Cascades, and west of the Cascades there had been none stationed north of the Columbia except for Reverend and Mrs. John P. Richmond at Nisqually in 1840 and an occasional Catholic priest or Church of England clergyman connected with the Hudson's Bay Company. A few months after the Whitman massacre, the Catholic missionaries returned to the Yakima area and continued their work with the Indians, and, as Americans continued to move north of the Columbia, they were visited by whatever ministers traveled through the region. For example, Reverend William Richmond, an Episcopalian, was sent to Oregon in 1851. His headquarters were in Portland, and his congregations were all south of the river. However, he did conduct church services north of the Columbia, the first being on October 26, 1851, at Cathlamet.

No Protestant church was built in Washington until 1853,[1] when the Reverend John F. DeVore was able to erect and dedicate a Methodist church at Steilacoom. DeVore, a missionary circuit rider sent to the territory of Washington, was very successful, partly because of his engaging personality and capacity for hard physical labor. An amusing story is told of DeVore's efforts to provide a church building in Olympia for a group of Methodists who had begun to meet in 1852. He went to the owner of a sawmill to ask for a donation of lumber, wearing a fine suit and kid gloves. The miller was convinced that DeVore considered himself above manual labor and therefore told him that he might have all the lumber he could carry from the mill to the Sound in one day. DeVore gladly started to work the following morning at dawn and worked until sunset, moving during that time enough lumber for both a church and a parsonage.

Bishop Demers, from Vancouver Island (mentioned earlier as one of the Catholic priests in the Willamette Valley in the 1830's and 1840's), preached the first sermon in Seattle in 1852. He held a service in the cook house of Yesler's Mill. In November, 1853, the Methodist Episcopal Church appointed Reverend David E. Blaine to Seattle. In 1854 he was successful in organizing a Methodist church, and in 1855 a church building was completed. In addition to clearing the land and helping build the church, Blaine acted as deputy county clerk and taught an evening school besides performing his regular ministerial duties.

In 1865, Reverend Daniel Bagley, one of the trustees of the recently created University of Washington, organized a Methodist Protestant church in Seattle (called the "Brown Church" because of its color to distinguish it from the "White Church," the Methodist Episcopal Church).

When Reverend George F. Whitworth came to Seattle as president of the University of Washington in 1866, he wished to found a Presbyterian church; consequently, Daniel Bagley offered to alternate with him as pastor of the Brown Church. This arrangement continued until 1877 when a Presbyterian church was built for the use of that part of the congregation.

[1] The dates used for the establishment of the early churches in Washington are those given by each church for the *Guide to Church Vital Statistics Records in Washington* (Preliminary edition, 1942), a publication of the Historical Records Survey, a federal WPA project.

East of the Cascades, the Methodist Episcopal church was again the first Protestant group to organize a local church. In 1859 the Methodist Conference for Oregon created the Walla Walla Circuit, naming Reverend J. H. Wilbur as presiding elder and Reverend G. M. Berry as pastor. The two men went at once to Walla Walla and held meetings in the homes of the few settlers in the area or in the log courthouse until a church was built in 1860.

The following year, 1861, a Catholic church was built with Father Yunger as the local priest. Later Father J. B. Brouillet, who had been one of the earlier Catholic missionaries, succeeded him. During the gold rush of the 1860's, the Seventh Day Adventist and Congregational denominations opened churches in Walla Walla, and in the 1870's the Episcopal, Presbyterian, and United Brethren groups were represented.

In the Yakima area the Catholic Mission on Ahtanum Creek, referred to earlier, continued with a few months' lapse after the Whitman massacre. In 1871 St. Joseph's Catholic Church was founded on the site of the mission, but in 1885 the church was moved to Yakima where the population had concentrated.

When Reverend Cushing Eells learned that the Spokane Indians were trying to continue with religious services and that a white settlement was developing rapidly in the same locality, he returned to Spokane in 1874 and conducted services for the white settlements at Chewelah, Colville, and Spokane and for the Indians at various points. In 1877 Eells organized a Congregational church in Colfax and spent most of his remaining life as a circuit rider, preaching and establishing churches in the Inland Empire. He was instrumental in organizing the first Congregational church in Spokane in 1879.

Catholic influence was also strong in the Spokane area, stemming from the missionary work done by Fathers DeSmet, Joset, Cataldo, and the other devoted priests who had come as missionaries to the Indians. Our Lady of Lourdes Cathedral was established in 1884, St. Aloysius Church in 1886, and St. Patrick's in 1898.

Other denominations which organized a church in Spokane during the 1870's and 1880's were: Baptist (1881 and 1889); Christian (1886); Church of God (1880); Evangelical (1887); Lutheran (Norwegian, 1888) and Augustana Synod (1888); Methodist Episcopal

(1879); Hillyard Methodist (1888) and First German Methodist (1887); Presbyterian (1883).

The history of the founding of churches in the other areas of the state follows the same general pattern of Methodist, Congregational, Presbyterian, Baptist, Christian, and Episcopal churches as the earliest Protestant groups and the Catholic church, if distinguished from Catholic missions, slightly later in most places.

Because a pioneer community could ordinarily not support more than one or two churches to begin with, often the state or regional administrative bodies of the various denominations would agree to place a church of one denomination in a town and one of another faith in a neighboring town. Interdenominational community churches were also common in the early days. The trend toward cooperation between or actual merging of churches of different denominations has continued since the pioneer period. In many towns one youth group or religious service agency is composed of members of all the denominations present.

Churches in Washington have been responsible for many programs of social service, including youth centers, recreation camps, rehabilitation of handicapped persons, and so forth. Such work was done largely by churches or religious groups like the Salvation Army before government agencies undertook public welfare to the extent that we now know.

The move toward consolidation of churches has been offset, to a certain extent, by the appearance of additional denominations or sects, particularly in our cities. The table on page 256 shows the names and membership of the various religious groups in our state.

NEWSPAPERS

Even though our early settlers had no way of getting international or even national news for weeks or months after an event happened, they wanted newspapers to give them current local news and information about outside events as soon as messages reached our region either by ship or by the difficult overland trails. Often a newspaper served locally as the best means of conducting a political campaign or of advertising commodities for sale. As a result of these needs, the *Oregon Spectator* was begun as a weekly newspa-

TABLE 1

CHURCH MEMBERSHIP IN WASHINGTON

	Both Churches and Membership Reported		Churches only Reported	Members only Reported
	Number of Members	Number of Churches	Number of Churches	Number of Members
All religious groups	*695,375*	*2,148*	*125*	*30,714*
Seventh-Day Adventist	14,612	123		
Assemblies of God	20,061	214		
American Baptist Convention	29,625	101	21	
Southern Baptist Convention	4,978	41	36	
Church of the Brethren	2,530	16		
Church of God (Cleveland, Tenn.)	374	13		
Church of God (Anderson, Ind.)	2,268	41		
Church of God in Christ			13	
Church of the Nazarene	6,251	91		
Congregational Christian Churches	21,629	111		
Disciples of Christ, International, Convention	31,682	103	3	
Greek Archdiocese of North and South America			4	
Evangelical and Reformed Church	728	8		
Evangelical United Brethren Church	3,455	28		
Jewish Congregations				10,882
Church of Jesus Christ, Latter-Day Saints				19,403
Reorganized Church of Jesus Christ of Latter-Day Saints	2,762	21		
American Lutheran Church	15,782	52		
Augustana Evangelical Lutheran Church	14,696	31		
Evangelical Lutheran Church	32,102	74		
Lutheran Church—Missouri Synod	21,598	71		
Evangelical Lutheran Joint Synod of Wisconsin and other states	2,034	22		
United Lutheran Church in America	11,034	26		
The Methodist Church	71,085	257		
Presbyterian Church in the United States of America	50,887	173		
United Presbyterian Church of North America	3,606	18		
Protestant Episcopal Church	38,337	97		
Christian Reformed Church	5,765	13		
Reformed Church in America	866	4		
Roman Catholic Church	267,632	172		429
Advent Christian Church	605	6		
Baha'i Faith			2	
Baptist General Conference of America	3,703	22		
North American Baptist General Conference	756	5		
Plymouth Brethren			23	
General Convention of the New Jerusalem in the United States of America	30	1		
Divine Science Church	75	1		
Evangelical Free Church of America	457	11		
Evangelical Mission Covenant Church of America	2,527	24		
Oregon Yearly Meeting of Friends Church	1,024	13	3	
International Church of the Foursquare Gospel	1,445	13		
Church of the Lutheran Brethren of America	155	2		
American Evangelical Lutheran Church	833	4		
Finnish Apostolic Lutheran Church of America	214	4		
Finnish Evangelical Lutheran Church (Suomi Synod)	275	5		
Mennonite Brethren Church of North America	176	1		
United Missionary Church	234	9	1	
Free Methodist Church of North America	3,546	50		
Holiness Methodist Church	45	2		
Pacific Yearly Meeting of Friends	179	1		
Wesleyan Methodist Church of America	38	2		
Open Bible Standard Churches, Incorporated	480	9		
Pentecostal Church of God in America			16	
The Pentecostal Holiness Church	35	1		
Pilgrim Holiness Church	191	10		
National Spiritualist Association of Churches	119	3	3	
Unitarian Church	943	9		
United Brethren in Christ	145	4		
Vedanta Society	35	1		
Volunteers of America	555	6		
Church of God of Prophecy	176	8		

Source: Division of Home Missions of the National Council of Churches of Christ in the U.S.A., *Churches and Church Membership in the United States*, Series B, No. 8 (1956).

per in Oregon City in 1846 before Oregon became a territory.

In what is now Washington, the first newspaper was the *Columbian,* published in Olympia, beginning in September, 1852, while the area was still a part of Oregon Territory. Its owners considered advertising the area north of the Columbia to be one of the main functions of the paper. They had a messenger take copies of the second issue (September 18, 1852) along the Oregon Trail until he met the incoming wagon trains through which he distributed copies of the paper. One editorial said:

> Come and let us reason together. The Willamette Valley is already full. All the first, second, third and fourth rate claims are occupied and being improved. Will you who have suffered the toil and privations of a 2,000 miles journey in search of a desirable home, consent to take the refuse lands of those who have gone before?

The editor continued to point out that there was plenty of choice, unoccupied land north of the Columbia; that the harbors on Puget Sound were excellent; that the future of the lumber trade was extremely bright; that the Sound would undoubtedly become the terminus of a transcontinental railroad and the location of a big navy yard. Such a statement of inducements for settling north of the river apparently was effective in persuading a number of prospective settlers to go to Puget Sound instead of the Willamette Valley.

Other early coast papers were: the *Puget Sound Courier,* Steilacoom, 1855-56; *Puget Sound Herald,* Steilacoom, 1858-64; *North-West* (Republican), Port Townsend, 1860-61; *Washington Standard,* Olympia, 1860-1922 (Democratic after 1868, supporting women's suffrage and prohibition). Nearly all of the early newspapers had similar histories, including numerous owners, many changes of politics, and frequent mergers with other small papers.

East of the Cascades, the first newspaper was the *Washington Statesman,* begun in Walla Walla in the fall of 1861 to take advantage of the tremendous influx of population that accompanied the mining boom. In 1866 W. H. Newell bought the paper and made it one of the few supporters in the territory of the Confederate side in the Civil War. Even though the war was over before he began publication, he used editorials to attack persons who had fought on the Union side and displayed a bitter attitude toward the Republican party. When Newell died in 1878, Colonel F. J. Parker bought the paper; in 1880 he turned it into a daily. He continued it as a Democratic paper, but not a violently pro-Southern one.

The first newspaper in Seattle was the *Puget Sound Gazette,* which appeared as a weekly in 1863. On October 26, 1864, it printed the first news received by telegraph, the line having been completed to Seattle that day. The *Gazette* was shortlived, however, and, although a number of successive owners tried to revive it, the paper was not continued on a permanent basis until 1867 when Samuel L. Maxwell, a printer from San Francisco, issued it as the *Weekly Intelligencer*. In 1876 it became the *Daily Intelligencer.* The *Alaska Times and Seattle Dispatch* was moved from Sitka to Seattle in 1869, and, in 1878, the *Daily Intelligencer* bought it as well as two other papers that had begun publication but were not succeeding. In 1881 the *Intelligencer* became the *Post-Intelligencer* when it was merged with the *Post,* a daily paper begun in 1878 as a successor to the *North Pacific Rural,* an agricultural monthly magazine.

From its beginning, Thomas W. Prosch managed the *Post-Intelligencer* so well that it soon came to be regarded as the leading paper of Washington Territory, having a circulation east and west of the Cascades. Leigh S. J. Hunt, who succeeded Prosch, perfected its organization still further. He was proud of continuing to publish the paper even at the time of the great Seattle fire of 1889, which destroyed his newspaper building along with much of the rest of Seattle. He had a small printing press in his home on which the staff printed the story of the fire while it was still raging, and the paper came out, as usual, on the following morning, June 7.

The second Seattle paper to continue to the present is the Seattle *Times,* which appeared in 1886 to make a social crusade on behalf of the Chinese who, as we saw, were being violently attacked on the coast. The previous year a newspaper, the *Call,* had begun with a rabid anti-Chinese editorial policy. Some Seattle businessmen who felt that the anti-Chinese agitation was morally wrong and also economically unwise founded the *Times* to express their viewpoint. The paper managed to maintain a satisfactory circulation, and the Alaskan gold rush boom of the late 1890's brought a new wave of prosperity which made Seattle well able to sustain two daily papers.

Spokane had a newspaper called the *Spokan Times,* published

Sulky racing in Spokane in the early 1900's. (Washington State University Library)

from 1879 to 1882 by Francis H. Cook, who spelled Spokane without the final *e*—"Spokan." In 1881, J. J. Browne, A. M. Cannon, and J. H. Glover established the Spokane *Chronicle,* giving the name its present-day spelling. People facetiously commented that the *Chronicle* was begun to fight a battle over the spelling of the city's name. It was a weekly at first, but became a daily in 1886 with H. T. Cowley as the publisher. The paper is still in existence.

The second Spokane paper to continue to the present time is the *Spokesman-Review,* begun in 1883 as a weekly by Frank M. Dallam who used a hand press in Cheney at first to print the paper, which he called the *Spokane Falls Review.* In 1885 it became a morning daily, and in 1893 W. H. Cowles bought it and another newspaper, the *Spokesman,* which had begun publication in 1890. He combined them under the present name of *Spokesman-Review.*

These are only a few examples of the origins of newspapers in the present state of Washington. In other parts of the state, newspapers were begun as soon as possible, and the influence of many of the editors extended far beyond the radius of their paper's circulation, as we shall see in regard to the impetus given to the building of Grand Coulee Dam by Rufus Woods, editor of the Wenatchee *Daily World.*

LIBRARIES

We have noted that books were a precious commodity in pioneer days, and, as they did with their other possessions, the early settlers tried to share their books with their neighbors. Even before Oregon Territory was formed, the residents of the Willamette Valley had organized the Multnomah Circulating Library, and, north of the Columbia, the early settlers followed a similar practice.

When Washington Territory was created in 1853, Congress appropriated $5,000 for a territorial library. Governor Stevens, with his usual speed of action, bought two thousand books before he left for the Pacific Northwest and had them shipped by sea to Olympia. They arrived within a year and formed a fine basis for the territorial library which, in 1889, became our state library with 10,448 volumes at that time. Since statehood, the legislature has also allowed county and city governments to establish public libraries financed from tax moneys.

In 1858, William H. Wallace, a Washington politician mentioned earlier, persuaded other civic-minded persons to join him in incorporating the Steilacoom Library Association to sponsor a subscription library. The members paid an admission fee of five dollars and dues of twenty-five cents a month. In less than a year the group had raised $300 for books. They also opened a reading room for the public and sponsored lectures and public debates. To make money for these projects, they gave public dances and other entertainments.

In 1865 the Vancouver Catholic Library Association established a library for Holy Angels College. By 1876 it had around three hundred volumes and was the only library in the territory besides the Washington Territorial Library to have that large a collection. In 1865 a library association was founded in Walla Walla along the same lines as the earlier one in Steilacoom, and in 1868 Seattle followed suit. In 1869 "Library rooms" were opened in Olympia, called "The Tacoma Library" of Olympia. In 1875 Mrs. D. S. Maynard set aside a room in her home in Seattle as a community reading room and furnished books, tables, and chairs for the use of the public. The following year this reading room became the nucleus for a YMCA organization with Dexter Horton as first president. Dayton followed with a free library in 1876, and Spokane in 1880. The Colfax academy, established in 1878, joined with the community in 1882 in providing public library service. Tacoma's public library was formed in 1886.

The University of Washington Library, which was founded in 1862, also served at times as a public library in addition to its primary function of providing books for the University's students and faculty. In the institution's 1881 catalogue, the statement is made that with the additional books from the Seattle City Library, eighteen hundred bound volumes and eight hundred pamphlets were available. Over the years, the universities and colleges in the state have developed noteworthy libraries, primarily for the use of their students and faculty. Of these, the University of Washington in Seattle and Washington State University in Pullman have the largest collection of books, the former having more than nine hundred thousand volumes and the latter more than seven hundred thousand. In both institutions, adequate sources for undergraduate and graduate research in most fields of learning are available. The special interest in both libraries has been Pacific Northwest history, and each has a distinguished collection of books and manuscripts in that field. Manuscripts sought are pioneer diaries, letters, photographs, account books, and other types of family papers throwing light on everyday life in the early period of settlement in this region.

NATIONALITY GROUPS

The type of music, art, and literature in a given locality depends on the nationality of the groups first settling in the area, the influence of later immigrants, the effect of the customs of surrounding countries, and the length of time these elements have had to fuse into a new regional culture. In the Pacific Northwest, our cultural background has been largely Anglo-Saxon with an addition of oriental touches. Certain localities, however, are heavily made up of Scandinavians, Germans, or Russians.

The first American settlers, beginning with the missionaries, were largely of Anglo-Saxon stock and represented families who had been in this country for more than one generation. With the exception of the English and French Canadians already in the Willamette Valley as ex-Hudson's Bay Company employees, this type of immigrant remained dominant during the 1840's. In 1850, for example, in the part of Oregon Territory north of the Columbia (Clark and Lewis counties), 629 of the adults were native-born whites, and nearly three fourths of these came from eleven states, seven of which were in the Middle West or upper South: Missouri, Illinois, Kentucky, Tennessee, Ohio, Indiana, and Iowa. The remaining native-born residents had been born in the Oregon country, Maine, New Hampshire, Vermont, Massachusetts, New York, Pennsylvania, Maryland, and Virginia.

Even in 1850, a small number of Oregon Territory's inhabitants were foreign born, but the countries so represented were all in the British Isles or northern Europe: England, Scotland, Ireland, and Wales accounted for 164; Germany for 82; France for 13; Switzerland for 3.

During the 1860's, the population of Washington Territory jumped from 11,594 to 23,955 in spite of the turbulent conditions produced in the East and South by the Civil War. In some instances, people migrated to the Pacific Northwest to escape the pressures of war. These immigrants still followed the earlier pattern of being largely native-born Americans. There was one different influx, however, during the 1860's—the Chinese who were brought in to do placer mining after the gold strikes began in the Clearwater River area in 1860. Many of them stayed on, as we saw in the section on the anti-Chinese riots of the 1880's in chapter 7.

After the coming of the railroads in the 1870's and 1880's, the immigration pattern changed. As we saw, the railroad companies advertised all over the United States and Europe that "free" land was available in the West. By 1883 over one hundred newcomers reached Seattle every day during a period of several months. Most of these were Norwegians and Swedes. Generally, they became log-

gers and fishermen to begin with, rather than farmers, and they settled largely in Seattle, Tacoma, Everett, Bellingham, and Aber-
deen-Hoquiam—places where lumbering and fishing were prominent occupations.

Poulsbo is still made up largely of fishermen of Norwegian
blood. It lies on an arm of the Sound that evidently seemed to the
first comers to resemble a Norwegian fjord. Until the Second World
War, the inhabitants observed some of the Norwegian holidays with
folk dances and games which had been popular in Norway when
the first generation left their homeland. On the east side of the
mountains, the Norwegians settled largely in Spokane, and a
significant Norwegian element still remains there.

Since 1900 the Norwegians and Swedes have been active in the
halibut and herring fishing industries, both as ordinary fishermen
and as owners and managers of commercial fishing operations. In
recent years, many Scandinavians have turned to dairy and truck
farming on the coast and to wheat farming in the interior of Washington.

German immigrants also arrived from the 1870's on. They came
to farm, for the most part, and were able to claim land in the more
arid parts of central Washington. In the Ritzville-Davenport-
Sprague section, there were a number of communities settled so
completely by Germans that the German language was almost the
only one spoken until early in the present century. In this same region, groups of Russians also took up claims. Odessa is an example
of a city that retains the name of the Russian city from which the
first group came. There were Russian settlements as far south as the
LaCrosse-Colfax area, too, but they were dispersed to a greater extent among the predominant English-speaking native and foreign
groups. One variation of the German and Russian immigrations
was a large German group that had migrated to Russia in the mid-
1800's and then to the United States around the turn of the century,
settling among the Germans in central Washington.

Some of the non-English-speaking groups did not come directly
from Europe. Scandinavians, Germans, and others who had settled
in the Middle West, particularly Iowa, Wisconsin, and Minnesota,
moved on to the Pacific Northwest when conditions here sounded
more promising. A group of Dutch families from Holland who had

settled in the Dakotas left there to come to the coast in 1894 because of a drought and a grasshopper plague that had ruined their farm lands.

During the early 1890's, too, financiers in Holland became interested in buying up land in Washington and then sending Dutch colonists to farm the land. In 1893 the agent of the Netherlands American Mortgage Company wrote back to Holland from Pullman, Washington, that the land was as fertile as the best areas of Holland and that farming here would be lucrative for Hollanders. As a result, a group of Dutch families came from Holland to Colfax where they were placed on the third floor of a hotel until they could be settled on farms. During their first night, a group of vigilantes among the neighboring ranchers hanged an alleged cattle thief just outside their hotel windows, and the Hollanders were so sickened by the sight and also frightened by the evidence of the "wild west" that they went straight back to Holland.

The Netherlands companies then decided that Spokane was a safer place for investment activities, and they put considerable capital into lumbering, banking, real estate ventures, and flour milling. By 1914 approximately $50,000,000 in Dutch capital was invested there. These activities did not call for colonists, however, and few Hollanders lived in Spokane. The Dutch who came as settlers in the 1890's and early 1900's went largely to Whidbey Island and other parts of the Sound where the lush pasture lands reminded them of the dairy farms in Holland. Lynden in Whatcom County became the largest Dutch settlement in Washington. One group tried farming in the Yakima Valley in 1896 and did so well with irrigation that in the early 1900's Dutch communities appeared at Zillah, Moxee City, and Prosser.

Finns and Italians came to our urban areas in the early 1900's as laborers of various kinds. The English-speaking residents of these cities were uneasy at first about these newcomers, fearing that they would cling together in their own sections of a city and remain apart from the life of the rest of the community. This did not happen in Washington. Both the Italian and the Finnish groups merged readily with the older Anglo-Saxon culture patterns, and their identity was therefore not retained so long as that of the German and Russian groups in our rural communities.

In 1920, of the 1,356,621 people in Washington, 1,319,777

Alki Point bathing beach, Seattle, 1912. (Original photo belongs to the Washington State Historical Society; courtesy of the University of Washington Library)

were white; 6,883 were Negro; 17,387 were Japanese; 2,363 were Chinese; 9,061 were Indian; and 1,150 were distributed among other countries, such as India, Malaya, Korea, and the territory of Hawaii. The distribution of the 250,055 foreign-born white residents in Washington was as follows: Canada, 17.2 per cent; Sweden, 13.9 per cent; Norway, 12.1 per cent; Denmark, 3.3 per cent; Germany, 8.9 per cent; England, 8.3 per cent; Ireland, 3.6 per cent; Scotland, 3.2 per cent; Finland, 4.7 per cent; Russia, 4.4 per cent; Italy, 4.3 per cent; Austria, 2.6 per cent; Greece, 1.7 per cent; Poland, 1.6 per cent; Switzerland, 1.5 per cent; Yugoslavia, 1.4 per cent; Netherlands, 1.2 per cent; France 1 per cent. The remaining 5 per cent were distributed among other countries, each sending fewer than 1 per cent. The Japanese were predominantly occupied in truck farming on the coast, with the heaviest concentrations on the outskirts of Seattle and Tacoma. Only 939 lived east of the Cascades—771 were engaged in irrigated farming in Yakima County, and the remainder had settled in Spokane. Approximately the same distribution existed for the Chinese, with only 139 living in Spokane.

During the Second World War, people of Japanese blood, both aliens and United States citizens, were evacuated from the Pacific Coast to relocation centers for the duration of the war. General John DeWitt issued the order for their removal on March 24, 1942, on the ground that if Japan attacked the United States mainland, as was expected, her main targets on the Washington coast would be the Boeing airplane factory, the Bremerton Navy Yard and other shipyards, docks on the Sound and the Columbia River, all of which were in the midst of truck gardening centers or fishing enterprises operated by Japanese, some of whom would probably be saboteurs aiding Japan.

A total of 14,559 Japanese were removed from Washington, mostly from the west side of the state. In addition, many Japanese left voluntarily, in order to be able to choose their new location, and some were exempted from the order. Minidoka Center in southern Idaho was the place to which most of the Washington Japanese were sent, and around two hundred went to Tule Lake Center in northern California. Both centers were in an area suited to truck gardening.

Some non-Japanese pointed out that, logically, Italian and German families should be removed since the United States was at war with their homelands, also, and feeling was bitter both on the part of those who feared any Japanese as a probable traitor to the United States and of those who felt that the damage to be done by a few might-be saboteurs was not worth the emotional harm done to the many whose loyalty was unquestionable. After the war, some of the Japanese remained in other parts of the country, but the majority returned to the area in Washington where they had previously lived.

During and after the Second World War, many Negroes came to the Washington coast cities to find work in industrial plants. When agricultural workers became scarce during the war, ranchers arranged to bring in groups of Mexicans as transient labor to pick fruit and hops in the central part of the state. The 1950 *Census* lists the national groups as follows: of the 2,378,963 inhabitants of Washington in 1950, 2,316,496 were white; 30,691 Negro; 13,816 Indian; 9,694 Japanese; 3,408 Chinese; and 4,858 represented other races.

UTOPIAN GROUPS

Sociologists find that the dominant culture pattern in an area is modified by the customs of different racial groups that come in after the first one is established. Some of these influences are apparent even to an untrained person, but the amalgamation of cultures in our state is considered particularly successful because no one nationality was firmly entrenched in an area before others began to appear. Some groups did not want to join this "melting pot," but they were not trying to perpetuate a set of national customs so much as some plan for an ideal society—to found a utopia. Because the Pacific Northwest was a region where a settlement could still be isolated from outsiders and yet have fertile land for farming, it became a mecca for such bands.

In Washington the first one was the Puget Sound Cooperative Colony, launched by George Venable Smith in Port Angeles in 1877. Land was to be held in common, and, from the sale of goods, each person would be guaranteed good wages, "free lands, free water, free lights, free libraries" and no taxes or rents. Housekeepers would be hired for wives who preferred to work outside their homes. For two years the colony ran with enough success to operate stores, factories, a hotel, and other businesses, and a newspaper, called the *Commonwealth*. Then the group broke up because the leaders began to accuse each other of fraud.

In the 1890's a socialist colony established itself at Edison, Washington. It was called Equality and was to be one unit of a series of cooperative commonwealths all over the country. One hundred people from Maine came to Washington and bought land on which they built a sawmill and other industrial concerns. Their plan was that each person was to do the type of work for which he was best fitted. Then as the group prospered, it would by example draw other communities into its system until the whole state would be a socialist commonwealth. Each person was also to have complete freedom in thought and behavior, and before long this emphasis on individuality made it difficult to secure sufficient conformity to any system to keep the industries going. After awhile the whole project became so disorganized that it collapsed.

The most famous of these utopian experiments was one called Home, which was founded in 1897 by three families who left another socialist community that had been operating in Tacoma. The Mutual Home Colony Association was planned as an anarchist settlement where there would be no governmental control beyond what the people had to accept from the state of Washington. The members chose an isolated spot twenty miles from Tacoma without roads or other settlements and hoped to avoid entanglements with the outside world. Within two years, over two hundred people belonged to the Home organization, and they were sufficiently devoted to their ideal of a free, peaceful community that they might have maintained it for a longer period if they had not advocated free love. This doctrine brought in an unstable group which did not care about the welfare of the colony and brought notoriety to the settlement.

In 1901 when President McKinley was murdered by an anarchist, many people in Tacoma became almost hysterical at the thought that Home also represented the hated anarchist philosophy. A mob chartered a steamboat and started for the settlement to burn it down. A minister and the owner of the steamboat who knew that the Home group had no intention of practicing violence were able to disperse the mob. The next year, however, the federal post office barred the newspaper *Discontent,* the Home publication, from the mails because it endorsed free love. This publicity brought all kinds of cultists to the community, and its days of peace seemed to be over.

The colony survived this intrusion, however, and in 1910 still operated its cooperative store and auditorium where speakers were free to present any cause. In that year, several of the members were arrested for indecent exposure because they practiced nude bathing, and they, plus the editor of their paper, spent some time in jail. Gradually the town became like any other, but the early residents who are still living are occasionally pointed out today as the leaders of one of our most devoted and long-lived utopian groups.

Industrial Development

9

AGRICULTURE

Early Farming

When we turn to study the development of many of Washington's industries, we have to begin with the Indians' use of a natural resource, such as wood or fish. This is not the case with agriculture, however. Neither the Coast nor the Plateau Indians cultivated the ground before the white men came. They merely gathered the roots, berries, seeds, and other vegetable products that they found growing wild.

The early maritime fur traders were not in one place long enough to plant crops or raise cattle until the Spaniards made their settlement at Nootka Sound in 1789 and at Neah Bay in 1792. They brought cattle to the former and poultry, hogs, sheep, and goats to the latter. The Canadian and British overland fur traders who followed experimented with small gardens around their post, but they used them only for a few items which they missed keenly—potatoes and occasional green vegetables.

The American fur traders paid more attention to raising food. We have mentioned that the Winships planted a garden as soon as they started their first post. Astor even planned for farming on a commercial scale, intending to sell food as well as lumber to the Russians in Alaska.

After the North West Company bought Astoria, the Canadian fur traders kept the livestock, which was not fenced in, and continued to raise potatoes for their own use. It was not until the North West and Hudson's Bay companies merged and Dr. McLoughlin became the chief factor at Fort Vancouver that raising food became an important occupation.

We have seen that George Simpson, the Hudson's Bay Company governor, who brought McLoughlin to Oregon in 1824, demanded that each fur-trading post be self-supporting. He forbade the brigades to bring to the posts food that could be raised there; and it became necessary for the fur traders to plant crops. The site for Fort Vancouver was chosen partly because it was suited to agriculture, and McLoughlin set out to follow Astor's plan of raising so much food that some could be exported for sale.

He ordered that no cattle be killed until the twenty-seven already there had increased to a sizable herd. By 1836 when the Whitmans and Spaldings arrived, he had 1,000 cattle, 700 hogs, 200 sheep, 500 horses, and 160 oxen at the various Hudson's Bay Company posts, with the greater percentage at Fort Vancouver. He was then ready to start using them as food, and, as we have seen, he lent cattle to the missionaries and other American settlers who were asked to repay him when their own herds had grown to sufficient size.

McLoughlin also had vegetable seeds sent to him from England, and he distributed them to the Hudson's Bay posts and to American settlers. Narcissa Whitman wrote in her diary that when she reached Fort Vancouver in 1836, McLoughlin had apples, grapes, peaches, figs, pears, melons, plums, and a large variety of vegetables, including cucumbers, beans, beets, cabbage, tomatoes, potatoes, turnips, and four thousand bushels of peas. He had raised that year an estimated four thousand bushels of wheat and around seventeen hundred bushels each of oats and barley. McLoughlin built a grist mill to grind flour near Fort Vancouver.

The Americans, too, brought in livestock and seeds since most of them intended to raise food for their own use, at least. Jason Lee brought the first cattle from Missouri to Oregon in 1834, and settlers who followed did also. Since the early immigrants usually were unable to bring more than three or four head of cattle, they still had to rely on the Hudson's Bay Company for additional ones. McLoughlin instructed the factors at Fort Walla Walla, Fort Boise, and Fort Hall to accept exhausted cattle at any of these posts and give the owners a receipt that could be used at Fort Vancouver to procure good livestock in their place.

By 1838 the Hudson's Bay Company posts had increased their agricultural interests to the point where they were more than self-supporting and were selling grain, butter, cheese, wool, and hides in Alaska and elsewhere. The company became concerned over the vastness of its agricultural business since its charter was based on

Stump puller, Grays Harbor County. This contraption, designed on wheels so it could be moved directly over the stump, was operated by horse power. (Courtesy of the University of Washington Library)

fur trading. Consequently, the company set up the Puget Sound Agricultural Company as a separate organization for farming. It had one large farm on the Cowlitz River and another on the Nisqually where thousands of cattle, sheep, and horses were raised in addition to large amounts of grain and vegetables. After the boundary was settled in 1846, the company was given time to dispose of its holdings, and it continued to operate in Washington Territory until 1869.

As we have seen, Michael T. Simmons with his party came north of the Columbia River to the outskirts of present Olympia in 1844. They farmed and in 1846 built a grist mill to grind flour from their wheat. However, their interest in agriculture was not primarily commercial. They raised food for their own use, to a large extent, and depended on lumbering, fishing, and other industries for their income.

As settlers spread out into other sections of Puget Sound during the 1850's, they planted orchards on a commercial scale, and grew other types of food, largely for the California market. Although the California gold rush stimulated the demand for all types of agricultural produce as well as for lumber, California's population remained large enough, even after the gold fever died down, to make it a continuing market for Washington products.

We saw earlier that Dr. Whitman used irrigation at his mission to raise vegetables and grains. In 1860 when miners began to move through the Walla Walla area to the diggings on the Clearwater and Salmon rivers, they needed an outfitting center where they could buy food and other supplies. Present Walla Walla (then called Steptoe City) was the logical point for one. The outfitters started to farm there, using irrigation, and others followed similar procedures at the junction of the Snake and Clearwater rivers where the town of Lewiston sprang up almost overnight. Walla Walla's population quadrupled during the 1860's, and the population west of the Cascades rose, too. In 1870 there were approximately three thousand farms in Washington Territory. Some statistics from the 1860 and 1870 Census show the consequent rise in agriculture: 1860, 27,767 head of livestock; 93,000 bushels of wheat; 158,000 pounds of butter; 1870, 106,708 head of cattle; 217,000 bushels of wheat; 407,000 pounds of butter. Fruit production had trebled, and eight times as much wool was raised in 1870 as in 1860.

During the 1870's and 1880's transcontinental railroads were completed from the East to Puget Sound and local feeder railroads increased. The new transportation had a tremendous effect on agriculture since the lack of a means of sending produce to market easily had been a vital factor in restraining farm development.

In Whitman, Spokane, Klickitat, and Yakima counties, large cattle ranches developed, and fruit raising in the river valleys in Walla Walla, Whitman, and Columbia counties became greater than that on the coast. Sheep ranches became numerous, too, in the Palouse and Klickitat areas.

Although early ranchers planted grains in river bottoms east of the Cascades, it was some time before they realized that the dry Palouse hills would raise grains as well as provide pasture for cattle.

There are many stories about the first experiment in wheat raising in this area. The usual account is that some rancher in digging a well noticed that the soil looked moist and rich to a considerable depth and wondered then if wheat would grow in it. He decided to plant a small amount as an experiment on the sides of a steep hill and, to his astonishment, found that it grew well and produced a high yield.

Undoubtedly such experiments did take place, and a number of ranchers may have had such an experience at about the same time. At any rate, during the 1870's and early 1880's, wheat ranching was begun in Whitman and neighboring counties, with Whitman emerging into the foremost wheat-producing county in the country, raising a $10,000,000 crop in 1910. The Palouse region is still largely devoted to wheat as a crop, although field peas for seed came into favor between 1940 and 1950, and on some farms the peas now bring in more money that wheat. However, wheat equalled nearly 49 per cent of the value of all field and vegetable crops for the period 1957-61. In 1962, 59,440,000 bushels of winter wheat were produced and 7,385,000 bushels of spring wheat, making a total of 66,825,000 bushels. Washington ranked third among the states in that year in the production of winter wheat, bringing in $115,908,000 to its growers. Whitman County ranked first among the counties of Washington in 1962 in the production of both wheat and barley. That year barley was our second largest field crop in acreage and third in value; it has shown marked increase recently because farmers have tended to plant barley instead of wheat when wheat acreage has been reduced in accordance with federal allotments.

Irrigation

Farmers east of the Cascades must irrigate most plants other than grains and seed peas. Since the 1890's the raising of irrigated fruits has been one of our large agricultural industries, particularly in recent years when the water from Grand Coulee Dam began to allow many more thousands of acres in the dry region around Moses Lake to be brought under cultivation.

Not only Whitman, but the Catholic priests on Ahtanum Creek

Early harvest scene in the Palouse country. (Photo in the Woodward Manuscript Collection of the Washington State University Library, Pullman)

in the Yakima region used irrigation ditches at their missions to bring sufficient water to their crops, and they taught the Indians to use water in a similar fashion. After the Yakima War, when white settlers began to come to the Yakima Valley, the farmers pooled their resources to build small dams and canals for more extensive irrigation. As early as 1877 the federal government recognized that some incentive was desirable to encourage prospective settlers to choose dry lands for their claims and attempt to irrigate them. Congress therefore passed the Desert Land Act (1877), which allowed an individual to take possession of as much as 640 acres of dry land for a nominal fee (usually $1.25 per acre). If he provided a water supply, he received title to the claim after a specified time.

In central Washington, the individual settlers could not afford to construct the works necessary to provide sufficient water. The demand for water was great enough, however, that private businessmen put up capital in the 1880's to build bigger irrigation systems from which they leased water to the farmers. The financiers found that the immediate return on the amount of money required to build large irrigation systems was limited, and many of the smaller companies could not continue to operate profitably. If such a firm was already supplying individuals with water, the existing system had to be maintained somehow or the farmers involved would be in a desperate situation. The depression of the 1890's increased the number of insolvencies among irrigation companies.

The state legislature then attempted to come to the rescue of the farmers on irrigated land by appropriating money to dig artesian wells and to buy up the bonds issued by irrigation companies that could not redeem them. In both of these instances, the legislature expected the money appropriated to constitute a revolving fund which would enable the state to get back at least part of the amount as the fees the farmers paid for water increased. When it became obvious that this would not happen, the legislature withdrew from direct financing of this kind.

Another plan that the legislature instituted in the 1890's, however, did prove successful—the creation of irrigation districts. These allow land holders in any part of the state to organize districts, with the approval of the state Department of Conservation, which build irrigation works from assessments paid by the land owners. Diking and drainage districts to control excess water may also be created by a similar procedure. The state legislature also passed laws regulating the way in which individuals may claim water rights.

Such districts could not raise enough money to build the big storage dams necessary for the increasingly widespread acreage under irrigation. In fact, the huge sums required for irrigation on a large scale were more than local or even state governments could provide. Therefore, people turned to Congress with the problem, and in 1894 the first tentative step toward federal construction of dams and accompanying irrigation works was taken when Congress passed the Carey Act, which provided that up to a million acres of federal land be given to any western state that would irrigate it. However, this plan still required too much money from the individual states, and Wyoming was the only state which had taken advantage of the offer by 1902. Therefore, in that year President Theodore Roosevelt appointed a committee, including Congressman Wesley L. Jones of Washington, to propose a bill that would have more local support. The result was the National Reclamation Act by which almost 95 per cent of all money received from the sale of federal lands goes into a fund to be used for the reclamation of arid lands. The Bureau of Reclamation (called the United States Rec-

lamation Service at first) within the United States Department of the Interior is in charge of the projects.

The Interior Department had to persuade one of the remaining private companies, the Washington Irrigation Company, to sell its irrigation system to the federal government in order to have control of sufficient water to form a successful irrigation project in the Yakima area, and the sale was made in 1905. The water users also had to give up their former leases if those leases represented more water than was actually being used. With the help of Representative Jones, the farmers agreed to substitute leases with the Reclamation Service, and the Yakima project got under way. Dams and distribution systems were added for the Tieton, the Wapato, Kittitas, and Okanogan units by 1911.

Grand Coulee Dam

At this early period, the prospect of using water from the Columbia River in the dry central part of the state was not considered feasible because the banks are so high and steep that the task of pumping the river water up to the level of the fields above the bed of the river seemed to be too formidable. Even at that time, however, the idea of utilizing the tremendous flow of water from the Columbia teased the imagination of certain far-sighted individuals, particularly Rufus Woods, editor of the Wenatchee *Daily World*. One day in 1918 when he was having lunch with two friends in Ephrata, they discussed the problem of irrigating the fertile but dry soil of central Washington. One of the men, William Clapp, suddenly proposed the plan of damming the Columbia and pumping the water back into Grand Coulee as a reservoir. Woods leaped at this proposal, rushed back to Wenatchee, and the next day used the following headline in his paper:

FORMULATE BRAND NEW IDEA FOR IRRIGATION
GRANT, ADAMS, FRANKLIN COUNTIES, COVERING
MILLION ACRES OR MORE . . . LAST AND NEWEST
AND MOST AMBITIOUS IDEA CONTEMPLATES

Modern harvest scene near Pomeroy, in Garfield County. (Photo by Washington State Department of Commerce and Economic Development)

TURNING OF COLUMBIA RIVER BACK INTO ITS OLD BED IN GRAND COULEE, THE DEVELOPMENT OF A POWER PLANT EQUAL TO NIAGARA AND THE CONSTRUCTION OF THE GREATEST IRRIGATION PROJECT IN THE WORLD—FIRST CONCEIVED BY WILLIAM CLAPP OF EPHRATA, WASH.

James O'Sullivan, also of Ephrata, joined in supporting the plan to utilize the Grand Coulee as a storage reservoir. Water from the lake would be used to raise the level of water in the river to a point where it could be easily pumped over the edge into the Coulee. Ditches could then run off from it.

We noted in our discussion of the geological formation of the Columbia Basin that the present Grand Coulee represents the bed which the Columbia used for several thousand years while its former route was blocked by a glacier. Then when the ice withdrew, the river returned to its old bed, leaving the temporary depression a huge dry ditch.

A rival plan was advocated by E. F. Blaine, a member of the Reclamation Service's staff for the Yakima Irrigation Project. He proposed using the north Idaho lakes (particularly Priest and Pend Oreille) as the reservoirs from which water would be siphoned by gravity to the Columbia Basin. Controversy as to whether this gravity plan or the one calling for a dam at Grand Coulee was preferable raged bitterly for many years. The crux of the debate was whether the system was to be almost entirely one for irrigation or whether the water held back by the dam should be used to generate electricity as well as to irrigate the surrounding country.

For hydroelectric power, a higher dam was needed than for irrigation alone. Army engineers pointed out that the power project could sell enough electricity to reduce the cost to irrigation farmers from $400 per acre (the figure for the gravity system) to $85.00 per acre. When the depression of the 1930's made gigantic public projects desirable, the construction of a high dam at Grand Coulee fitted beautifully into the scheme, and work was begun on it as a P.W.A. project in 1933.

By 1941 electricity was available for sale, and since this coincided with the unprecedented spurt of industrial activity all over the country in supplying arms and equipment for our armed forces in World War II, the hydroelectric function of the Grand Coulee project rather than its irrigation potential was the first one emphasized. In 1937 Bonneville Dam had been completed on the Lower Columbia, and the Bonneville Power Administration was created by Congress to sell the power generated there to public and private power agencies. After Grand Coulee and other local federal dams were completed, authority to sell their power was added by Congress to BPA.

During the war, we could not produce enough electricity to supply the demand. In 1943, for example, our regional per-capita use was 3,500 kilowatt-hours in contrast to 1,410 kilowatt-hours for the whole country. Grand Coulee and Bonneville dams produced 63 per cent (1,336,400 kilowatts) of the electricity in the Columbia Basin. Plants owned by other governmental units produced an additional 3 per cent, leaving 34 per cent to be generated from privately owned plants.

Northwest Power Pool

In order to make more efficient use of the power available, in 1942 the public and private utility companies in parts of Oregon, Montana, Washington, Idaho, and Utah made an agreement, called the Northwest Power Pool arrangement, in which they accepted allocations of power according to a formula for firm and interruptable power. Since the area covered two time belts, peak loads came at different hours, and transmitting local surpluses from one time zone to the other increased the power capacity of the Pacific Northwest by three hundred thousand kilowatts without installing any more generating equipment. By the end of the war, general consumption of electricity had increased to the point that the pool was still necessary. Such a voluntary arrangement represented a new development in power distribution.

Planning agencies were concerned about a threatened power shortage in 1965-66, but it has now seemingly been averted by a new development of salable power at the Hanford Atomic Works. The reactor at Hanford generates steam as a by-product of its production of plutonium, and in 1962 Congress authorized the Atomic Energy Commission and the Bonneville Power Administration to make contracts with any public or private agency (other than the federal government) to use this waste steam for the generation of electricity. The Washington Public Power Supply System, which is a group of sixteen Washington State public utility districts, received the contract to build and operate the necessary facilities for producing the electric power. By this means, more than nine hundred thousand kilowatts of firm power will be added to that available for sale to public and private power companies through the Bonneville Power Administration. Experts believe that this will make the total amount of electric power sufficient to meet the present demand. In addition, it will bring an estimated $125,000,000 back into the United States Treasury and reduce the cost of the Hanford project to the government by that amount.

An additional source of power for the future will be the dams authorized in a treaty recently ratified by the United States and Canadian governments. Canada intends to construct three large storage dams in British Columbia, and the United States will add the Libby Dam in Montana. Its reservoir will extend forty-two miles into Canada; consequently it could not be built without Canadian consent. Additional kilowatts produced at our present dams as a result of this proposed storage will be shared on an equal basis by the two countries. Our share of the additional power will amount to approximately two million salable kilowatts.

The Bonneville Power Administration anticipates an increase of 7.1 per cent a year in energy requirements. Since it started operations in 1938, it has sold 363 billion kilowatt-hours of hydroelectric energy. This would be enough to meet the present power requirements of the whole country for more than six months. In 1962 the power sales amounted to 29.2 billion kilowatt-hours for $69,000,000.

Columbia Basin Project

At the end of the war, the Bureau of Reclamation was able to concentrate its attention more fully on putting into effect the irrigation phase of the Columbia Basin program. In 1947, 7,750 acres were irrigated directly from the Columbia River, whereas when the maximum volume of water from the Coulee Dam irrigation system is in use, the Department of the Interior envisages having 1,330,000 acres in the Basin under irrigation. The state Department of Conservation says that as of 1962, 450,886 acres of land have been irrigated from water made available by the Columbia Basin Project. The United States Department of the Interior analyzed the prospective cost of the entire system in 1947 as totaling an estimated $5,598,494,000. Over four billion of this figure will be used for water-resource development and over one billion for hydroelectric power transmission. Potential revenue from the sale of electricity will be more than $560,000,000 above the percentage planned as reimbursable, 84 per cent or $4,728,066,000. This is the portion to be devoted to phases covered through the Department of the Interior—irrigation, power development, and domestic water supply. The nonreimbursable features are those covered through the War Department and other agencies of the federal government—flood control, navigation, pollution control, and wildlife maintenance.

One major problem has been to keep the size of individual farms small enough to prevent speculators from building up large acreages for sale at high prices and to prevent a few large landowners from buying all of the new land in the Columbia Basin put on sale by the federal government. The original law specified that water would not be delivered to units of more than 160 acres held by any one family. However, the farmers maintained that machinery for use on an irrigated farm cost so much that a family could not make a profit from the crops raised on that small an acreage in view of the initial investment required. Consequently, in 1957 Congress modified the law to allow a family buying land after September 1, 1957, to receive water on an amount of land up to 320 acres. People who already held more than one unit at that time (chiefly those having had large acreages for many years under dry farming) are pressing for the removal of the date restriction.

In 1960 water was available for 430,982 acres in the Columbia Basin Project; 440,064 acres in 1961, and 450,886 acres in 1962. Land actually under cultivation during those years was: 283,900; 307,800; and 340,200 acres. From 1952 to 1962 the population in the Basin had risen from thirty thousand to seventy thousand.

Water was available to 425,500 acres in 1962, and 299,364 acres were under cultivation. The gross value of the crops produced in that year was $40,912,096. In 1952 potatoes represented 59 per cent of the value of all crops grown; by 1960, although the percentage had dropped to less than 28 per cent, potatoes were still the most valuable single crop. Other main ones are dry beans, sugar beets, and grains for feed. Many agricultural economists predict that the expansion of agriculture in the Basin to its full capacity will depend for financial success on the increased population of the area inasmuch as our distance from markets in the Middle West and East is still a deterrent to the sale of produce there on a competitive basis.

Crop Summary

Preliminary total of the gross value of farm production in 1962 was $644,512,000, a rise of approximately $41,000,000 from the final figure for 1961—$603,442,000. The volume of production for all farm commodities in 1962 was the largest on record—nearly 9,800,000 tons, 7 per cent greater than in 1961. Except for certain livestock and fruit, prices were enough higher than those for 1961 to bring the increase in value for the year to 10 per cent.

The preliminary estimate of total tonnage and corresponding value for 1962 is: field crops, 7,164,699 ($276,911,000); fruit crops, 727,630 ($75,597,000); berry crops, 39,120 ($10,615,000); vegetable crops 461,950 ($29,034,000). Livestock and livestock products added 1,386,546 tons, having a value of $223,679,000. Of the total value of farm production in 1962, field and seed crops accounted for 43 per cent; fruit, nuts, and berries for 13.4 per cent; vegetables for 4.5 per cent; specialties for 4.4 per cent, and livestock and livestock products for 34.7 per cent. Our state ranks first in the country in the production of hops, late summer potatoes, spearmint, dry field peas, and commercial apples; second in peppermint, processing of green peas, Bartlett pears, apricots; third in pears other than Bartlett, prunes, asparagus, strawberries, sweet cherries, winter wheat, alfalfa seed; fourth in cranberries, grapes, barley; fifth in rye; and sixth in spring wheat, excluding durum.

Within the state, the value of the top twenty specific commodities

Hop harvest near Yakima. Washington ranks first in the United States in the production of hops. (Photo by Washington State Department of Commerce and Economic Development)

in 1962 had the following order: wheat, milk, cattle and calves, apples, hay, eggs, barley, sugar beets, potatoes, dry field peas, hops, chickens and broilers, green peas, all pears, strawberries, all cherries, asparagus, hogs, alfalfa seed, and grain corn.

Industrial Revolutions

The need for expensive equipment has increased greatly for farmers both on irrigated land and on dry-farming ranches. The wheat farmer needs many heavy tractors and other mechanized vehicles, just as water pipes, sprinkling systems, and other types of machinery are essential for irrigation. Practically all farmers use electricity for milking machines, brooders, extra lighting in chicken houses and barns, and countless other needs.

For eastern industries, the invention of the steam engine brought about such tremendous changes in working methods that it is said to have produced an "industrial revolution" in the late 1700's. A century later the use of electricity increased speed and variety of industrial processes in even greater proportions and so is said to have brought about the second industrial revolution. Then the financial world changed from predominantly individual or small-company ownership of a business to the control of an industry by a large corporation. The change is often referred to as the "commercial revolution."

In the East, these "revolutions" occurred in succession, and business people could adjust to them one at a time, for the most part. However, by the time our region was settled sufficiently that its industry was well under way, both steam and electric power were available for businesses in our cities, and corporate financing was becoming general. Until the end of the First World War, farming in our state was not done on a scale large enough to allow for the purchase of expensive steam- or gasoline-driven machines by the average farmer. During that war, however, the demand for wheat and other foodstuffs increased farming prosperity to such an extent that a farmer could begin to mechanize his farm. By the beginning of the Second World War, government aid to farmers through the Rural Electrification Administration and other agencies and the extension of private power lines had made electricity available for most farmers who wanted to electrify their farms. Postwar agricultural prosperity has allowed them to expand all types of mechanization until agriculture qualifies as the second biggest industry in the state, manufacturing being first, tourist expenditures third, lumbering fourth, mining fifth, and fishing sixth. For our farmers, then, all of these developments have been compressed into such a small space of time that they are actually confronted with the three revolutions at once, and their adjustment has been much more difficult for that reason.

FISHING

Early Methods

The Indians were our first fishermen, and their methods of taking fish ranged from killing whales with harpoons thrown from the ocean-going canoes of our northern Coast Indians, to the spears, small traps, and weirs used on our rivers. For a review of these techniques, see chapter 2.

The white traders and settlers at first bought fish from the Indians, or they did their own fishing. During the eighteenth century and the first half of the nineteenth, however, a satisfactory means of commercial canning had not been devised, so that it was difficult to preserve fish long enough to sell them at any great distance from the fishing grounds.

Salted Salmon

Some of the American maritime fur traders did salt a few barrels of salmon for use on their ships, and the extra supply was sold in the East. It was this practice which gave Nathaniel Wyeth the idea of setting up a salmon factory near the mouth of the Columbia River where salmon could be salted on a large scale for sale in Boston. When his project failed, no further attempts were made by Americans to sell cured salmon in large quantities until settlement was well under way. The Hudson's Bay Company, however, exported salted salmon to Hawaii, the Orient, and England.

Canning of Salmon

In 1866 William Hume, an American, built a salmon cannery at Eagle Cliff about forty miles above the mouth of the Columbia. It was only the second cannery in the entire United States. Four thousand cases were produced the first year, eighteen thousand the second, and twenty-eight thousand the third (1868). William Hume plus his three brothers built most of their canneries on the Columbia because it was close to the Oregon markets which, in turn, forwarded many cases of canned salmon to California. In 1881 there were thirty-five canneries on the Columbia (almost half of which belonged to the Hume family) and only two on Puget Sound, both at Mukilteo. In the 1890's the supply of salmon in the Columbia began to decrease, and the population on the Sound had increased greatly. Therefore, the favored location was reversed, and Puget Sound became the center of the fishing industry. The peak load from the Columbia was 634,000 cases in 1895. By 1952 almost four times as much fish was packed on the Sound as on the Columbia—611,823 cases for the former and 165,045 cases for the latter.

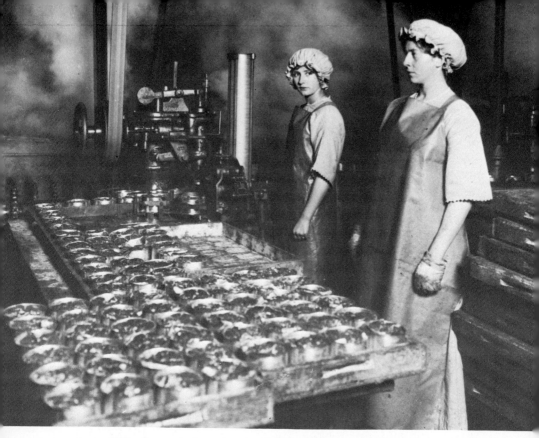

Apex Fish Company's cannery, 1913. (Original photo belongs to the Washington State Historical Society; courtesy of the University of Washington Library)

The Sound reached its peak production in 1913 when over 2,500,000 cases were packed. The runs then became so much smaller that the canneries had to look to Alaskan fishing grounds for much of their catch, but Seattle has remained the base of the main fleet. Salmon is still the most important item in the state's fishing industry. Washington salmon had a value of $7,615,471 in 1962. Halibut and shellfish came next with a value of $5,300,976 and $3,159,229, respectively.

In common with our other industries, the techniques of fish preservation have gone through radical changes. In the early days, a few men went out in small boats with traps, gill nets, and seines of various kinds and brought the catch back to the canneries (often houseboats along the shore) where the fish were cleaned by hand. One of the Hume brothers began to hire Chinese to do this disagreeable job, for white people did not want that kind of work when times were good.

The cans were usually made in the cannery, and their construction was a laborious process, involving soldering the edges of a cylinder together and then attaching a bottom with solder. At the same time, workers cleaned the fish and cut them into the proper sizes for the cans. When the cans were filled, the lids were soldered on, and the cans were set in a hot-water bath for cooking.

In 1902, E. A. Smith of Seattle invented a machine for cleaning salmon which, with improvements, soon took the name of the "iron chink" because it did the work previously performed by many Chinese. This machine greatly speeded up the preparation of fish, and, when tools were devised by 1915 to make cans and to cut the fish into pieces to fit, the mechanization of fish canning was almost complete.

Fresh Fish

There were, however, many problems of preserving the fish before the canning took place. Prior to the invention of the gasoline motor, fishing boats were largely powered by sails and oars, there being only a few propelled by steam engines. Because these early boats were slow, the crews could not go far from shore or the fish would spoil before they could get to the canneries.

The use of gasoline engines in fishing boats revolutionized commercial fishing. Soon after the first of these engines reached the Sound in 1903, firms on the coast were building power boats for use as purse seiners that were highly successful. Living quarters were added for the crews so that the boats could go out to sea for halibut and other fish.

Frozen Fish

At first, fish were preserved in ice as the radius of the fishermen's trips increased, but the invention of mechanical refrigeration was such an improvement over ice-packing that it produced what amounted to another revolution in the preservation and shipping of fish. The use of refrigerated railway cars, trucks, and storerooms on fishing boats and steamships meant that there was no limit to the distance fish could be shipped. As refrigerating techniques were improved to allow for quick freezing of food, Washington's output of frozen fish became increasingly important.

Many fishing vessels are now floating canneries where the fish are cleaned and canned. A large amount of the catch is also kept packed in ice and sold fresh. The halibut vessels from Seattle, for example, may go as far as the Aleutian Islands for their catch, and, to avoid going all the way back with each load, they often take what is to be sold fresh to Prince Rupert, British Columbia, where wholesale firms buy the fish and complete the distribution. What is to be sold as frozen fish is cleaned and packaged on board ship.

Shellfish

In addition to salmon, halibut, cod, sole, and other similar fish, shellfish represent an important part of the state's economy. It was pointed out in chapter 1 that the native Olympia oysters found on the Sound (particularly on Willapa Peninsula) are famous throughout the country for their flavor and delicate texture. In addition to the Olympia oyster, which is once again reaching commercial status after severe depletion, Japanese oysters, called Pacific oysters, continue to be raised for canning. On Willapa Peninsula alone, one hundred thousand cases or more are canned each year.

The Pacific razor clam, which has to be dug out of the sand by hand, has been so much desired that the stock was nearly wiped out during the 1930's. The state Department of Fisheries then forbade commercial operators to take them; but a small number may now be sold from Copalis Beach. Canneries for hard-shell clams operate at various points on the Sound.

Our crab and shrimp production is also of value, although our shrimp grounds were almost depleted by overfishing at the time of the First World War. A new series of beds have now been developed twenty to thirty miles off Westport, however, which has resulted in a jump from seventy-six thousand pounds to two million pounds in 1957. In 1962 the catch had fallen to 1,398,964 pounds. The industry has been made possible by the invention of a new peeler that shells the shrimp, for they are too small to be profitably processed by hand.

LUMBERING

Early Methods

The history of lumbering, until recently our state's leading industry, goes back to the Indians' use of wood. In chapter 2, we discussed the methods by which the Coast Indians made houses, canoes, boxes, eating utensils, and other items from wood.

The early white maritime traders who came toward the end of the eighteenth century likewise had many uses for wood. We mentioned earlier that John Meares in 1788 built a post at Nootka and constructed the first ship in the Pacific Northwest, the *Northwest America*. This lumber had to be cut and sawed by hand. The overland traders set up wooden buildings, too, and Astor planned to ship lumber as one of the commercial products for sale to the Russians in Alaska.

As with agriculture and fishing, however, it was the Hudson's Bay Company that actually started lumbering on a commercial scale. In 1827 John McLoughlin built a sawmill at Fort Vancouver which turned out about three thousand board feet per day at first. Until waterpower was used to run the saws, the logs were sawed by hand, with one man in a pit sawing from the under side and one man above sawing from the top. By 1833 the company was selling fifty thousand feet of lumber to China in a year.

Michael T. Simmons, who was one of the first group of Americans to defy the Hudson's Bay Company and settle north of the river, built the next sawmill in the present state of Washington in 1847. He bought the machinery for his sawmill from the Hudson's Bay Company, which had purchased newer equipment.

A. D. Abernethy constructed a sawmill on the north bank of the Columbia in 1848, and in 1851 another was built at the mouth of the Nisqually River by James McAllister. By that time the California gold rush had brought so many miners to the San Francisco area that the demand for lumber enabled sawmills on the Sound to export lumber to California. It was mentioned earlier that before the Denny party had located a site for their cabins at Seattle, ships from California appeared in the Sound looking for lumber.

To satisfy this demand, the incoming settlers built mills as fast as possible. Henry L. Yesler built the first steam sawmill in 1853 at Seattle, and by 1860 there were thirty-two sawmills in Washington Territory, twenty-five of which were on Puget Sound.

As the lumber market expanded, California and eastern capitalists began to build sawmills in Washington Territory. An example of the activity of eastern capitalists is the Puget Mill Company, situated at Port Gamble. Its owners bought up huge tracts of timberland, some of which sold at that time for around $1.25 an acre. They also ran their own steamship line so that they could carry their lumber cheaply by transporting other cargo, in addition, on a commercial basis.

By 1869 all of the sawmills, employing 474 men, were cutting around 128,743,000 board feet of lumber, and the figures did not increase much during the 1870's. Tacoma, Seattle, Port Gamble, Port Discovery, and Port Madison were lumbering centers. Portable mills were used most frequently east of the Cascades since that region lacked adequate water facilities. However, a permanent mill was built in Spokane in 1871. In 1889 there were 310 sawmills which cut 1,064,000,000 board feet of lumber. By 1934, 419 sawmills cut lumber valued at $16,332,586. In 1962, 5,051,344,000 board feet of lumber was cut in the state, according to the state Department of Natural Resources.

Mechanical Improvements

The great increase in the amount of lumber cut was partially due to mechanical improvements. At first, trees at the edge of a stream were cut by hand with an axe. The loggers cut them into logs small enough to be pushed into the water where they floated down to the mill which had to be placed on a river.

As the demand for lumber remained at a high level and desirable timber near the streams had been cut away, some means had to be found for using trees farther away from water. Teams of oxen were introduced for this purpose since they could pull much greater weight than men could. As a further aid, skid roads, consisting of heavy wooden slabs laid across the road in the fashion of railroad ties except much farther apart, were built in the woods. The timbers were greased so that the logs would slide over them more easily. Cordu-

Oxen pulling logs on Corduroy Road. (Washington State Historical Society)

roy roads were skid roads having smaller planks laid close together.

The next step was the construction of a logging railroad with wooden rails that carried flat cars on which logs were loaded. Until the 1880's, however, the cars were pulled by horses. As far as is known, the first steam locomotive for pulling logs was used in 1883 by Blackman Brothers at Marysville. Later, the logging operators bought used standard engines, such as one at Port Blakely Mill which in 1896 pulled seventy-six logging cars thirty miles. After 1900, special logging locomotives and tracks came into general use.

Steam engines were also used to run strong pulleys or winches, called donkeys. From a crude type available in the 1880's, the steam donkey quickly developed into an efficient machine for hoisting and loading logs, being replaced in the 1900's by the present-day gasoline and diesel varieties. Power chain saws, tractors for pulling logs, huge tongs for grasping logs, and many other devices are now gasoline-driven. Trucks are used largely to carry logs to the mills or to the nearest shipping point.

Within the mills, there were the same types of radical changes in methods as in the woods. Circular saws and power carriages were

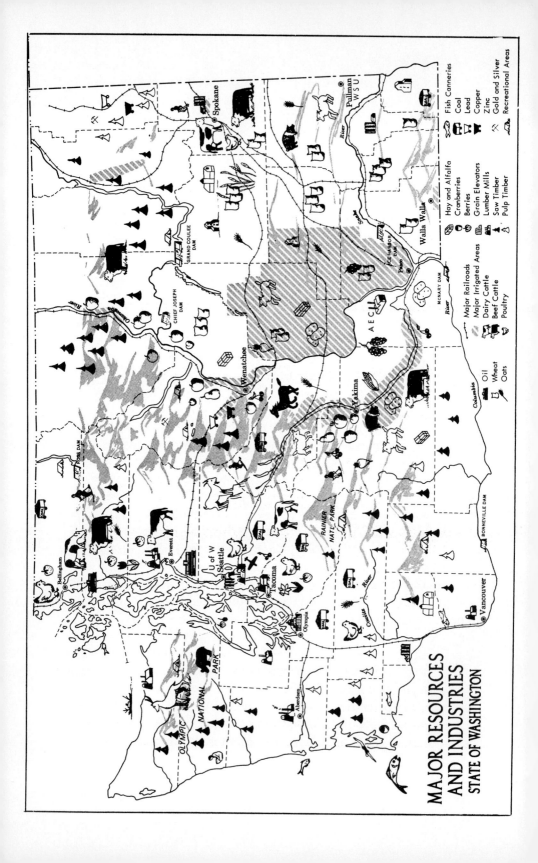

MAJOR RESOURCES
AND INDUSTRIES
STATE OF WASHINGTON

among the first devices to be mechanized. A power carriage is a frame that pushes a log under a saw which then cuts through it at the proper place, and the carriage moves forward again for the desired thickness of the slab. Trimmers, edgers, and many other lumbering tools followed.

As steam, gasoline, and finally electric power were introduced, lumbering became one of our most highly mechanized industries. In a modern mill, the bark is usually first removed from a log by a hydraulic hose which forces water under such tremendous pressure against a log that its bark is stripped off. Saws then cut it into chunks which are graded and reduced further in size to strips of high-grade lumber, or to rough timbers for railroad ties, posts, or other purposes. The chips and other waste parts of the log are sold to pulp and paper mills for use in making paper, cardboard, boxes, and wallboard, a few of the items derived from waste wood and from trees of insufficient size or quality for lumber.

Plywood is another major industry based on wood. Douglas fir is particularly adapted to its production since it can be peeled easily by electric lathes into sheets as thin as one-tenth of an inch. When three or more sheets are glued together, they form a strong, light panel, which is in increasing demand for building purposes. If these strips of veneer are glued together under steam heat and pressure, they form hardboard, a substance much like plywood and having the added advantage that it can be made from chips left as waste material from lumbering.

Washington's manufacture of furniture and other finished wooden articles has grown into an important industry for our state. For a review of the centers of such manufacture as well as the areas for various types of lumbering, see chapter 1.

MINING

Early Gold Strikes

The effect of the gold discoveries in the Pacific Northwest has been mentioned earlier in connection with the Colville and Orofino strikes, both of which stimulated settlement in those areas and caused outfitting centers to develop along the way. There are many

Steam engine for logging, early 1900's. (Photo in the Woodward Manuscript Collection of the Washington State University Library, Pullman)

fascinating stories about the finding of gold and about the adventures and hardships of the miners.

The most commonly told version of the Colville gold discovery is that in 1852 Angus McDonald, the Hudson's Bay Company agent at Fort Colville, showed a sack of gold-bearing sand from California to his men at the fort. When one of them later stooped down to drink from the Columbia River, he saw some sand that looked like the black California dirt. He took off his hat and scooped up some of the gravel and water at the edge and shook it gently for a minute or two. When he carefully poured off the water and sand, he saw some tiny flakes of gold left in the bottom of his hat.

Since the Hudson's Bay Company wanted to keep Americans out of the area as long as possible, the officers did not publicize their discovery; however, they did send word to some of their personal friends in the Willamette Valley, the ex-Hudson's Bay Company employees who, as we saw earlier, had settled there when they retired. By the following spring, a few French Canadians from that section of Oregon were at Colville taking out gold.

By the summer of 1855, therefore, sufficient word of the gold deposits had reached the public that an occasional group of miners was trying to push through central Washington to the Colville area. As we have seen, the Yakimas, who had just signed a treaty which promised them that white people would stay off their reservation, were angered. A miner on his way from Puget Sound to Fort Colville was murdered near the Yakima country in August, 1855. Governor Stevens in his *Railroad Reports* tells of meeting some miners from Colville at Antoine Plante's in the Spokane country on his way back from the Blackfoot Council in November, 1855. Later he enrolled eighteen of them in a Spokane volunteer unit. On the basis of accounts left by people who were in the Colville country at that time, however, one competent present-day scholar thinks that there was no real rush for the Colville diggings before 1856 when General Wool closed the eastern part of Washington Territory to settlement because of the Yakima War.

Although miners were exempted from Wool's order, it was so dangerous to be in the area that not many dared to cross from the Sound to Fort Colville. A number of those who did reach Colville went on to the Fraser River area where gold had also been found.

At the close of the Yakima War in 1858, eastern Washington and Idaho were reopened to settlement, and interest in the Colville gold fields was revived. However, in March, 1858, reports from British Columbia were so alluring that the main mining rush went in that direction, both from Colville and directly from the Sound. Activity by the miners and their outfitters was heavy enough in the northeastern section of Washington Territory, even then, that the legislature in its 1858-59 session created Spokane County. So few of the incoming miners remained, however, that it was not until 1863 that the population seemed to warrant the creation of a second county in the region—Stevens. By that time Spokane County was not sufficiently populated to maintain a county organization and in 1864 the legislature attached it to Stevens County. It was not recreated until 1879.

The Fraser River mines were not the only ones to compete with

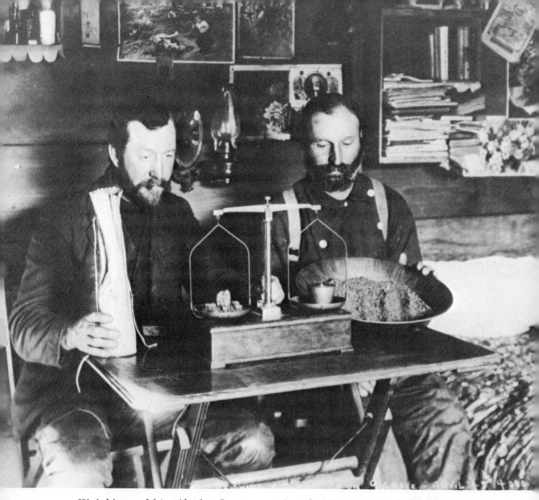

Weighing gold in Alaska: It was a serious business to weigh $4,000 worth of gold. The gold dust in the pan was weighed and then packed into the leather bag for shipment to the nearest assay office. Similar scenes took place inside the cabins of lucky prospectors during gold rushes in the Pacific Northwest. (Seattle Historical Society)

those around Colville for people's attention. In 1860 E. D. Pierce discovered gold on Orofino Creek, a tributary of the Clearwater River. Pierce had been a prospector in the California gold rush and then had come to the Nez Perce country in 1852 to trade for horses and cattle, which he took back to California to sell. As he traveled through the Snake River country, he looked for gold. In 1857 he returned to the Walla Walla area to trade and remained there since the Yakima War made it unwise to prospect in the Nez Perce country. In 1860 he gathered a small group of prospectors in Walla

Walla, and they headed for the Nez Perce region despite the protests of Indian agents. They found evidence of gold all along the Clearwater River, and in October the group decided that Orofino Creek was the place where they wanted to place their mining camp.

After a few days, the men went back to Walla Walla and reported what they had found. A month later (November, 1860), thirty-three men returned to Orofino while Pierce went to Olympia to try to persuade the legislature to grant him and his friends a charter to build a wagon road from Walla Walla to the mines. In the spring, Pierce took additional men to the diggings, and the combined group brought out $800 in gold dust which was shipped to Portland. This immediately produced a "gold fever" that resulted in a rush of prospectors and outfitters who soon made a flourishing town out of Walla Walla.

By June, 1861, newspapers in Portland reported that farms in the Willamette Valley were suffering because so many farmers had left for the gold fields. Prices for labor had gone up even in California because miners from there, too, had gone to the Clearwater-Salmon region as prospectors. Two new steamboats were built to carry the traffic on the Columbia and Snake rivers as far as the mouth of the Clearwater where in 1861 the town of Lewiston sprang up as a second outfitting center. Pierce City, Elk City, and Florence were some of the other boom towns to develop. Twenty-five hundred men were reported to be prospecting at that time, and four or five thousand more were making a living in other ways connected with supplying the miners. As the result of this particular boom, Portland developed rapidly into the financial center where the gold dust was brought and shipped on to San Francisco.

Placer Mining

These early miners practiced placer mining, techniques used for securing gold found on the surface of the ground, usually in dry beds of streams or at the edges of flowing creeks. The simplest method for retrieving such gold was "panning." The pan was ordinarily about twelve inches wide and six or eight inches deep, used both for dipping up gold-bearing gravel and for baking bread.

The prospector dipped up the gravel, sand, and water where he thought gold existed and shook the pan gently in order to force any gold particles to the bottom. He would pour off a top layer, shake the pan further, pour off another layer, and repeat the process until, if he was lucky, gold flakes were left at the bottom. The miner usually poured in quicksilver to bring the gold together; that way more gold could be secured than if he tried to pour it out without amalgamation.

The next step in order of complication was the use of the rocker, which looked like a cradle with a perforated iron sheet at one end. One man shoveled dirt into it while another man poured water on top and rocked it back and forth to separate the gold which would then fall to the bottom of the rocker.

A more complicated device was the sluice, which consisted of boxes arranged on an incline so that water could run from the top one to the ones below. Water from a stream would be diverted to run through the sluice, and a greater percentage of the gold was secured by this method since the gravel was washed more than once. After the use of hydraulic power was possible, a great amount of dirt could be sluiced by a powerful stream of water, and large-scale dredging operations came into use.

One person could pan gold, and there were examples of lone prospectors during the early days. However, even this type of mining was much faster and safer with a group of men, and a mining company was the rule. When a member of such a group found a spot that seemed rich enough in gold to warrant digging, he was allowed one claim by virtue of having discovered the strike and another as a member of the party. The claims ordinarily ran across the gulch or stream bed from bank to bank and were usually one hundred feet wide.

Since many of our miners had already prospected in California, the organization of mining groups here followed the California pattern. Each party at once held a miners' meeting at which they elected a judge, sheriff, and recorder and adopted strict rules. The officers then enforced the rules. The "miners' court" passed on disputes or charges that somebody had broken the rules. Although a mining camp is often thought of as a lawless place, this judgment is seldom applicable to the first group of prospectors in a given area. The prospectors' success in getting the gold out safely depended on an orderly process, and usually the "hangers-on" who came later and tried to prey on the miners once a strike was successful made up the violent element.

The rules adopted by most mining parties concerned the duties of the group. One of these was always the amount of work required to hold a claim, called the "representation" that the prospector had to make. Each member must work one or more days at the site, whatever figure was voted by the majority of miners themselves. Sometimes, a miner was not allowed to hold his claim if he left the site for more than seventy-two hours. Required work consisted of clearing brush from the claim, bringing in provisions, building a cabin, or other acts for the welfare of the group. The miners also decided the length of time when the claim would be laid over, that is, when work would be halted because of either snow or lack of water. During such a time, no one could jump a person's claim because of his absence. Moreover, a skeleton crew had to stay to saw lumber, make sluices, and protect the site.

Soon Chinese laborers were brought into the Idaho area largely for the purpose of going through the gravel already washed by the white prospectors to take out the small amounts of gold still remaining. Some came direct from China; some from California. Ordinarily, a Chinese contractor would buy a washed-out claim from a group of white prospectors and send in Chinese to work it again. One record exists of forty Chinese having been sent to one Idaho camp by a Chinese firm. They worked patiently through the tailings (the washed gravel) for a much smaller return than the white miners would accept, and, when they had paid to the owner the amount stipulated, they became laundry workers, fruit pickers, or servants. In Canada they were treated like all other workers, but at diggings in the United States' part of the Pacific Northwest, they were forced to pay a special tax and in a number of instances were mistreated. Economists now point out that in spite of such discrimination, the Chinese miners saved for the area several millions of dollars in gold dust that would otherwise have been lost.

Quartz Mining

In addition to gold particles found in surface gravel, there are much more substantial deposits of gold in veins deep underground. Such quartz-lode mining requires an individual or firm with sufficient capital to pay for mining machinery. Consequently, as soon as an early prospector found indications of a rich vein, he tried to interest a financier in putting up sufficient money to mine the ore. Portland capitalists began to invest money in such projects in the early 1860's almost as soon as the first placer mining began. New York capitalists were responsible for much of Montana's development of quartz mining, so that again the complaint was made that the use of "foreign" capital in such enterprises meant the draining off to the East of another of our natural resources.

Quartz mining of ore near the surface of the ground could be done by an arrastra, a machine used by the Spaniards for mining gold in Central and South America. It consisted of a post with an attached sweep set in the middle of a circle paved with rocks. A block of granite was fastened to the sweep, and chunks of the quartz were laid on the rocks. A mule (or other animal) then dragged the granite over the quartz as it walked round and round the circle, hitched to the sweep. The granite block crushed the ore finely enough that the gold could be removed with quicksilver. This method took little capital, and many miners were able to set up such a machine.

It was too slow, however, to satisfy most of the early prospectors if they could interest a capitalist in constructing a mill. Water wheels were used at first to provide power to raise heavy weights, called stamps, which would fall with great force on chunks of quartz placed in a box. The stamp would crush the ore to bits, and, as fine particles of gold were pressed against the sides of the box, they would pass through a fine screen provided for that purpose. As steam and electricity were used for the power to crush the ore and extract the precious metals, the mills became very expensive.

In the area of Blewett Pass in the Cascades, remains of several of these various stages of mining were still visible a few years ago. Along Squak Creek there was placer mining; also wooden water wheels used to move the sweep for an arrastra could be seen. On the east bank of Peshastin Creek at Blewett an arrastra was cut out of the rock wall itself. Farther down the creek was the first stamp mill in the state and the Blewett Mill, which contained twenty stamps.

Gold was discovered in that general area in 1860, the year when, as we have seen, prospectors located the Clearwater-Salmon fields.

At that time, goldseekers were combing all accessible areas of the Pacific Northwest for evidence of the ore. In the Cascades and Okanogan Highlands, however, the proportion of surface gold was smaller than that underground, so that there was more quartz than placer mining.

The Holden mines in the Cascades at the tip of Lake Chelan are an example of a large-scale company operation. The outcrop was first noticed in 1887, and in 1892 J. H. Holden staked it out on a grubstake. Various companies tested it, but plans for its exploitation did not materialize until the 1930's, and then the depression halted the construction of a mill. In 1937 the Howe Sound Company of New York, the holding company for the Britannia Mining and Smelting Company, formed a Chelan Division, built a mill, and began treatment of ore.

Ore Refineries

As was the case with agriculture and lumbering, most of the minerals produced were shipped out of the Pacific Northwest for final reduction until electrolytic processes were discovered. Then our hydroelectric capacity made it advantageous for more companies to use the electricity produced here to refine ores completely.

There were a few smelters on the Sound even before the electrolytic era. In 1889, for example, W. R. Rust built the Tacoma Smelter to treat ores, and in 1893 the Puget Sound Reduction Company built a plant in Everett in which it smelted ores of lead, gold, silver, and arsenic and refined the furnace products. In 1901 the Tacoma Smelter was treating four hundred tons of ore a day, and in 1902 its output was increased by the addition of a copper blast furnace. Electrolysis was begun there in 1907, and by 1939 the smelter employed 1,338 men, smelted 535,697 tons of ore per year, and burned 49,913 tons of Washington coal. It made 101,745 tons of electrolytic copper, 10,020 tons of refined arsenic, and 704,297 ounces of gold alloyed with 10,269,777 ounces of silver as *doré* bars. The total value of the product during 1939 was $51,040,000.

No other modern smelter in the world has drawn its ore supply from as many distant points as has the Tacoma one. Shipments have come from Alaska, British Columbia, Washington and the whole Pacific Slope, Lower California, Central and South America, the St. Lawrence River, Norway, Sweden, Holland, Portugal, Burma, Australia, New Zealand, the Philippine Islands, Korea, Russia, and the north coast of Africa.

Although gold is our most glamorous mineral resource, other metals are of greater economic importance to the state. In fact, where gold does exist in a lode, ordinarily copper, lead, and zinc are also present in the ore, as well as a small amount of silver. The Holden mines, for example, produce zinc and copper as well as gold.

Since 1954 uranium ore has been mined in Stevens and Ferry counties, and in 1947 a $3,000,000 uranium processing plant was built at Ford in Stevens County. In 1957, for the first time, enough petroleum was recovered from a well near Ocean City in Grays Harbor County for a commercial venture, and in 1959 a major mercury mine, extending over two thousand acres, was located near the Green River gorge in western Washington.

Nonmetallic Minerals

The nonmetallic minerals—such as coal, sand, gravel, limestone, and clay—are, in turn, of more economic value to the state than the metals. It was mentioned in chapter 1 that most of our coal is not of sufficient quality to produce coke. What we do have, however, is of considerable importance to our economy.

In fact, coal was the first mineral product noticed by our pioneers and was extensively used in the early days. Dr. William Tolmie, the Hudson's Bay Company factor at Fort Nisqually, mentioned in 1833 that he had noticed coal deposits on the Cowlitz River. In 1853 settlers began to mine coal in the Seattle area, and during the 1850's and 1860's other deposits from Bellingham Bay to the Olympia region were opened.

In 1863, for example, a bed of coal was found on the north bank of what became Coal Creek, on the eastern side of Lake Washington. This was a part of the Newcastle coal fields of King County, which have been productive since. The mining possibilities were great enough to stimulate agitation for the construction of a railroad to carry the coal to market. The difficulties of transportation at that time may be seen from the fact that in the Squak Valley near Seattle the miners had to haul coal by team a mile and a half to Lake Sammamish, then by scow along Squak Creek to Lake Washington, across the lake by scow, and then by wagon into Seattle. This difficult passage made the cost prohibitive.

For the Seattle region, it was decided to use Lake Union as much as possible. The plan was to load cars at the mines, let them down a tramway to Lake Washington where they could be towed across the lake on barges to a point where the present crew house of the University of Washington stands. From there a second tramway would carry the cars across a portage to Lake Union where they would again cross the lake on barges. A third tramway would then carry them to the coal bunkers which would be built on a dock on the waterfront of Elliott Bay. This kind of project took more capital than individual local citizens could provide, and California capitalists formed companies to carry out the scheme. By 1872 operations had actually begun, and the first steam locomotive on Puget Sound went into operation between Lake Union and the Seattle harbor on Elliott Bay.

In 1875 an engineer of the Black Diamond Coal Company of San Francisco investigated the Puyallup coal fields and opened what has since been known as the Pierce County field. It included the Carbonado mines, which by 1883 were the second largest in Washington Territory. The Northern Pacific Railroad in 1878-79 built a branch railroad up the Puyallup Valley. With the addition of other branches and the mainline in the 1880's, coal throughout the Cowlitz and Chehalis valleys was utilized.

The Black Diamond Company also established a mine in the Bellingham region, but an explosion and fire destroyed so much of it that the company sought a substitute vein and tried bituminous coal near Green River in King County. This mine proved so valuable that the region became known as the great Ravensdale-Franklin-Black Diamond area. It was necessary to extend the Columbia and Puget Sound Railway from Renton to the town of Black Diamond. By 1885 the mine was operating.

In 1885 the Kittitas mines on the east side of the Cascades were opened by a subsidiary of the Northern Pacific Railway. The field had been discovered a few years previously and was one of the biggest inducements to the Northern Pacific to finish its Puget Sound extension. Kittitas County has exceeded any other county in yearly production of coal for over half of the years since 1905. From 1890 to 1900 new fields in Whatcom and Skagit counties were added.

Both world wars provided very strong impetus to mining, and the state Department of Conservation and the United States Bureau of Mines still attempt to locate additional coal sites, particularly coal of sufficient hardness to produce coke. At present, our only known deposits of such coal are in Pierce County.

For a review of the outlook for the use of the natural magnesium deposits in northeastern Washington and for the manufacture of aluminum either from imported bauxite or from the natural clays, see chapter 1.

Statistics

Statistics from *The Minerals Yearbook* published by the United States Bureau of Mines indicate that in 1962 the mineral production value in Washington was 3 per cent more than in 1961. Since 1952 there has been an average increase of 2 per cent per year. This has been caused by a greater output of sand, gravel, and stone, which in 1962 equalled 53 per cent of the total value of mineral production—$68,500,000. The mining of zinc increased, but the output of gold, lead, and uranium was smaller than that in 1961. The amount of coal had been declining in recent years, but it increased in 1962. The production of cement was lower.

One encouraging feature of the metal-processing industry was the rise in the demand for aluminum in spite of the cutback by the federal government in several airplane and missile projects at Boeing. The amount of aluminum produced in 1962 was 372,000 tons for a value of $178,200,000, an increase of 12 per cent in amount and 6 per cent in value. Most of the raw material for the manufacture of aluminum (bauxite) is shipped to Washington from plants located in the South and Southwest. For prospects for extracting aluminum from the clays in northeastern Washington, see chapter 1.

Average daily employment in mining increased from 2,646 in 1961 to 2,708 in 1962. The distribution of the latter number was:

902 in quarries and mills, 196 in nonmetal mines and mills, 908 in sand and gravel operations, 497 in metal mines and mills, and 205 in coal mines. Total wages paid in mining and mineral manufacturing were $195,210 in 1962. The figures in the following table from the 1962 *Minerals Yearbook* show the comparative value of the various minerals mined in the state for that year by counties.

TRANSPORTATION

By Water

As we have seen, the first explorers and traders reached our coast by the sea. Even the later overland settlers built their villages on the Columbia River or its tributaries or on parts of the Sound where they could use the water as a highway for their own travel and for shipping out produce and bringing in supplies.

During the maritime fur-trading period, oars or poles of some kind propelled small boats, and sails powered larger boats and ships. Meares built the *Northwest America* at Nootka in 1788, the first ship constructed in the Pacific Northwest; it was a sailing ship, as were the *Adventure,* built by Gray in 1792, also at Nootka, and the third ship, the *Vancouver,* built at Fort Vancouver in 1826 by the Hudson's Bay Company.

In 1836 the first steamship reached our coast, having been built in England for the Hudson's Bay Company. Appropriately named the *Beaver,* it had come across the Atlantic and around South America, by sail rather than steam, however. When it reached Fort Vancouver, the side wheels were put on, and the *Beaver* operated as a steamship between Fort Vancouver and Alaska for many years, carrying employees, produce, and furs for the Hudson's Bay Company, and Americans or other persons who wished to go as passengers to any of the points touched. The first American steamer to enter the Columbia was the United States troopship *Massachusetts,* bringing reinforcements for the Cayuse War.

The California gold rush, as we have seen, increased population to such an extent that the people needed an enormous amount of additional food and equipment. These commodities had to be transported in ships. From 1849 to 1852, over a hundred ships were

TABLE 2

COMPARATIVE VALUE OF WASHINGTON MINERALS

County	Value, 1962	Minerals produced in order of value
Adams	$194,000	Sand and gravel, stone
Asotin	16,000	Sand and gravel
Benton	108,000	Stone, sand and gravel
Chelan	1,043,000	Gold, stone, sand and gravel, silver, pumice, copper
Clallam	242,000	Sand and gravel, stone, gold
Clark	560,000	Stone, sand and gravel, clays
Cowlitz	158,000	Sand and gravel, stone
Douglas	217,000	Sand and gravel, stone
Ferry	Confidential	Gold, silver, stone, copper
Franklin	874,000	Sand and gravel, stone
Garfield	102,000	Stone
Grant	1,687,000	Stone, diatomite, sand and gravel, lime
Grays Harbor	352,000	Sand and gravel, stone
Island	393,000	Sand and gravel
Jefferson	337,000	Stone, sand and gravel
King	11,363,000	Cement, sand and gravel, stone, coal, peat, clays
Kitsap	219,000	Sand and gravel, stone, peat
Kittitas	1,373,000	Coal, sand and gravel, stone
Klickitat	4,290,000	Stone, sand and gravel, carbon dioxide
Lewis	618,000	Stone, sand and gravel, coal
Lincoln	318,000	Stone, sand and gravel
Mason	15,000	Sand and gravel, stone
Okanogan	126,000	Sand and gravel, stone, epsomite, silver, copper, gold, lead
Pacific	303,000	Stone, sand and gravel
Pend Oreille	Confidential	Zinc, cement, lead, stone, sand and gravel, silver, copper, barite, uranium
Pierce	3,402,000	Sand and gravel, stone, clays, peat, coal
San Juan	5,000	Sand and gravel
Skagit	3,323,000	Cement, stone, olivine, sand and gravel, talc and soapstone
Skamania	341,000	Stone, sand and gravel
Snohomish	4,106,000	Sand and gravel, stone, peat, clays, copper, gold, silver
Spokane	3,540,000	Cement, sand and gravel, stone, clays, uranium
Stevens	3,938,000	Uranium, stone, magnesite, sand and gravel, zinc, lead, barite, silver, clays, copper, grinding pebbles, gold
Thurston	496,000	Stone, sand and gravel, coal, peat
Wahkiakum	116,000	Stone
Walla Walla	855,000	Sand and gravel, stone
Whatcom	Confidential	Cement, stone, sand and gravel, clays
Whitman	437,000	Stone, sand and gravel
Yakima	1,798,000	Sand and gravel, stone, pumice, lime, clays
Undistributed	21,236,000	(This is the figure for the amounts kept confidential at the request of individual companies plus that which cannot be assigned to specific counties)

Port Blakeley mill about 1900. The many ships indicate the importance of lumber as an export product. (Original photo belongs to the Washington State Historical Society; courtesy of the University of Washington Library)

built in San Francisco alone, and many of them carried produce from our coast to California.

In 1850 a group of businessmen in Astoria instituted steamboat transportation on the Columbia with a ninety-foot side-wheeler, the *Columbia,* which they built and operated between Astoria and Oregon City. The next year a number of ships began operating on the Willamette. Also in 1851, three steamers were running between the Cascades and The Dalles. Goods on the ships below the Cascades had to be unloaded and carried around the rapids and loaded on the ships running above the Cascades. In 1851, F. A. Chenoweth built a wooden portage railroad, using mules to pull a loaded car around the Cascades.

In 1851 the *Lot Whitcomb* began carrying passengers and freight from Cowlitz Landing on the Cowlitz River across the Columbia and up the Willamette to the towns along that river. Additional ships followed suit. From Cowlitz Landing north to Olympia, the settlers used a wagon road made on an ox-cart trail cleared by the Hudson's Bay Company. Canoes and boats ferried people and goods up and down the Cowlitz.

In 1859 the famous steamship, the *Colonel Wright,* was put into service above The Dalles, another portage being made at that point by wagons. The *Colonel Wright* went as far as Fort Walla Walla at first, carrying freight for the troops stationed there. The next year, 1860, the men operating the steamers on the various sections of the Columbia and its tributaries merged their holdings and produced the Oregon Steam Navigation Company, which held a monopoly of river transportation for many years.

The company was almost immediately swamped, of course, with passengers on their way to the Clearwater and Salmon gold fields, and other ships were added until by 1865 the Oregon Steam Navigation Company had twenty-nine passenger boats, thirteen schooners, and four barges on the Columbia.

The runs lay between portages, as we have seen. On the Columbia itself there were five such divisions: from Astoria to the Cascades; from the Cascades to The Dalles; from The Dalles to Priest Rapids; from Priest Rapids to Colville; from Colville into British Columbia, sometimes as far as present Revelstoke. On the Snake River, the *Colonel Wright* went first as far as Wallula; then to Lewiston; then up the Snake almost to Hell's Canyon. The section above Asotin, however, was too difficult and was abandoned after the *Colonel Wright* was severely damaged by the trip back down the river. The current was so fast that she did in eight hours coming down what it had taken her eight days to do going up. After wheat and cattle ranching succeeded the mining era on the Snake, the company's boats carried agricultural produce between Asotin and Riparia.

During the mining boom, the Oregon Steam Navigation Company also sent steamboats up the Clearwater River from Lewiston almost to the forks of the river. When the mining trek moved on to Montana around 1865, the company tried to establish a route for transporting the miners there. It ran a stage from Wallula to Lake Pend Oreille where it had built boats to take the miners across the lake and up Clark Fork River to Thompson Falls, but this run lasted only a short time. Its distance plus that traveled on the Willamette, Columbia, Snake, and Clearwater, equaled 1,730 miles.

Steamship Annie Faxon *loading wheat on Snake River. (Washington State University Library)*

Passengers, wheat, lumber, and other produce continued to keep the river boats operating even after the mining booms declined until the coming of the transcontinental railroads in the 1880's. New areas served by boats for shipping agricultural produce in the 1880's were the Columbia River region from Wenatchee to the mouth of the Okanogan and White Bluffs to Celilo.

With the coming of the railroads, the passenger boats were largely abandoned, although freight barges continued to operate, particularly for lumber and wheat. After the First World War, barges supplanted the earlier steamships since double the cargo of a ship could be pulled on a barge by one tug. The Panama Canal, which was completed in 1915, gave a further impetus to maritime shipping from our coast to eastern markets since it eliminated the long sea route around South America.

The development of truck transportation in the present century increased the effect that railroads had had in supplanting river freighting. Now, however, with the building of dams at the points where the worst rapids made portages necessary, river freighting is increasing again, at a rapid rate. Statistics for McNary Dam show that during the first three months of 1963 the rate of increase for freight carried on the Columbia was 1.7 per cent, and in August of that year 3,377,333 bushels of grain moved downstream past the dam. This broke all previous monthly records. When the remaining dams on the Columbia and Snake rivers are completed, the quantity of freight carried will probably increase by more than ten million tons annually. It will be carried on big ocean freighters as far as Wenatchee on the Columbia and Lewiston on the Snake. For imperishable commodities like lumber and wheat, water transportation remains feasible because their tremendous bulk and weight can be carried more cheaply by water.

By Road

The inland areas with no access to water transportation had to rely for many years on horse-back trails or crude wagon roads. Many of the latter followed Indian trails that had been used over the years as paths to hunting or fishing grounds or to other villages. The first settlers in a given area improved such trails to whatever degree they could. Then as soon as they became a part of a governmental unit, they urged it to raise taxes to build and improve roads. We have seen that road laws were among the first ones passed by the legislature of the Oregon Provisional Government, the territory of Oregon, and the territory of Washington.

The federal government as well as the territory and counties provided roads in Washington Territory. At first, Congress appropriated money for specific roads on the theory that they were needed as military roads, ones which United States and territorial troops would use in their campaigns against the Indians. The Washington residents, however, regarded them primarily as a means for opening up the Sound to the immigrants coming along the Oregon Trail. Even in the 1850's, these incoming settlers had to follow the Columbia to Portland (a village smaller than Oregon City) and then go south to the Willamette or north to the Sound. Since the Willamette Valley was easy of access, whereas the trip to the Sound was difficult, as we have seen, nearly all of the settlers chose to go south.

In 1853 while Washington was still a part of Oregon Territory, Congress appropriated money to build a road from Walla Walla to Steilacoom, thus opening a route across the Cascades. When Washington Territory was created shortly afterwards, Secretary of War Jefferson Davis instructed the newly appointed governor, Isaac Stevens, to direct the building of the road. As we have seen in an earlier chapter, Captain George B. McClellan was assigned the job of choosing a good route through the mountains and constructing a road along it. He was expected to be finished by the fall of 1853 so that immigrants of that year could use the new road to get to the Sound, but he failed in this task, and the settlers succeeded in building a makeshift road themselves.

The first territorial legislature in 1854 authorized the building of roads from Steilacoom to Seattle; Steilacoom to Clark County; Seattle to Bellingham Bay; Olympia to Shoalwater; Cathlamet to Thurston County; Shoalwater to Grays Harbor; Olympia to the Columbia River; Seattle to the immigrant trail, and so forth. These roads were poor, at best, and pioneer journals contain many references to the terrible conditions. Ezra Meeker says, "And such mud holes! It became a standing joke after the road was opened that a team would stall with an empty wagon going down hill." Mrs. Isaac Stevens wrote apropos of her first glimpse of Olympia, "Below us, in the deep mud, were a few low, wooden houses, at the head of Puget Sound. My heart sank, for the first time in my life, at the prospect. . . . After ploughing through the mud, we stopped at the principal hotel."

In addition to the almost impassable local roads, there was an early one built by the federal government, the Mullan Road, which was to run from the mouth of the Walla Walla River (Wallula) to Fort Benton, the end of navigation on the Missouri River. Governor Stevens left John Mullan in the Coeur d'Alene Mountains to find out what the weather was like during the winter in preparation for planning a road. Mullan crossed and recrossed the Continental Divide six times during the winter and learned as much as he could from the Indians and the Catholic missionaries in the area. Congress appropriated money for the road in 1854, but the Steptoe defeat intervened.

As soon as peace was restored, Mullan reorganized his construction gang and started from the mouth of the Palouse River at the beginning of June, 1859. At this time, as we have seen, the "pig and potato" incident on San Juan Island brought to a head the friction between the United States and Great Britain over the ownership of the islands. When in the fall of 1859 news of the fracas reached Washington, D. C., the possibility of war made the federal government eager to have the road completed as fast as possible.

Mullan reached the east side of the Divide in the St. Regis Borgia Valley by December, 1859, and camped there. In the spring, 150 men spent six weeks cutting a six-mile stretch through the mountains near present Missoula, and by August, 1860, they reached Fort Benton. Mullan stayed until 1862, making improvements on the road.

By that time, the Indian scares were over, the San Juan situation was quiet, and the gold rushes were beginning. Consequently, the road never was used in the way it had been intended, as a military road, but miners coming from the East traveled it en route to the Montana gold fields. It was used to a lesser extent for our own gold strikes, which by that time, as we have seen, had started in the Salmon and Clearwater areas, and the Fraser River region was replacing the Colville locality as important diggings.

Stagecoach days are a colorful part of our transportation picture, although the tales of daring holdups of the Wells Fargo and other lines, which we see dramatized on television and in western movies, were more typical of the gold fields of Nevada and Montana than of our own sections. Our stagecoach period is a part of the whole development of wagon freighting. It was first important in Oregon, being on a permanent basis in the Willamette Valley by 1849. By 1852 advertisements were appearing in the Olympia newspaper for the Cowlitz and Willamette valleys. In 1864 a wagon road reached the Boise wagon trail, and the wagon freight business to the East then began.

A firm called Stewart's Express operated in 1854 between Portland and Olympia. It boasted that even with "stoppages," its messenger had covered the 180-mile distance within thirty-six hours. It used steamboat, canoe, and wagon. When the gold rush to Colville began in 1855, the proprietor extended his services to that point, and in 1856 he joined Wells Fargo and had regular stops for

St. Helena, Rainier, Monticello, Cowlitz Landing, Steilacoom, Seattle, Port Townsend, and Vancouver Island. Wagon freighting both for mail and private goods continued along with water transportation until the coming of the railroads in the 1880's.

In 1905 when the office of highway commissioner was created by the legislature, there were twelve state roads of varying mileage and in various stages of construction. They were still wagon roads, many just the somewhat improved trails over which the pioneers had come forty or sixty years before. By 1907 the Commissioner reported that there were 124 miles of improved roads, but only Yakima County had as much as eighteen miles of improved road. In 1960-62 Yakima County had 180.72 miles of primary state highway and 100.24 miles of secondary state highway. In addition, there were approximately 1,600 miles of county roads in Yakima County in 1962. For the entire state in 1962, there were 4,190 miles of primary state highways and 2,431 miles of secondary state highways. A study called *Priority Programming for Washington* made by the Automotive Safety Foundation predicts that by 1975 there will be more than two million cars to be accommodated on roads in the state. Since the present four-lane highways in urban areas mean traffic congestion even now, new roads and improvement of existing ones are constantly needed.

By Railroad

It has been mentioned that as early as 1854 when Governor Stevens left the East for Washington Territory, he was commissioned by the United States government to survey a route for a northern railroad. His survey was excellent, and many years later the Northern Pacific Railroad was built along the line he proposed. However, the Civil War occurred before any transcontinental railroad got under way. At the close of the war, the Union Pacific Railroad was the first one built, running across the central part of western United States and reaching San Francisco in 1869.

After that time, travel on the overland routes to the Pacific Northwest dropped off greatly because it was easier to take the train to California and then a ship up the coast from that point. California was the greatest user of Northwest products, with the Orient being a slowly expanding market. The completion of the railroad to California had the following effect: it made emigration into the Pacific Northwest easier, so that our population increased from twenty-four thousand in 1870 to sixty-seven thousand in 1880; and by thus increasing our population, it also increased the amount of produce which we could sell. New markets were therefore needed, and the people began to demand a more direct and serviceable route of communication with the big eastern cities.

In our own region, we did not wait for the transcontinental railroads, but built local ones as fast as possible. Dr. Dorsey S. Baker built a railroad from Walla Walla to Wallula between 1872 and 1875, and the Oregon Steam Navigation Company had built the portage roads, which were mentioned earlier, between the Cascades and The Dalles in 1863. These, in turn, had superseded makeshift railroads built in the 1850's. Both of these became an integral part of the Columbia River navigation system. Baker had come out as a forty-niner, and he built his railroad with his own limited funds, using scrap iron on wooden rails, extending the track mile by mile as the section already laid down brought in revenue. Hauling wheat by wagon was so laborious that farmers would use the railroad in order to have it carried even a few miles since, in addition, the railroad rates were much cheaper than wagon-freighting rates. We have already seen that Walla Walla had become a fertile agricultural belt after the 1860 gold rush, and the railroad enabled that area to expand enormously. It moved produce only to the Columbia, however; it did not provide overland transportation to the East.

John M. Murphy, an Englishman who visited the Pacific coast in the late 1870's, gives an amusing account of his ride on Baker's railroad in his *Rambles in North-western America from the Pacific Ocean to the Rocky Mountains:*

> The next stoppage was made at Wallula, a post town and shipping point claiming the distinction of supporting neither lawyer, physician, nor minister, and only one schoolteacher. It is 240 miles from Portland, and may be called the head of navigation on the Columbia proper, as no other hamlet is met with until Idaho is reached.
>
> I went ashore there, intending to go to Walla-Walla, in Eastern Washington Territory. On landing, I was informed that the stage had left in the morning, and that the only means of reaching my destination was to hire a farm wagon, or secure a seat in a goods truck

attached to a miniature train that ran fifteen miles into the interior on a wooden line of rails. Having secured an interview with the president, secretary, conductor, and brakeman of the road, he informed me that he would book me as a passenger on the payment of 2 dollars, and that sum being paid, I was placed on some iron in an open truck and told to cling to the sides, and to be careful not to stand on the wooden floor if I cared anything about my limbs. I promised a strict compliance with the instructions, and the miserable little engine gave a grunt or two, several wheezy puffs, a cat-like scream, and finally got the car attached to it under way. Once in motion, it dashed on at a headlong speed of two miles an hour, and rocked like a canoe in a cross sea. The gentleman who represented all the train officials did not get aboard, but told the engineer to go on and he would overtake him in the course of an hour. Before I had proceeded half a mile, I saw why I was not permitted to stand on the floor of the truck, for a piece of hoop-iron, which covered the wooden rails in some places, curled up into what is called a "snake head," and pushed through the wood with such force that it nearly stopped the train. After this was withdrawn the engine resumed its course, and at the end of seven hours hauled one weary passenger, with eyes made sore from the smoke, and coat and hat nearly burnt off by the sparks, into a station composed of a rude board shanty, through whose apertures the wind howled, having made the entire distance of fifteen miles in that time. The route of this famous railway ran through a sandy alkaline desert, capable of producing nothing but wild sage and kindred useless shrubs; hence, houses were scarce, and those seen were perched on the banks of some stream. Life was active enough there, however, for immense prairie schooners, as the waggons are called, drawn by teams of seven or eight pairs of mules or horses, or ten of oxen, wound in long serpentine lines over its bluish surface; and some of their drivers had the temerity to challenge the president of the railway line to run a race with them in his old machine, but he scorned their insinuations, and kept quietly walking beside his train.[1]

Portland, and the Oregon Steam Navigation Company, in particular, tried for years to interest the Northern Pacific Company in building a railroad along the bank of the Columbia River into Portland, but by 1870 it was apparent that some city on Puget Sound was going to be the terminus for the northern road. That year an

[1] John M. Murphy, *Rambles in North-western America from the Pacific Ocean to the Rocky Mountains* (London: Chapman and Hall, 1879), pp. 152-54.

agent for the Northern Pacific visited Olympia, Nisqually, Steila-coom, Tacoma, Seattle, Port Townsend, and Bellingham Bay, and each city was excited, hoping that it would be the favored site. By 1873 all of them except Seattle, Mukilteo, and Tacoma were elim-inated, and the commission appointed to make the final decision chose Tacoma.

Seattle residents were disappointed and furious, and Portland de-termined to stop the railroad if possible. Henry Villard, along with some Portland financiers, had acquired control of the old Oregon Steam Navigation Company and renamed it the Oregon Railway and Navigation Company. They set about to prevent the Northern Pacific from taking the Columbia River trade away from the Ore-gon company. The Northern Pacific's plan was to run a branch line from Tacoma through Kalama to Portland and also a branch from the Inland Empire down the Columbia to the ocean. Its main line east from Tacoma would absorb much traffic that would ordinarily go to the Columbia. Villard began to buy up land for the construc-tion of a line from the Palouse country down the Columbia to fore-stall the Northern Pacific in that region.

The residents of Seattle, too, determined to have a railroad in spite of the Northern Pacific and started building a railroad (called the Seattle and Walla Walla Railroad and Transportation Compa-ny) from Seattle to Walla Walla. It had reached the Renton coal mines, as we saw, by 1875. Villard bought this road in 1880, re-named it the Columbia and Puget Sound Railroad, and was author-ized to extend it to Walla Walla over Snoqualmie Pass. Then in 1881 he secretly bought a controlling interest in the Northern Pacific.

In the meantime the Northern Pacific was extending slowly west-ward, having reached Bismarck, North Dakota, in 1873. The branch line from Kalama up the Sound was within twenty-two miles of Tacoma when the Jay Cooke Company failed in the financial panic of that year. Although the whole enterprise was endangered by this crisis, the Kalama branch was completed to Tacoma by 1873.

After Villard became the controlling force of the Northern Pacific, he was able to command sufficient capital, in spite of his losses in the depression of the 1870's, to push construction rapidly. In 1883 the Northern Pacific reached the mouth of the Snake River, having come along the Clark Fork River to Spokane and then running southwest to the Columbia River, connecting with the tracks of the Oregon Railway and Navigation Company, which by that time had been completed along the south bank of the river to Portland. From Portland, people used the Kalama branch of the Northern Pacific to Tacoma.

In the early 1880's, Villard managed to finance the Oregon and California railroad south from Portland to California, and in 1884 the Union Pacific completed its line to Portland from the east through Idaho. It then leased the North Coast or Strahorn road to obtain an outlet to Spokane. In 1888 the main line of the Northern Pacific was completed from Pasco to Tacoma through the Yakima Valley and Stampede Pass.

The Great Northern Railroad followed in 1893, using the Marias Pass through the Rocky Mountains, which Stevens had looked for but had failed to find. Its route also lay through Spokane since, as we have seen, it lies in the "trough" that represents the easiest route from the northern Rockies to the Sound. Seattle was made the terminus for the Great Northern. James J. Hill of the Great Northern later built the Spokane, Portland and Seattle Railroad down the north bank of the Columbia, but now it too is operated by the Northern Pacific. The Milwaukee Railroad was the last transcontinental road to be run through Spokane, being completed in 1909.

After the 1880's, produce could be shipped by rail to the East in greater and greater quantities. To begin with, this increase caused a drop in the freight business of the water transportation companies. Rail passenger service increased as well since people much preferred the shorter, more comfortable train trip to the long and difficult sea voyage. The element of time was important, too, in the shipping of many commodities. However, the development of railroads in the Northwest stimulated water commerce between our coast and the Orient inasmuch as more produce was sent to Seattle by rail for shipment across the Pacific. Also, the growth in our population caused a big increase in coast traffic, and this local commerce plus the greater oriental trade actually made a rise in the quantity of materials carried by our merchant fleet.

In many cases in the oriental trade, the railroads and transpacific steamship lines cooperated. The first steamship service from the Pacific Northwest to China, Japan, and the Philippines was from Vancouver, British Columbia, the terminus of the Canadian Pacific Railroad. It remained for a railroad company, the Great Northern, to inaugurate American transpacific transportation from a Washington port. The *Minnesota* and the *Dakota,* the two largest merchant vessels built in the United States up to that time, were placed on the run to the Orient in 1904.

The motor truck and bus also are competitors of the railroads, but at the same time, they, too, feed produce into them. On long hauls between cities which do have boat or rail connections, they are definitely competitors. We know how many people, for example, take the bus from Seattle to Spokane, or even from Seattle to Chicago, instead of the train because of the cheaper bus fares. However, many people could not travel at all if there were no buses; consequently, the trains do not lose the entire number, by any means, who travel by bus.

Competition is also keen between commercial trucking companies and railroads for freight transportation, and in recent years the railroads have been trying to find some means of increasing their freight volume. One innovation in this attempt is the trailer-on-flatcar transportation, called piggyback service, in which loaded trucks are placed on flat cars and carried by rail to the area where the produce is to be sold. The trucks are then driven to the purchaser's plant, saving the time necessary to load the produce onto a freight car at the point of origin and unload it onto a truck at its destination for transfer to the owner's premises. In 1959 the piggyback type of railroad freight hauling was used for new automobiles for the first time, beginning in Oakland, California.

The issue of *Railway Age* for July 15, 1963, states that during the first six months of 1963, 319,118 trailer-carrying flat cars had been loaded. For the same period in 1962, the figure was 344,814 cars. For a number of years, some railroad companies have bought trucks to use for the shuttle runs from the railroad freight station in a city to the factories where merchandise is to be delivered, but such a system still requires the double loadings onto and off railroad cars, avoided by the piggyback method.

By Airplane

Airplanes are the most recent additions to the transportation pattern, and they present competition for both passenger and freight service to the older railroads and motor vehicles. The appeal of greater speed by air has made inroads on passenger travel on both railroads and buses, and, where the advantage of speed in transporting perishable merchandise offsets the greater cost of air freight, planes are used increasingly to carry such items. The various types of transportation are now in the phase of making adjustments so that each one may find the best way of giving the service suited to it and at the same time of operating profitably.

In the state of Washington, the development of our airplane industry has been almost synonymous with the development of the Boeing Airplane Company. It was mentioned in chapter 1 that the Boeing Company stemmed from William Boeing's interest in flying, a hobby he developed before the First World War. Because so few planes were being constructed in the country, he decided to build his own; consequently, he and an associate, Conrad Westervelt, ordered motors, body, and other parts from various shipyards and machine shops on the coast and hired men to put them together in a hangar on Lake Union. Before the first one was completed in June, 1916, Westervelt had left for naval duty. Called the B & W in honor of the builders, the plane had 125 horsepower, a wing span of 52 feet, and took off from water on pontoons.

With the successful completion of the B & W, Boeing felt that he was ready to begin manufacturing planes commercially. Therefore, in July, 1916, he with two other trustees formed the Pacific Aero Products Company and started to produce a Model C, also attached to pontoons. By April, 1917, when the United States entered the war, Boeing was ready for a war contract. He and his partners changed the name of their company to the Boeing Airplane Company, moved their plant to the site on the Duwamish River where the Boeing Number One plant is still maintained, and, during the summer of 1917, received a contract from the Navy for fifty Model C's.

At the close of the First World War in 1918, although the armed services continued to order airplanes for peacetime use, Boeing realized that, if he were to continue to expand production, he would need to develop commercial planes. His first one was called the B-1 flying boat, with space for a pilot and for mail bags or two passengers behind him. By this time, however, the Boeing Compa-

The Boeing B & W of 1916: The first airplane built by William E. Boeing had a speed of 75 miles per hour, a range of 320 miles, and was powered by a 125-horsepower Hall-Scott A-5 engine. (Photo by Boeing Airplane Company)

ny was in competition with a growing number of other airplane manufacturers, and Boeing did not receive enough orders to operate profitably. In fact, in 1920 his company had a deficit of $300,-000, a loss which Boeing made up from his private income. He was faced with the prospect of giving up the business when in 1920 he was awarded a government contract to build two hundred pursuit planes, MB-3A's, and his company was saved for the time being. Boeing decided to have his engineers keep hard at work on models for better planes in order to be ready at the end of one contract for a new one on a different type of plane.

In 1926 the United States Postal Department announced that it would accept bids from private firms to carry air mail from New York to Chicago and from Chicago to San Francisco instead of continuing to have government agencies operate the air mail service as it had done since 1918. Boeing felt that he had a plane, the 40-A, capable of making the trip. Therefore, he asked a friend, Eddie Hubbard of San Francisco, to join him in bidding on the San Francisco–Chicago route. Since 1920 Hubbard had been running an air mail service between Seattle and Vancouver, using a Boeing plane. The two men secured the contract and set up a separate company, the Boeing Air Transport, to carry the mail.

On June 30, 1927, Boeing and Hubbard had twenty-five planes stationed along the line for their first air mail flight from Chicago to San Francisco, to begin at midnight. Only a little more than a month before, Charles Lindbergh had made the first transatlantic flight, and the future of air transportation was very much in people's minds. Even at this time, however, planes were not yet designed for passenger transportation. From the beginning, Boeing had envisaged them as carriers of both people and freight and had specified in the articles of incorporation for the Pacific Aero Products Company that it was formed "to act as a common carrier of passengers and freight"; but in 1916 people, in general, had not even considered the plane as a means of passenger transportation.

In 1927 the 40-A had a tiny cabin for two people between the wings, with the pilot in an open cockpit behind the cabin. The trip from Chicago to San Francisco took twenty-three hours with stops at many cities along the way for mail delivery. At first the planes did not have even radio communication with ground stations, let alone radar. At the landing stations, the pilots were advised of weather conditions ahead by telegram, but, if fog or storm came on suddenly, they could only get low enough to follow railroad tracks or other landmarks or make a sudden landing, if possible, in an open place.

In spite of the hazards and discomfort of these flights, individuals began to ask to ride with the mail, and soon there was hardly a trip made without two passengers being squeezed into the cabin, either for the entire flight or to intermediate points. By the end of 1927, the company had carried 525 passengers and 230,000 pounds of mail. In 1926 the Post Office Department also made a contract with the Pacific Air Transport Company to carry mail between Seattle and Los Angeles, via Portland and San Francisco. Boeing Air Transport bought Pacific Air Transport in 1928, but operated it as a separate company. It, too, was besieged with requests from would-be passengers, particularly after Boeing was making the San Francisco–Chicago run. However, Pacific Air Transport did not encourage passenger travel until 1931, because, before that time, it used open-cockpit planes. After 1931 passenger transportation became a major part of the business.

The determination of people to ride in the mail planes reminds one of the similar insistence shown by an earlier generation to use the local freight railroads as they were built. The hazards and discomforts of Murphy's ride on Dr. Baker's railroad, mentioned earlier in this chapter, must have seemed to him almost as great as those experienced by the first passengers on the mail planes. Just as people's desire for the greater speed represented by trains as compared with horses enabled railroad companies to extend their tracks until transcontinental railroad travel was possible, people's eagerness to take advantage of the superior speed of airplanes as compared with railroads made transcontinental air travel also inevitable.

Other parallels are noticeable. The first railroad to reach the Pacific from the East was the Union Pacific in 1869 with its San Francisco terminal. People in the Pacific Northwest then made their way to San Francisco, as best they could, by ship and, later, by branch railroad lines, to reach the main one. The same pattern appeared in airplane travel. At first, people from the Pacific Northwest had to reach San Francisco by some other means to take advantage of the plane from there to Chicago, unless they could persuade the Pacific Air Transport Company to accommodate them on its Seattle–Los Angeles mail planes. In the meantime, people in the Pacific Northwest agitated for plane service between Seattle, Portland, or other cities in the area and San Francisco, where they could use the main air line from the Pacific coast eastward. Such moves would correspond to the efforts to build local railroad lines in this area.

Even before the United States Post Office Department decided in 1926 to turn over to private airplane companies the entire task of carrying the mail, it had made contracts with private individuals to carry the mail along certain stretches of a route. One such instance occurred in 1926 when Walter T. Varney of San Francisco began to carry mail by air from Pasco, Washington, to Elko, Nevada, where it was transferred to a government mail plane. The following year when Boeing secured the contract for the San Francisco–Chicago run, his company made Salt Lake City rather than Elko a stop, and the Post Office Department then changed the southern terminus of Varney's run to Salt Lake City, also, in order to keep the connection between the two routes.

No records have been found that passengers were carried on Varney's early mail runs. In 1929, however, when he and some associates had formed Varney Air Lines, Incorporated, they were eager to combine mail and passenger service. Therefore, when in June, 1929, the Post Office Department advertised for bids for air mail service between Pasco and Spokane and between Pasco and Seattle via Portland, the Varney company got the contract on a very low bid, intending to make a profit from passengers rather than from the mail. It bought Boeing 40-B-4 single-engine airplanes with seats for four passengers, and in 1930 passengers, as well as mail, were carried from Spokane to Pasco and from there to Seattle, Portland, or Salt Lake City. At Salt Lake City, they could continue east on the Boeing Air Transport line to Chicago.

In 1928-29 the Boeing Airplane and Transport Corporation was formed as a holding company for Boeing Airplane Company (the manufacturing division), Boeing Air Transport, Incorporated, and Pacific Air Transport. In 1929 the directors changed the name of the holding company to United Aircraft and Transport Corporation, which by 1934 had secured control of these additional companies: the Pratt and Whitney Aircraft Company, Chance Vought Corporation, the Hamilton Standard Propeller Corporation, Stout Air Services, National Air Lines, Varney Air Lines (1930), United Air Lines, and United Airports Company of California. Stout Air Services and National Air Lines operated lines in the East and Middle West. In 1933 Northwest Air Lines began operations between Spokane and Billings, Montana, and gradually extended its lines to Seattle and to the East Coast.

In 1934 because the Postmaster General believed that private companies carrying the mail had conspired together to prevent competitive bidding for the routes, he canceled all mail contracts with them. Since United Air Lines, which had acted as a management company for the transport units within the Boeing organization up to that time, had not been involved, the holding company made United into an operating company quickly, changing its name to United Air Lines Transport Corporation, in order that it could bid to carry mail. It secured air mail contracts shortly.

While litigation went on between the federal government and the companies affected, the Army Air Corps carried much of the mail.

The Postmaster General wished to return the mail service to private companies, but he wanted to avoid the future possibility of the kind of abuses which he felt the airplane companies had engaged in previously. Therefore, through President Roosevelt, he urged Congress to pass new air transportation legislation. Congress complied with a law forbidding a company to carry mail if it was also engaged in building airplanes. Boeing and his close associates preferred to continue with constructing planes rather than with operating them. Therefore, they decided to withdraw from the transportation phase of airplane activity. The stocks of Boeing Air Transport and the other subsidiary firms making up United Aircraft and Transport Corporation were sold to form a new company, United Air Lines Transport Corporation. Boeing then reincorporated the Boeing Airplane Company to continue building airplanes.

In the 1930's the state of Washington had another famous representative of aviation, Clyde Pangborn, whose family lived in Wenatchee. Pangborn Air Field there now is named for him. During the First World War, he taught flying at Ellington Field in Houston, Texas. He was then employed by the Northwest Aircraft Corporation of Spokane to do exhibition flying in Washington and Idaho. In 1920 he bought a Curtiss JN4d and made the first flight from California to Washington with a commercial plane. In 1921 he formed the Gates Flying Circus with Ivan R. Gates, acting as chief pilot and operating manager for the company. It operated from three to six planes and carried 1,500,000 passengers in the next nine years, going from one town to another to take people for short air rides.

Although there was hardly a year from 1931 through the Second World War that Pangborn did not win some coveted aviation award or establish a record of some kind, the one of most interest to Pacific Northwest residents is probably his nonstop flight in 1931 from Japan to Wenatchee, where he was given a hero's welcome. He and Hugh Herndon headed across the Atlantic from New York on July 28, 1931, in a Bellanca monoplane for a round-the-world flight. They were attempting to break the record established earlier that summer by Wiley Post and Harold Gatty who flew around the world in eight days, fifteen hours, and fifty-one minutes. The Post-Gatty plane was faster, but Pangborn's could carry more fuel and thus save time by avoiding stops. Also, Post had done all of the piloting on their flight, whereas Pangborn and Herndon intended to take turns as pilot, allowing one to catch some sleep while the other was at the controls. Both flights, of course, were made in machines almost toy-like in size by today's standards, without radio, landing fields (except in a few cities), or instrument flying.

By the time Pangborn and Herndon reached Khabarovsk, Siberia, they had been delayed so long by torrential storms and a damaged wing that they knew it was impossible to equal the Post-Gatty record. They therefore decided to stop in Tokyo and arrange to try for a $25,000 prize offered by a Japanese newspaper to the first aviators to fly the Pacific nonstop. When they reached Japan, officers on Hokkaido Island notified their government that the plane had flown over that area, a forbidden zone because of military fortifications. Their plane was seized. Clyde and his partner were able to convince the Japanese authorities that they had no idea where they were, until an official found Herndon's camera in the plane with pictures of what appeared to be military fortifications. Again Herndon maintained that photography was his hobby and that he had taken pictures of most of the areas they had crossed. Patriotic societies, however, made such a commotion about the American spies that the men were arrested, detained for several weeks, and finally fined $2,500.

The newspaper, however, continued its prize offer, and the two men took off from a sandy beach near Tokyo on October 3 headed across the Pacific. They had too much weight to maintain necessary speed and altitude; so they threw off their landing gear completely. Then ice on their wings almost brought them down. Their single engine stopped running at one point, when the gasoline unexpectedly ran out, and they were dangerously low before they could hook up an extra gas tank. Their calculations were off, and they were afraid they were heading out over the open ocean when they finally spotted land along Queen Charlotte's Island and later saw the glow of Seattle and circled Mount Rainier before heading for Wenatchee, where they arrived at 7:14 A.M., October 6, 1931.

Pangborn's mother, brother, a reporter for the Wenatchee *World,* and a group of friends had waited all night at the airport, and when they saw that the plane had no wheels, they feared the

worst as it came in to land. However, Clyde eased it down as best
he could; it screeched along for several yards, tipped over on its
nose, then settled back, slid along slowly in a cloud of dust, and
came to rest on its left wing. The only damage was that the propeller was smashed.

The representative of the Japanese newspaper was there with the
$25,000 check, and later that day, after a few hours' sleep, the men
were treated to a big parade and a tremendous outpouring of pride
and affection by the entire Wenatchee area. After they had rested,
the two men flew on to New York to complete their circle of the
globe. Two years later in Ripley's "Believe It or Not" column, the
item appeared that one of the wheels dropped to lighten the load
had drifted forty-four hundred miles and was found less than two
hundred miles from Wenatchee. Clyde Pangborn continued with his
flying exploits until his death in 1958.

By the 1940's, when the Second World War began, Boeing had
designed planes which became famous bombers used by our armed
forces—the B-17, B-29, B-47, and others. In 1940 the company
employed four thousand persons, and in 1944 the figure had risen
to over forty-five thousand. An additional plant was built in Seattle,
one in Renton, two in Tacoma, and one each in Everett, Bellingham, Chehalis, and Aberdeen. Over two hundred other firms
acted as subcontractors for Boeing during the war, the local ones
making even a greater impact on our regional economy.

Since the war, Boeing's expanded commercial aircraft production, including the development of the 707 jet airliner, has combined with continued manufacture of military planes to boost the
level of employment even higher at times than it was when defense
needs were greatest. The production of airplanes and spacecraft of
all kinds, including work on missiles and various phases of satellite
construction, has been the main factor in the economic growth of
the state since the early 1950's. Twenty-three per cent of total primary employment in the state in 1962 was in this field, whereas the
same figure for 1950 was 7 per cent, and 3 per cent in 1940. The
State Department of Commerce and Economic Development adds
the following details on the state's air industry for 1962: 73,800
people were employed in the aerospace programs, almost all of
them working for the Boeing Company. Products stressed during

A Boeing jet airliner in flight. (Photo by Boeing Airplane Company)

that year were the Minutemen ICBM, the Dyna Soar space glider, the Saturn rocket booster, and jet transports, including the 707, 720, and the Air Force KC 135. Cutbacks in several of these programs by the federal government resulted in a drop in employment in 1963 which is expected to continue through 1964. Boeing hopes to offset this decline partly by increasing its output of commercial planes for passengers and, particularly, air cargo traffic, which is expected to increase greatly between the United States and Europe and the United States and Asia. For example, Pan American World Airways in 1963 ordered five additional 707-32OC all cargo jets, bringing its total fleet to eight. Boeing is also encouraging the organization of firms to supply it with commodities discovered through its research facilities. A new laminated vinyl material, called Boelite, will be manufactured by a company in Hoquiam. Besides being used in the interior of airplanes, it will also be sold for Venetian blinds, doors, and parts of boats, trucks, and other vehicles and equipment.

Air transportation by United Air Lines, Northwest Air Lines, and the other companies giving service to this area at the time of the Second World War has also increased greatly since that time. Feeder service to transcontinental lines throughout central and eastern Washington was extended in 1952 when West Coast Air Line and Empire Air Lines merged under the former name.

General Manufacturing

Both governmental and private economists are concerned with the great dependence of the state's industrial level on employment by the Boeing Company. When its contracts for production of aircraft are reduced and employees are dismissed, unemployment in the state rises sharply and remains high until Boeing can again absorb the work force. In the meantime, the rise in our local population and the increase in immigration into the Pacific Northwest from other parts of the country have made the number of job applicants greater, so that the demand for jobs is still ahead of the number available. Doing away with this lag is the primary goal of private business and welfare agencies.

To get a more diversified manufacturing base, not only new industries but new outside markets will have to be secured. Such moves are becoming more necessary because with more types of machines in existence to do farm work and the processing of our agricultural commodities, fewer workers are needed on farms and more rural young people are therefore leaving their home communities when they finish high school and college to find nonfarming jobs, usually in cities. This group is added to city graduates, already unemployed, who are in search of jobs. Automation is also reducing the number of workers needed in practically all other fields. The *Annual Review; Summary of Pacific Northwest Industries* for May, 1963, contains a useful summary of the following possible solutions to the problem of providing new jobs for the excess workers for whom the earlier occupations are no longer available.

One tremendous potential for the Pacific Northwest coast is increased foreign trade. In 1962 an estimated 78,000 people in Washington were working in industries depending on exports and 25,500 in ones depending on imports. The volume of trade through the customs offices in the state amounted in 1962 to $540,000,000 in exports and $450,000,000 in imports. Canada represents our biggest single customer and seller. For example, Alberta ships crude oil in pipes to Puget Sound refineries, and British Columbia sells newsprint, fertilizer, limestone, and copper ore to our firms which use them in further processing of commodities. Our major exports to Canada and more than fifty other nations are jet aircraft, paper products, scrap metal, off-highway trucks, refined copper, lumber, wheat, apples, and processed foods. If additional foreign markets can be secured, the increase in exports, with resulting additional employment and industrial gain, will be a great economic boon. Because we are near the ocean, we can in many cases sell more profitably to foreign countries by transporting our produce on water than we can to the eastern section of our own country. There we have to compete with the firms in large cities which are near both raw materials for manufacturers and the big markets for the finished products.

Finding new products which can be manufactured from our local raw materials (primarily timber and food materials) is the chief purpose of much research done by private and governmental agencies in the state. Securing new business firms to utilize present inventions is one major task of the State Department of Commerce and Economic Development which lists many of the new manufacturing ventures in its periodical, *Progress*. Samples are: de-tinning plant in Seattle to recover tin from scrap; paperboard tube processing plant in Longview; folding paper carton plant in Spokane; factory to make wirecloth for the paper industry in Tumwater; new machine for sorting potatoes and bulbs to be used in Quincy plant; firm to manufacture lime products in Tacoma; plant to build large aluminum cargo containers in Spokane; plant to make machines for closing plastic bags in Yakima; new process for producing levulinic acid from forest raw materials (used in printing inks and protective finish for can linings, and so on) in Port Townsend.

Airplane and space vehicle manufacture; shipbuilding; furniture, paper and plywood products and other commodities from wood; food processing, including canning and freezing of fish; aluminum manufacture, and metal refineries are the main categories of our basic manufactures. For a discussion of the specific placement of such industries in a given area, see chapter 1.

Suggested Readings

CHAPTER 1

Books listed are largely recent publications which are still obtainable.

Impressions of Washington:

Binns, Archie. *Northwest Gateway, the Story of the Port of Seattle.* New York: Doubleday, Doran and Co., 1945. Selected events in Seattle's history told as entertaining anecdotes.

———. *The Roaring Land.* New York: Robert M. McBride and Co., 1942. The life of Mr. Binns's father as a stump farmer in western Washington and reminiscences of his own boyhood, plus chapters on our earlier history.

———. *Sea in the Forest.* Garden City, N.Y.: Doubleday and Co., 1963. Geology and impressionistic sketches of colorful events in the history of Puget Sound and the Olympics.

Holbrook, Stewart Hall. *The Columbia.* New York: Rinehart and Co., 1956. History of the Columbia River from its early geology to the present time.

———. *Far Corner: A Personal View of the Pacific Northwest.* New York: Macmillan Co., 1952. An attempt through description and historical anecdote to give the flavor of the Pacific Northwest as a region.

Morgan, Murray. *The Dam.* New York: Viking Press, 1954. History of the construction of Grand Coulee Dam.

———. *The Last Wilderness.* New York: Viking Press, 1955. Sketches of the Pacific Northwest based on Mr. Morgan's personal experience as well as accounts of earlier historical occurrences.

———. *Skid Road: An Informal Portrait of Seattle.* New York: Viking Press, 1951. Early history of Seattle's waterfront.

Morgan, Neil. *Westward Tilt; the American West Today.* New York: Random House, 1963. Chapter 12 deals with this state ("Washington, the Gentle People"). Excellent readable sketches of the social and economic tone of the western states.

Sundborg, George. *Hail, Columbia: The Thirty-Year Struggle for Grand Coulee Dam.* New York: Macmillan Co., 1954. Report of the controversies over what type of dam should be built to irrigate central Washington and where it should be located.

Geology (all of the books in this section are popular accounts written by specialists in the field):

Brockman, C. Frank. *The Story of the Petrified Forest, Ginkgo State Park, Washington.* Seattle, Wash.: State Parks and Recreation Commission, 1952.

Campbell, C. D. "Washington Geology and Resources," *Research Studies* (Pullman, Wash.), XXI, No. 2 (1953).

Danner, Wilbert R. *Geology of Olympic National Park*. Seattle, Wash.: University of Washington Press, 1955.

Daugherty, Richard D. "Archeology of the Lind Coulee Site, Washington," *Proceedings of the American Philosophical Society,* C (June, 1956), 223-78.

Ekman, Leonard. *Scenic Geology of the Pacific Northwest*. Portland, Ore.: Binfords & Mort, 1962. Descriptive geology for the general reader; organized around designated tours.

Livingston, Vaughn E. *Fossils in Washington*. Olympia, Wash.: State Printing Plant, 1959. This contains suggestions of places where amateur naturalists can ordinarily find fossils, along with instructions for handling and reporting them. Order from State Department of Conservation, Olympia.

Resources and Industrial Development:

Bonneville Power Administration. *Twenty-five Years of Growth: 1962 Report on the U. S. Columbia River Power System*. Portland, Ore., 1962.

Cohn, E. J. *Industry in the Pacific Northwest and the Location Theory*. New York: Columbia University Press, 1954. An analysis of the advantages and disadvantages of the Pacific Northwest in regard to its industrial development.

Freeman, Otis W., and Howard Martin (eds.). *The Pacific Northwest: An Overall Appreciation*. 2nd ed. New York: John Wiley and Sons, 1954. Present and potential use of natural resources.

Highsmith, Richard M. *Atlas of the Pacific Northwest: Resources and Development*. Corvallis, Ore.: Oregon State College, 1953. Map showing location of each natural resource.

Washington (State) Department of Commerce and Economic Development. *Facts to Help You Know Washington* [1963].

Washington (State) Secretary of State. *Historical Highlights*. Olympia, Wash., 1961.

―――. *This Is Washington*. Olympia, Wash., 1962.

CHAPTER 2

Unless otherwise specified, the following works are by competent anthropologists, but written in a sufficiently popular style for students as well as teachers.

Origin and Migrations of the American Indian:

Daugherty, Richard D. *Early Man in the Columbia Intermontane Province*. (University of Utah Anthropological Papers, No. 24.) Salt Lake

City, Utah, 1956. Scholarly bulletin of interest to the general reader.

Lafarge, Oliver. *A Pictorial History of the American Indian.* New York: Crown Publishers, 1956. Chapter ix describes Pacific Northwest coast culture in addition to a discussion in chapter i of the coming of the Indian to this continent.

Culture of Pacific Northwest Coast Indians:

Durham, Bill. *Indian Canoes of the Northwest Coast.* Seattle, Wash.: Copper Canoe Press, 1960.

Drucker, Philip. *Indians of the Northwest Coast.* (American Museum of Natural History, Anthropological Handbook, No. 10.) New York: McGraw-Hill Book Co., 1955.

Hawthorn, Audrey. *People of the Potlatch: Native Arts and Culture of the Pacific Northwest Coast.* Vancouver, B.C.: Vancouver Art Gallery with the University of British Columbia, 1955.

McCurdy, James G. *Indian Days at Neah Bay,* ed. Gordon Newell. Seattle, Wash.: Superior Publishing Co., 1961.

Underhill, Ruth. *Indians of the Pacific Northwest.* (Indian Life and Customs, No. 5.) Washington, D.C.: U.S. Office of Indian Affairs, 1944.

Washington (State) Secretary of State. *Indians in Washington.* Olympia, Wash.: State Printing Plant, 1955. This pamphlet is largely based on Underhill, *Indians of the Pacific Northwest.*

Culture of Plateau and Coast Indians:

Daugherty, Richard D. *Early Man in Washington.* (State of Washington Department of Conservation, Information Circular No. 32.) Olympia, Wash.: State Printing Plant, 1959.

Gunther, Erna. "Indian Life of the Pacific Northwest," chapter ii of *The Pacific Northwest, An Overall Appreciation,* ed. W. Freeman and Howard H. Martin. 2nd ed. New York: John Wiley and Sons, 1954.

Smith, Allan H. "The Indians of Washington," *Research Studies* (Pullman, Wash.) XXI, No. 2 (1953).

Indian Legends:

Clark, Ella E. *Indian Legends of the Pacific Northwest.* Berkeley: University of California Press, 1954. Indian legends told from the standpoint of folklore and literature rather than from that of anthropology.

CHAPTER 3

Anderson, Bern. *Surveyor of the Sea: The Life and Voyages of Captain George Vancouver.* Seattle, Wash.: University of Washington Press, 1960.

Aumack, Thomas M. *Rivers of Rain, being a Fictional Accounting of* the *Adventures and Misadventures of John Rogers Jewitt, Captive of the Indians at Friendly Cove on Nootka Island in Northwest America.* Portland, Ore.: Binfords and Mort, 1948. The original narrative of Mr. Jewitt's adventure as written by himself is long out of print.

Cook, Captain James. *The Journals of Capt. James Cook on his Voyages of Discovery,* ed. J. C. Beaglehole. Cambridge, Eng.: Hakluyt Society, 1955. Vol. I containing Cook's *Journal* for his first voyage in the South Pacific has appeared; Vol. II will treat his second voyage to the South Pacific; Vol. III will contain his voyage to the Pacific Northwest coast, and Vol. IV will consist of essays on his accomplishments. This is intended as the definitive edition of Cook's works. The following entry is a condensed version suitable for the general reader.

————. *The Voyages of Capt. James Cook round the World, Selected from his Journals and Edited by Christopher Lloyd.* London: The Cresset Press, 1949. See note on preceding entry.

Fuller, George W. *History of the Pacific Northwest.* New York: Alfred A. Knopf, 1941, chapter iii. One of the older standard histories of the Pacific Northwest.

Goodhue, Cornelia. *Journey into the Fog; the Story of Vitus Bering and the Bering Sea.* Garden City, N.Y.: Doubleday, Doran and Co., 1944. Dramatic tale of Bering's adventures.

Howay, Frederic W. *The Dixon-Meares Controversy.* New York: L. Carrier and Co., 1929. Detailed account of events up to and through the Nootka Sound controversy.

———— (ed.). *Voyages of the "Columbia" to the Northwest Coast, 1787-1790 and 1790-1793.* Boston: Massachusetts Historical Society, 1941. Annotated edition of primary sources for Gray's two voyages to the Pacific Northwest coast.

Johansen, Dorothy, and Charles M. Gates. *Empire of the Columbia.* New York: Harper and Brothers, 1957. Recent history of the Pacific Northwest, particularly helpful for economic and social history.

Marshall, James S. *Adventure in Two Hemispheres.* Vancouver, B.C.: Printed by Talex Printing Service, 1955. Main emphasis is on Vancouver's voyages, but the English, Spanish, and American explorers are treated, also.

Munford, Kenneth. *John Ledyard: An American Marco Polo.* Portland, Ore.: Binfords and Mort, 1939.

Schurz, William. *The Manila Galleon.* New York: E. P. Dutton and Co., 1939. History of the Spanish trade between Acapulco and the Philippines.

CHAPTER 4

Arntson, Herbert. *Adam Gray: Stowaway*. New York: Franklin Watts, 1961. Fictional account of the Astor expedition.

Davidson, Gordon Charles. *The North West Company*. Berkeley: University of California Press, 1918.

DeVoto, Bernard. *Across the Wide Missouri*. Boston: Houghton Mifflin, Co., 1947. Colorful account of the American overland fur trade.

————— (ed.). *The Journals of Lewis and Clark*. Boston: Houghton Mifflin, Co., 1953. A version compiled from the various journals of the Lewis and Clark Expedition.

Dryden, Cecil. *Up the Columbia for Furs*. Caldwell, Ida.: Caxton Printers, 1950. "The Journals, rewritten, of Ross Cox and Alexander Ross originally published under title, *Adventures on the Columbia River*, and *Fur Hunters of the Far West*, respectively." Quoted from book jacket.

Irving, Washington. *Adventures of Captain Bonneville*. Portland, Ore.: Binfords and Mort, 1954. Reprint of the popular Irving account of Bonneville's experiences in fur trading.

—————. *Astoria*. Student's ed. New York: Putnam, n.d. History of the Astorian venture told from Astor's viewpoint.

Jennings, John. *River to the West: A Novel of the Astor Adventure*. Garden City, N.Y.: Doubleday and Co., 1948. Fictionized version of the Astor story.

MacKay, Douglas. *The Honourable Company: A History of the Hudson's Bay Company*. Indianapolis, Ind.: Bobbs-Merrill Co., 1936. Detailed history of the company; good for reference work.

Mirsky, Jeannette. *Westward Crossings: Balboa, Mackenzie, Lewis and Clark*. New York: Alfred A. Knopf, 1946. Accounts of the trips of these explorers in a readable form.

Montgomery, Richard. *The White-Headed Eagle, John McLoughlin, Builder of an Empire*. New York: Macmillan Co., 1934. Popular biography of McLoughlin.

Morgan, Dale L. *Jedediah Smith and the Opening of the West*. Indianapolis, Ind.: Bobbs-Merrill Co., 1953. Story of Smith's life and account of the Rocky Mountain Fur Company.

Spaulding, Kenneth A. (ed.). *On the Oregon Trail: Robert Stuart's Journey of Discovery*. Norman: University of Oklahoma Press, 1953. Modernized version of Stuart's trip to the East through South Pass.

Stewart, Edgar I. *Washington: Northwest Frontier*. New York: Lewis Historical Publishing Company, 1957. Vol. I, chaps. vii-xii give a detailed treatment of the fur-trade period.

White, M. Catherine (ed.). *Journals of David Thompson Relating to Montana and Adjacent Regions, 1808-12*. Missoula: Montana State University Press, 1950. Critical edition of extracts from Thompson's journals.

CHAPTER 5

Bischoff, William N., S. J. *The Jesuits in Old Oregon*. Caldwell, Ida.: Caxton Printers, 1945. History of the early Catholic missionary movement in the Oregon country.

Brosnan, Cornelius J. *Jason Lee, Prophet of the New Oregon*. New York: Macmillan Co., 1932. Account of the Methodist mission in the Willamette Valley.

Drury, Clifford M. *Elkanah and Mary Walker, Pioneers among the Spokanes*. Caldwell Ida.: Caxton Printers, 1940. Dr. Drury's biographies of the Protestant missionaries in the Oregon country are scholarly works with sufficient portrayal of the human drama involved to appeal to the general reader.

————. *First White Women over the Rockies; Diaries, Letters and Biographical Sketches of the Six Women of the Oregon Mission Who Made the Overland Journey in 1836 and 1838*. Glendale, Calif.: A. H. Clark Co., 1963.

————. *Henry Harmon Spalding*. Caldwell, Ida.: Caxton Printers, 1936.

————. *Marcus Whitman, M. D., Pioneer and Martyr*. Caldwell, Ida.: Caxton Printers, 1937.

Jones, Nard. *The Great Command: the Story of Marcus and Narcissa Whitman and the Oregon Country Pioneers*. Boston: Little, Brown, and Co., 1959. Recent account of the missionaries, shown as real people reacting with both courage and pettiness to their unusual hardships.

Magaret, Helene. *Father DeSmet, Pioneer Priest of the Rockies*. New York: Farrar and Rinehart, 1940. Readable biography of DeSmet.

Paden, Irene. *The Wake of the Prairie Schooner*. New York: Macmillan Co., 1943. Charming account of the retracing of the Oregon Trail by Mrs. Paden and her family, with wealth of detail concerning trail experiences from published and manuscript sources.

Salisbury, Albert and Jane. *Here Rolled the Covered Wagons*. Seattle, Wash.: Superior Publishing Co., 1948. Photographs of points along the Oregon Trail with short explanation of the significance of each.

CHAPTER 6

There are innumerable pioneer narratives, some written many years ago and some very recently, telling of the experiences of a particular family in settling in some part of the Pacific Northwest. Samples of both older and current accounts are included in the following reading list. Copies of some which are out of print can still be located occasionally in libraries of relatives or friends of the author.

The Bureau of Research and Community Development of the University of Washington has helped individual towns or rural areas to gather materials for a local history, and some of these projects have resulted in the publication of a history of the community plus one or more pioneer narratives. Local county historical or pioneer societies sometimes sponsor a writing program of this kind, and they are all interested in locating and having preserved family papers or pioneer reminiscences. A number of high school classes in Washington History and Government have enjoyed cooperating with such programs and have benefited the community as well as themselves in learning to be on the lookout for diaries, letters, photographs, scrapbooks, early business records, or other manuscripts from earlier periods of the region's development.

Brown, William C. *The Indian Side of the Story*. Spokane, Wash.: Hill Printing Company, 1962. Indian version of Indian battles as told to the late Judge Brown of Okanogan.

Buchanan, Nina O. *Tall Tales of a Teacher*. New York: Vantage Press, 1962. Autobiography of an outstanding Seattle school teacher.

Cochran, John E. *Pioneer Days in Eastern Washington*. Spokane, Wash.: Knapp Bookstore, 1942.

Davidson, Bertha G. *Parade of Pioneers*. Vaughn, Wash.: Peninsula Gateway Printers, 1961.

Denny, Arthur A. *Pioneer Days in Puget Sound*. Seattle, Wash.: A. Harriman Co., 1908. Reminiscences of prominent Seattle pioneer.

Fort Vancouver Historical Society. *Clark County History*. The Society issues an annual reprint of a pioneer narrative. Example: Vol. II, 1961, Arline A. Cairns, *A Daughter of Uncle Sam,* account of life at the American military post in Vancouver by the daughter of an army officer.

Haines, Francis. *Red Eagle of the Northwest: The Story of Chief Joseph and His People*. Portland, Ore.: The Scholastic Press, 1939. Story of Nez Perce War intended for students.

Harder, Annine. *Opportunities of the Golden West*. Spokane, Wash.: Ross Printing Co., 1960. Reminiscences of pioneering in Palouse country.

Hazard, Joseph Taylor. *Companion of Adventure: A Biography of Isaac Ingalls Stevens, First Governor of Washington Territory*. Portland, Ore.: Binfords and Mort, 1952. Recent biography of Stevens.

Judson, Katharine B. *Early Days in Old Oregon*. Chicago: A. C. Mc-
Clurg and Co., 1916. Reminiscences of author's childhood.

McCurdy, James. *By Juan de Fuca's Strait: Pioneering along the North-
western Edge of the Continent*. Portland, Ore.: Binfords and Mort,
1937. Sketches of historical events on the Pacific Northwest coast.

McWhorter, L. V. *Hear Me, My Chiefs*. Caldwell, Ida.: Caxton
Printers, 1952. Versions of Nez Perce War related to the author by
Nez Perces; very useful for reference in regard to controversial points
of the war.

————. *Yellow Wolf, His Own Story*. Caldwell, Ida.: Caxton Printers,
1940. Reminiscences of the Nez Perce warrior as told to Mr. Mc-
Whorter.

Mills, Nellie Ireton. *All Along the River*. Montreal, Canada: Payette
Radio, Ltd., 1963. Stories of settlement of the Boise Valley.

Randall, L. W. *The Mountain that Moved*. New York: Pageant Press,
1952. Reminiscences of author's childhood in Montana and stories
of father's experiences as freighter.

Sheller, Roscoe. *Blowsand*. Portland, Ore.: Metropolitan Press, 1963.
Pioneering in the Yakima Valley.

Tobie, Harvey E. *No Man Like Joe: The Life and Times of Joseph L.
Meek*. Portland, Ore.: Binfords and Mort, 1949. Readable biography
of Meek.

CHAPTER 8

Almost all of the written material on our political and social history
later than the territorial period is in the form of magazine or newspaper
articles not usually available to high school libraries. In addition, most
of the books dealing with those subjects in the early days are now out of
print. Therefore, the titles listed in the reading list for chapter 1 under
the headings "Impressions of Western and Eastern Washington" probably represent the best sources obtainable which give a picture of the
cultural or political life of a particular area at a given time.

Bowden, Angie Burt. *Early Schools in Washington Territory*. Seattle:
Lowman and Hanford, 1935.

Building a State: Washington, 1889-1939. (Washington State Historical
Society Publications, Vol. III.) Tacoma, 1940.

Johannsen, Robert W. *Frontier Politics and the Sectional Conflict*.
Seattle: University of Washington Press, 1955. Territorial period.

Richardson, Elmo R. *The Politics of Conservation; Crusades and Controversies, 1897-1913*. Berkeley: University of California Press, 1962.

Spencer, Lloyd, and Lancaster Pollard. *A History of the State of Wash-*

ington. New York: American Historical Society, 1937. Chapters on cultural growth.

Stewart, Edgar I. *Washington, Northwest Frontier.* Vol. II. New York: Lewis Historical Publishing Co., 1957.

Warren, Sidney. *Farthest Frontier: The Pacific Northwest.* New York: Macmillan Co., 1949.

CHAPTER 9

The Washington State Resources Committee, Seattle, published a book, *Washington State Resources* (1957), edited by Otis Freeman and Rolland H. Upton to give a popular, yet authoritative, account of the development and present status of our industries based on our natural resources. A booklet issued in 1963 by the United States Department of the Interior called *Natural Resources of Washington* is also helpful in bringing some of the information more nearly up to date.

High school libraries may also receive publications from the various state executive and administrative departments that contain helpful data on the industries relating to the work of the department. Annual or biennial reports of the state departments of agriculture, conservation, fisheries, game, and natural resources publishes a similar publication called *The Totem.* Copies are sent free to individuals who have a good use for them.

The reading list for chapter 1 has some references to standard works on our industries. Other publications that are helpful are: BPA 1962 Report, *U.S. Columbia River Power System.* Portland, Ore., 1963. British Columbia Natural Resources Conference. *British Columbia Atlas of Resources,* ed. J. D. Chapman and D. B. Turner. Vancouver, B. C., 1956. Maps showing location of the various natural resources in British Columbia.

Bryan, E. A. *Orient Meets Occident.* Pullman, Wash.: Students' Book Corp., 1936. History of railroads in the Pacific Northwest.

Dodds, Gordon B. *A Pygmy Monopolist.* Madison: University of Wisconsin, 1961. Autobiography of R. D. Hume; of interest for details of early fish canning.

Hult, Ruby El. *Steamboats in the Timber.* Caldwell, Ida.: Caxton Printers, 1952. History of steamboating on Lake Coeur d'Alene and the St. Joe River.

King, William Ad., and Elmer D. Fullenwider. *The Pacific Northwest, Its Resources and Industries.* Cincinnati, Ohio: Southwestern Publishing Co., 1935. An analysis of the industrial position of the Pacific Northwest as it was in the 1930's.

League of Women Voters. *The Great River of the West: The Columbia River.* Eugene, Ore.: Koke-Chapman Co., 1959. Summary of various phases of the development of the river with a helpful bibliography. Order from the League, 7615 Sand Point Way, Seattle 98115.

Mansfield, Harold. *Vision: A Saga of the Sky.* New York: Duell, Sloan and Pierce, 1956. Narrative history of the Boeing Airplane Company.

Mills, Randall. *Stern-Wheelers up Columbia: A Century of Steamboating in the Oregon Country.* Palo Alto, Calif.: Pacific Books, 1947.

Spencer, Lloyd, and Lancaster Pollard. *A History of the State of Washington,* Vol. II. New York: American Historical Society, 1937. Chapters on the lumber industry; agriculture; the fishing industry; mining and its effects; transportation.

Trimble, William J. *The Mining Advance into the Inland Empire.* (Bulletin of the University of Wisconsin, No. 638; History Series, Vol. III, No. 2.) Madison, Wis., 1914. This is excellent as a reference work on our mining advance.

United States. Army. *Columbia River and Tributaries, Northwestern United States.* 8 vols. Washington, D. C.: U. S. Government Printing Office, 1952. Extremely comprehensive report on all phases of the development of the Columbia Basin. This is often referred to as the "308 Report" and is issued as House Document No. 531 of the 2nd Session of the 81st Congress.

————. Reclamation Bureau. *Columbia Basin Project, 1950.* Washington, D. C., 1950. Summary for visitors from the National Reclamation Association during its convention in Spokane, November, 1950.

————. Reclamation Bureau. *The Columbia River: A Comprehensive Departmental Report on the Development of the Water Resources of the Columbia River Basin,* February, 1947. Washington, D. C.: U. S. Government Printing Office, 1947. Extensive report on work accomplished through the Reclamation Bureau in the Columbia Basin.

————. Reclamation Bureau. *Reclamation Project Data: A Book of Historical, Statistical, and Technical Information on Reclamation Projects, 1948.* Washington, D. C.: U. S. Government Printing Office, 1948. Summary of Columbia Basin projects completed and in prospect, pp. 97-108.

Winther, O. O. *The Old Oregon Country: A History of Frontier Trade, Transportation, and Travel.* Stanford, Calif.: Stanford University Press, 1950.

Index

Aberdeen, Wash.: geography of, 19-20; depression hits, 225; IWW in, 234; Grays Harbor College in, 263; Boeing plant in, 326

Abernethy, Alexander, 289

Abernethy, Alexander S., 206-7

Abernethy, George, 161

Acapulco, Mexico: Spanish base, 65, 72

Adams County: geology of, 11; geography of, 24-27

Adventure (ship), 305

Africa: on trade routes, 6, 74, 82; mentioned, 73, 74, 96; ore from, 302

Agriculture: value of, 4; in western Washington, 4-5, 18-20, 23; in eastern Washington, 4; in Olympic Peninsula, 18-19; in Willapa Hills, 19-20; in Puget Sound, 20, 21, 168; in Cascade Mountains, 23; in Okanogan Highlands, 23-24; in Columbia Basin, 25-27; in Blue Mountains, 27; Indians' lack of, 44, 269; at Fort Vancouver, 116; missionaries teach Indians, 134-35; by fur traders, 269-70; history of, 269-84; by irrigation, 273-82

Ahtanum Creek: Catholic mission on, 150

Airplane industry, 7, 21, 318-28

Air travel, 5-6, 318-28

Alaska: fisheries in, 4; relationship to Pacific Northwest of, 5-6, 8; gold rush in, 5; effect of glaciers in, 13; *prairies* in, 13; on Indian migration route, 28; Indians in, 32; Bering's trip to, 69-81; Russian control of, 71; Cook reaches, 73; Meares reaches, 76; boundary of Oregon country, 95; Ledyard tries to reach, 95-96; Astor's plan for trade with, 107, 114; gold rush affects Seattle, 231-32; ore from, 302; ships on run to, 305

Alaska Times and Seattle Dispatch, 258

Alcohol, industrial: production of, 18

Aleutian Islands: Indians reach, 28; Bering sights, 70; halibut fishing in, 288

Alki Point, 170-71

Alumina, 25

Aluminum: lack of ore for, 6; manufacture of, 7-8, 21-22, 329; ores in Okanogan Highlands, 23; plants in Spokane area, 25-27

Amanda Park, Wash., 3

American Board of Commissioners for Foreign Missions: establishes missions, 128-29; sends agricultural implements, 135; orders missions closed, 139-40; abandons missions, 147

American Federation of Labor: joins Washington Commonwealth Federation, 228; growth of, 233, 239-40; merges with CIO, 240

American Fur Company: competes with Bonneville, 119; escorts missionaries, 129, 131, 135

American Legion, 238

American Revolution: effect on trade of, 82, 84, 107

Americans: in maritime fur trade, 81-85; in overland fur trade, 117-23; settle in Willamette Valley, 153-63; move north of Columbia, 164, 168; racial composition of, 261-66

Anarchist settlement, 268

Anchorage, Alaska: trade with Seattle, 5

Anian, Strait of, 66, 67-73

Anti-Chinese Congress, 211-12

Antitreating ordinance, 220

Apocryphal voyages, 67-68

Apples: in Wenatchee Valley, 25; at Fort Vancouver, 270; current production, 282-83

Arctic Ocean: on trade routes by air, 6, 8; effect on Indian migration of, 28; Bering sails in, 69-71; Mackenzie reaches, 89

Arrastra, 300

Artesian wells, 275

Asia. *See* Orient

Asotin, Wash., 308

Asotin County: geography of, 27

Asparagus: in Columbia Basin, 25

Astor, John Jacob: plans Pacific Northwest fur trading operation, 92, 94; establishes fur trading posts, 106-15; plans agricultural posts, 107; competes with North West Company, 107-15; operates American Fur Company, 119

Astoria, Ore.: founded, 108; Hunt

Shellfish: in state's economy, 4, 20; Indians catch, 32
Shelton, Wash.: geography of, 18
Shenandoah (ship), 189
Shepard, Cyrus, 26-27, 245
Sheridan, Phil, 183-84
Sherman Anti-Trust Act, 220-21
Shields, John, 100
Shipbuilding, 6-7, 21, 289, 305
Shoreline Community College, 252
Shoshone Indians: Sacajawea captured from, 98; Sacajawea meets, 101-2; aid Lewis and Clark, 102
Shoudy, W. H., 210
Showalter, Noah, 226
Siberia, 28, 68-71, 96
Silver deposits: in Cascade Mountains, 22; in Okanogan Highlands, 23; cause agitation for free silver, 214
Silver Republicans, 217
Silver shirts, 227
Simmons, Michael T., 164, 167-68, 203-4, 271-72
Simpson, George, 116, 124
Sioux Indians, 111
Sitting Bull, Chief, 194
Skagit County: geography of, 20, 22-23
Skagit Valley College, 252
Skamania County: geography of, 22-23
Skiing, 22-23
Slacum, William, 164
Slaughter, W. A., 180-81
Slavery: laws of Oregon provisional government concerning, 163-65; national issue, 165; attitude toward, Washington Territory, 204-8
Smith, George Venable, 267
Smith, Jedediah, 117-18
Smith, Mr. and Mrs. A. B., 135, 139
Smith, Solomon H., 245
Snake River: cattle ranches along, 25-27; Indian dwellings on, 62; Lewis and Clark reach, 103; Astor plans fur trading posts along, 106; Henry's Fork of, 111; Hunt tries to navigate, 111-12; in beaver country, 116-23, 141; missionaries on, 133; Oregon Trail along, 150; Stevens crosses, 183; Steptoe crosses, 186-87
Snohomish County: geography of, 20, 22-23
Snoqualmie Indians, 169
Snoqualmie Pass, 175-76
Social life, 242-68
Socialist-Labor party, 224
Socialist party, 234

Society Islands, 73, 121
South America: on trade routes, 5, 66; bauxite imported from, 8; first Indians reach, 28, 30; Drake at tip of, 72-73; Astor plans sea route to Pacific Coast around, 106; missionaries supplies sent round, 126
South Carolina, 207
South Dakota, 111, 202
South Pass, 113, 118, 130, 150
South Sea Company, 75-77
Southwest (U.S.): bauxite imported from, 8; Jedediah Smith in, 117-18; Kelley in, 122
Spain: horses brought to Mexico from, 11; involved in Nootka Sound Controversy, 75-81; claims Louisiana Territory, 95; disputes England's claim to Oregon country, 95; cedes Louisiana to France, 96
Spalding, Eliza Hart: chosen as missionary, 130; comes overland, 131-34; teaches at Lapwai Mission, 135, 245
Spalding, Henry Harmon: chosen as missionary, 130; comes overland, 131-34; directs Lapwai mission, 134-48 *passim;* mission activities, 135-48 *passim;* devises Nez Perce alphabet, 135; escapes Whitman massacre, 146; returns to Lapwai to organize church, 147
Spaniards: trade with Philippines, 65-66; restrict trade, 66; drive Jedediah Smith out of Southwest, 117
Splawn, A. J., 178
Spokane, Wash.: aluminum plants in, 7, 21-22; lava flows around, 8; glaciers near, 10; center for Inland Empire, 25-27; near Spokane House, 93; Tshimakain mission near, 136; Turner's home, 215; center of Free Silver forces, 215-16; Whitworth College in, 249; churches in, 254; newspapers in, 258-59; libraries in, 261
Spokane Community College, 252
Spokane County: geography of, 24-27; created, 197
Spokane Falls Review, 259
Spokane House, 93, 113-15
Spokane Indians: taken to Red River school, 124-25; Gray visits, 135; Walkers and Eells with, 136-47 *passim;* Spalding visits, 147; aid Stevens, 182-83; in Battle of Rosalia, 186-87
Spokane River, 93, 109, 186-87
Spokan *Times,* 258

4; in eastern Washington, 4-5; in Okanogan Highlands, 23, 24
Tumwater, Wash., 168
Tuna: processing of, 19
Tungsten deposits: in Cascade Mountains, 22; in Okanogan Highlands, 23
Turner, George, 215
Twisted-Hair, Chief, 103, 104
Tyler, John, 140

Umatilla Indians, 133
Umatilla River, 145
Umpqua River, 117, 157
Unemployed Citizens' League, 226, 228
Union Pacific Railroad, 198
United Brethren church, 254
United States: position of Washington industries in, 4; Oriental goods in, 82; in War of 1812, 113-15; claim to Oregon country, 81, 105, 143; Kelley urges seizure of Oregon on, 152
U.S. Atomic Energy Commission, 27
U.S. Census Bureau, 4
U.S. Civilian Conservation Corps, 228
U.S. Congress: authorizes Hanford production of electricity, 24; creates Washington Territory, 46; appropriates funds for Lewis and Clark Expedition, 97; debates Linn Bill, 160; creates Oregon Territory, 165; asked to create Walla Walla Territory, 198; admits Washington as state, 200
U.S. Dept. of the Interior, 231
U.S. Forest Service: regulation of logging by, 15
U.S. government: commissions Boeing to make planes, 21; sends Wilkes to Oregon country, 137; signs 1818 Treaty, 153
U.S. Public Works Administration, 228
U.S. Weather Bureau, 3
U.S. Works Progress Administration, 228
University of Washington, 249-51, 261
Upper Nez Perces, 193-94
Uranium deposits: in Okanogan Highlands, 23
Utah, 7
Utopian groups, 267-68

Valerianus, Apostolos, 67-68
Van Asselt, Henry, 169
Vancouver, B.C., 80

Vancouver, George: explores Puget Sound, 79-81, 84-85; journals of, 84-85; misses Mackenzie, 90
Vancouver, Wash.: aluminum plants in, 7, 21-22; named for Captain Vancouver, 80; Broughton reaches site of, 80; site of Fort Vancouver, 116; troops sent to Yakima War from, 180; Wool in, 182-83; troops sent to Seattle from, 212; Clark College in, 252; Holy Angels College in, 260
Vancouver Catholic Library Association, 260
Vancouver County (Oregon provisional government), 164
Vancouver Island: Meares builds ship on, 7; Indians on, 32, 39; Perez reaches, 71; named for Capt. Vancouver, 80; Mackenzie near, 90; *Tonquin* at, 108; channel in dispute, 190-92
Vantage, Wash., 9
Venetian blinds: production of, 18
Victoria, B.C., 175
Vizcaino, Sebastian, 66
Volunteer Infantry, First Washington Territory, 190
Voyageurs, 87-88, 117

Waddell, James I., 189
Wahkiakum County: geography of, 19-20
Waillatpu: Bridger's daughter attends school at, 130; Whitman mission established at, 133-34; wagons reach, 139
Walker, Elkanah: overland trip, 135-36; at Tshimakain, 136-40, 146; settles in Willamette Valley, 147, 248
Walker, Mary: overland trip, 135-36; at Tshimakain, 136-40, 146; teaches Indians, 138-39, 245; settles in Willamette Valley, 147
Walker, William, 125
Walker's Prairie, 248
Wallace, Leander, 169
Wallace, William Henson, 203, 260
Walla Walla, Wash.: in irrigated area, 25; Whitman mission near, 133; outfitting center for gold rush, 193, 199, 249; Whitman College in, 248-49; Walla Walla College in, 249; newspapers in, 257-58; libraries in, 260-61
Walla Walla College, 249

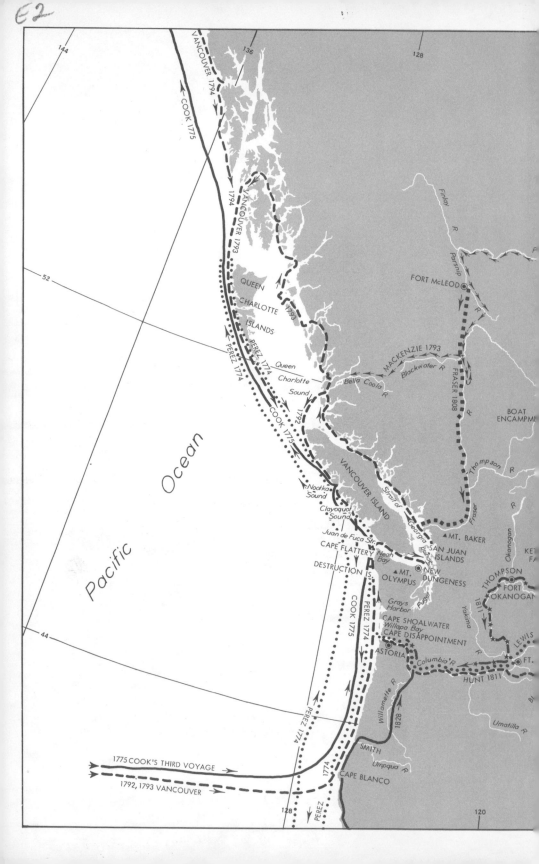

E2

VANCOUVER 1794

COOK 1775

144

136

128

52

QUEEN
CHARLOTTE
ISLANDS

Queen
Charlotte
Sound

VANCOUVER 1793

PEREZ 1774

VANCOUVER 1793

COOK 1775

PEREZ 1774

1792

Finlay R

FORT McLEOD

Parsnip R

MACKENZIE 1793

Blackwater R

Bella Coola R

FRASER 1808

BOAT
ENCAMPME

Thompson R

Pacific

Ocean

Nootka
Sound

Clayoquot
Sound

VANCOUVER ISLAND

Strait of

Georgia

MT. BAKER

SAN JUAN
ISLANDS

KET
FA

Okanogan R

Juan de Fuca Str.

CAPE FLATTERY

DESTRUCTION IS.

Neah
Bay

Puget

MT.
OLYMPUS

NEW
DUNGENESS

THOMPSON
FORT
OKANOGAN

Yakima R

LEWIS

44

COOK 1775

PEREZ 1774

Grays
Harbor

CAPE SHOALWATER
Willapa Bay
CAPE DISAPPOINTMENT

ASTORIA

Columbia R.

FT.

HUNT 1811

PEREZ 1774

Willamette R.

1828

Umatilla R.

BL

SMITH

Umpqua R

CAPE BLANCO

1775 COOK'S THIRD VOYAGE

1792, 1793 VANCOUVER

1774
PEREZ

128

120